THE GREAT AMERICAN DESERT

THEN AND NOW

THE GREAT AMERICAN DESERT THEN AND NOW

W. EUGENE HOLLON

UNIVERSITY OF NEBRASKA PRESS · LINCOLN

To Fred and Elsa Schonwald

First Bison Book Printing: 1975

Most recent printing indicated by the first digit below:

1   2   3   4   5⁻   6   7   8   9   10

Library of Congress Cataloging in Publication Data

Hollon, William Eugene, 1913–
   The Great American Desert then and now.

   Reprint of the ed. published by Oxford University Press, New York,
with a new "Addendum" by the author.
   "A Bison book."
   Includes bibliographical references.
   1. The West—History   2. The West—Description and travel—1951–
   3. Deserts—The West   I. Title.
[F591.H73   1975]   978   75–5512
ISBN 0–8032–5806–2

Published by arrangement with Oxford University Press, Inc. The Bison
Book edition, except for the Addendum, is reproduced with some emenda-
tions from the 1966 Oxford edition.

PREFACE

I first became aware of the Great American Desert in the 1930's, while living in a small west Texas town near the Pecos River. This was the period of the Dust Bowl, and I remember the eerie feeling of looking out each morning to see the sun blotted out by dust clouds rolling in from New Mexico or down from Colorado. On some days the sky turned black, and on others a dull red. As the ground baked harder and the arroyos and stream beds turned to powder, the only vegetation that survived was the hardy sotol plant and the thorny cactus. Old-timers recalled other droughts, but none as prolonged or as depressing. By the end of the decade things got better, however, and the country came back—as the natives say. I left the rim of the desert about this time and did not again venture beyond the 98th meridian for almost ten years.

The next time I saw the West was on a vacation trip to the mountains of New Mexico and Colorado. By then nearly all traces of the Dust Bowl had disappeared and the Great Plains were covered with a carpet of green grass, irrigated cotton fields,

and miles of ripened wheat. Farmers and ranchers were enjoy-
ing a cycle of heavy rainfall, and were getting high prices for
cotton, wheat, and beef. The country looked prosperous, and
any suggestion that the desert might return some day was un-
thinkable.

Since 1950 I have visited the Mountain West many times, on
vacations and on research and business trips. I have come to
know firsthand almost every settlement, back road, wilderness
area, and national park and forest from southern New Mexico
to northern Montana. I have witnessed the growth of cities and
the disappearance of small towns, the moving in of industry,
the expansion of interstate highways, and the opening and improvement of new camp grounds and recreational facilities.
Sometimes the landscape has been lush and green, but during
the dry years the plains and mountain slopes have reverted to
the conditions of the mid-1930's.

In a sense I started writing this book a full decade before Oxford University Press suggested the idea in 1960. Therefore, it
is the product of considerable personal experience, academic
and otherwise. Finding a new approach has been difficult, for
so much has been written about the American West that few
trails remain unexplored. I have tried, nevertheless, to center
emphasis at all times upon the problems of aridity, though it
has been impossible to avoid completely what J. Frank Dobie
often referred to as "moving dry bones from one graveyard to
another."

I am indebted to several people who have contributed in one
way or another to make this book possible. First of all is the
late Professor Walter Prescott Webb, whose many articles,
speeches, and books relating to the problems of aridity inspired
the original idea. In addition, four of my graduate students deserve mention for their tedious work in searching for materials
and evaluating voluminous secondary publications, scientific
articles, and government reports. John Ferrell accompanied me
on the journey "around the rim," and helped clarify the confused story of reclamation. Watson Parker's ability to synthesize

research materials saved countless hours, as did the library leg-work of Gerard Reed and Robert Bridwell.

Professors John Caughey of the University of California at Los Angeles and John Alexander Carroll of Texas Christian University read the entire manuscript and offered excellent criti-cism and advice. Professors Oakah Jones and Gilbert Fite read individual chapters relating to their special fields of knowledge. Moreover, this study would have been far more difficult with-out the efficient typing of Mrs. Jo Soukup, whose eye for the misspelled word is uncanny. Errors that inadvertently appear are my own responsibility.

The American West has held a peculiar interest for the Amer-ican Philosophical Society since the latter part of the eighteenth century, when Thomas Jefferson served as president of the or-ganization. Financial assistance from the Society in the form of a grant-in-aid made it possible for me to make two extensive research trips into and around the Great American Desert. I wish especially, therefore, to express my deep appreciation of the Society's continued support in behalf of this and other his-torical projects relating to my special field of interest.

W. Eugene Hollon

Norman, Oklahoma
October 1965

ADDENDUM

Much has happened in the intervening years since this book originally appeared in print. In the meantime I have become a resident of Ohio, but the mountains and deserts keep drawing me back—both physically and spiritually. Ten years ago I wrote that the key to the development of the arid West has been and always will be water. The statement is even more obvious today than it was in 1965, or 144 years earlier when Stephen H. Long expressed the same idea. Three generations after Long first labeled the region between the 100th meridian and the Rocky Mountains as "The Great American Desert," the famous geological explorer John Wesley Powell spoke to all Westerners when he warned members of the Montana Constitutional Convention that "the great values of this region . . . [will] ultimately be measured by you in acre feet."

In August 1974, I arranged an interview in the Department of Interior Building in Washington with representatives of the

Office of Saline Water, the Bureau of Reclamation, and the Bureau of Engineers in hopes of ascertaining their thoughts on the major water developments in the arid West during the past decade. The following comments represent a synthesis of the results of the two-hour meeting:

In the early '60s, all of us around here were confident that we would soon be providing an unlimited supply of water for the western states. Not only would we be desalinating millions of acre feet of sea water each year for West Coast cities and farms through cheap atomic power, but we also would soon tap the great surplus of fresh water in Alaska. By means of a one-hundred-billion-dollar engineering project known as NAWAPA (North American Water and Power Alliance), we could channel enough water from the North to convert the entire Great Plains and northern Mexico into another Garden of Eden. It also seemed beyond doubt that cloud-seeding would be so perfected that the drought-stricken areas of the West would be a thing of the past. At the same time, the Bureau of Engineers had grandiose plans for additional dams and reservoirs similar to Boulder, Glen Canyon, Lake Mead, and Lake Powell on the lower Colorado. We all believed then that we would soon eliminate, or at least control, rapid evaporation on large bodies of impounded water by covering the surface with a harmless chemical film.

But all of these hopes and great expectations have more or less been shattered and we are down to reality. We have less underground water today in the arid West than a decade ago, and what we have in our streams and reservoirs is much more polluted. At the same time, the demand for water today is far greater than it was in 1964. The NAWAPA plan turned out to be a pipe dream and as dead as the proverbial dodo bird. We have had no significant breakthrough in desalinization of sea water or brackish water, while the tremendous increase in the cost of energy has further complicated the problem. As for atomic power, we are not much better off here either, primarily because of strong opposition by environmentalists.

We engineers and scientists working for the federal government always considered ourselves conservationists, and it there-fore came as a shock when we suddenly became the guys in black hats. But charges by Ralph Nader, members of the Sierra Club, and Friends of the Earth have forced us to think ideas and plans through more carefully. These groups now have considerable power and can no longer be dismissed as "cranks," "crackpots," or "butterfly chasers." They also have made it extremely difficult for corporations to construct new power plants operated by coal or atomic energy. Moreover, it is equally difficult to obtain con-gressional approval for any new multipurpose dams on western rivers. Although most of the easy sites are already developed, one should not forget that hydroelectricity is still the cheapest source of energy available.

As far as cloud-seeding goes, there is no question that under certain conditions, clouds can be artificially triggered to release their moisture. In fact, the Bureau of Reclamation plans to spend twenty million dollars in 1975 seeding the clouds over the eastern slopes of the Rockies. This will be the most comprehen-sive weather-making program ever undertaken in the United States. But we have learned that the system has limited possi-bilities, especially since its wide-scale application in Vietnam proved anything but overwhelmingly successful. And among other disappointments is our failure to check evaporation effec-tively. This represents a fantastic loss of precious moisture, since more water evaporates in the huge reservoirs of the Colorado River than is used to power the giant turbines that generate hydroelectricity. A chemical film spread over the surface of Lake Mead, for example, will do wonders, but it takes only one motor boat at high speed to ruin everything.

Among the many reports that have been issued recently by the Department of the Interior, perhaps the most significant was released in January 1975, entitled *Westside Study: The Critical Water Problems Facing the Eleven Western States*. This 355-page document is better at defining particular problems than in offering solutions—other than the monotonous refrain that "further research and study on this matter is urgently needed." But the tone of the study is generally pessimistic and leaves no doubt that the water crisis is far worse in 1975 than a decade earlier.

For one thing, the Colorado River, which is to the arid West what the Nile is to Egypt, has about reached its limits for irrigation purposes. This is particularly true in the lower basin states, and no small cause of the problem is the fact that the upper basin states are now dumping an average of 70 tons of salt per square mile into the stream. When combined with what is picked up as the Colorado winds its way through the Grand Canyon and on to the Gulf of Mexico, the problem of sedimentation is compounded. The last United States user gets water of 900 ppm (parts per million) and the first users in Mexico get water of 1240 ppm—or 240 ppm beyond the limit for most crop growth.

On August 30, 1973, the United States signed an agreement with Mexico calling for the construction by this country of a desalting complex west of Yuma, Arizona, and a bypass drain, or canal, from the Wellton-Mohawk Irrigation District to the Gulf of California. The purpose is to reduce the salt content of the waters of the Colorado which Mexico receives to a level suitable for crops. By the time the two projects are completed in 1978, the cost probably will have exceeded two hundred million dollars.

What has happened to the Colorado is what will happen sooner or later to the Arkansas, Platte, Rio Grande, Yellowstone, and Missouri. Half of the causes of pollution of these streams are due to natural phenomena, but irrigated farming uses 80 per cent of the available water in the West and exceeds all other man-made causes combined. Cities are relatively minor causes in comparison to fertilizers and pesticides used by farmers and ranchers or salts brought to the surface by irrigation wells. Other recent contributors result from overgrazing, excessive cutting of timber, and the tremendous increase in feedlots. According to the Office of Environmental Protection, one cow or steer in a feedlot produces an average of 3.6 tons of waste. And anyone who has driven past Sterling,

Colorado, or any of literally hundreds of other western feedlots in recent years without a gas mask will not argue the point. Serious warnings were heard a decade ago that agriculture at best is a marginal use of water, and now more and more residents of the arid West are beginning to get the message. Thousands of once productive acres throughout the desert and desert-rimmed states have become so leached of minerals and saturated with salts that they have been abandoned. Tumble weeds, juniper, and desert shrubs have taken over where vegetables, fruits, and cotton once grew in abundance. In other sections of Arizona, western Texas, and eastern New Mexico, water levels have dropped so low that farmers no longer can afford to operate their pumps. Some are returning to dryland agriculture, letting their lands lie fallow, or shifting to feedlots or other operations. At the same time, the upper basin states of the Great American Desert are rapidly expanding irrigation acreage, thus increasing the problem of salinity for the lower basin states.[1] Irrigation is bound to suffer even more as the growing cities and new energy plants demand more and more of what is available. Approximately twenty-five transmountain systems have been constructed to divert water from the western slope to the cities and farms of eastern Wyoming, Colorado, and New Mexico.

As Denver and other cities along the Front Range draw off more water from the western slope, the quality and quantity left is becoming increasingly inferior. Trout can no longer survive in thousands of miles of once fresh streams in Colorado, New Mexico, and Arizona. Even worse is the pollution of the atmosphere by new coal gasification and electrical power plants. Until recently the complex of five giant plants in the Four Corners region released approximately 350 tons of nitrogen dioxide and other fine particulates into the southwestern at-

[1]By the mid-1970's, the upper basin states still were only using half of the water allotted to them under the Colorado River Compact of 1922 (pp. 166–67).

mosphere each day.[2] This represented more pollution than experienced by New York and Los Angeles combined. Meanwhile, the Tetons in northwest Wyoming presently are being covered by a dirty veil of pollutants coming from phosphate plants in Idaho and steel mills in Utah. Trees, vegetation, and wildlife are suffering severely, but little is being done about the situation.

Among the many problems this country faced in the mid-60's was farm surpluses, particularly of wheat and corn, a situation which prevailed in spite of acreage restrictions placed on farmers. Today with millions of people throughout the world facing starvation and with all acreage allotment controls removed, American farmers cannot keep up with demands. Thus, the stage could be set for another "lesson in consequences" (Chapter X), and Robert W. Long, Assistant Secretary of Agriculture, sees the possibility of a modern Dust Bowl developing. In their rush to produce more food and fiber, Westerners naturally will be tempted to ignore good soil and water conservation practices.

In October 1973, Dr. Walter Orr Roberts of Boulder, Colorado, predicted a severe drought for Colorado, Kansas, Nebraska, and other parts of the West for 1974 or 1975. He based the observation on recent recurring sun spots, a prophecy which unfortunately came true with serious effects upon world food

[2]Overwhelming public opinion, plus the passage of the Clean Air Act in 1970 by Congress, eventually forced El Paso Natural Gas and Utah International to install electrostatic precipitators and scrubbers on their plants in the Four Corners area. Whereas both companies originally argued that filters would not reduce the amount of fly-ash spewed into the southwestern atmosphere, by mid-1974 they were boasting in TV and radio advertisements that they had reduced air pollution by 99.6 per cent. According to Dr. John R. Bartlett, a chemical engineer at Los Alamos and an authority on atmospheric pollution, fly-ash at the five plants complex had only been reduced to approximately one hundred tons per day, but that when the installation of the remaining precipitators and scrubbers is completed, the content should be no more than approximately fifteen tons per day.

conditions.[3] The drought of 1974 was another reminder that
the Great American Desert has the capacity to expand and contract; it might be dormant for a generation, but man can never
completely conquer it. (To paraphrase a well-known TV commercial, "You can't fool Mother Nature.")

Whereas western boosters a few years ago were trying to
attract people and industry, they are now more willing to
sacrifice some development in behalf of environmental quality.
New residents and industry are frequently being resented,
especially by those who originally came from the outside themselves. In 1970, Idaho voters selected Cecil D. Andrus as its
first democratic governor in twenty-four years. His platform
called for protection of the state's legacy of natural beauty,
and he has since vowed that any more dams in Hell's Canyon
will have to be constructed over his dead body. Andrus also
has declared that people and industry who wish to settle in
Idaho in the future will do so in accordance with a new set of
ground rules. He was reelected for a second term in 1974 by
an unprecedented 73 per cent of the votes cast. Indeed, in
each of the eight desert states, ecology was the key issue in the
gubernatorial and Senate races, and the candidates who won
were those with the strongest environmental protection platform.

Closely related to the environmental issue are the subdividers, currently one of the most powerful pressure groups in
the West. In state after state worthless land is being sold at
exorbitant prices and the habitat of endangered species is being
threatened or destroyed. Between 1965 and 1971, the number
of subdivisions in Colorado increased from thirty to more than
three hundred, which represents enough individual lots for

[3]"Weathermen are suspicious of any rule of thumb for measuring conditions
that produce drought, yet there is some basis for the crackerbarrel assertion
that this country goes through a dry cycle every 20 years or so. Two decades
after the dust bowl of the 1930s came the racking drought of the 1950s.
Now another 20 years later, drought-cracked fields and withered corn are
back in the news. And there are warnings of increased wind erosions in the
Southwest." (*New York Times*, August 18, 1974, p. E3.)

twelve million newcomers. The state had virtually no control over the hundreds of ski lodges before 1975, and the legislature refused to pass an effective land-use law. On the other hand, a young legislator named Richard Lamm led the successful fight in 1973 against Colorado's hosting the 1976 Winter Olympics. In the subsequent election he defeated the popular incumbent, Republican John Vanderhoof, for the governorship of the state, primarily on the issue of protecting the environment.

Until mid-1973, Colorado had been invaded at the rate of approximately 1,400 people per week by Easterners and Westerners anxious to escape blight, sprawl, and crime. To most, the environment represented the overwhelming issue, more so than it previously had to the natives. Ironically, the newcomers have helped create the same type of conditions which they left elsewhere. Meanwhile, the more water Denver pipes through the mountains, the more people and automobiles it attracts, and the poorer the quality of water which is left behind for irrigation. The city now has the dubious distinction of possessing the nation's highest level of carbon monoxide pollution, followed closely by Phoenix, Tucson, Albuquerque, and Salt Lake City.

In nearby Utah, ski lodges, vacation homes, and condominiums spread along the slopes of the Uinta and Wasatch Mountains near Salt Lake City. And historic Bear Lake in the extreme northeast corner of the state, formerly one of the most beautiful and unpolluted bodies of water in North America, is overrun by new condominiums and second homes. At the opposite corner of the state in southern Utah, subdividers have bought up mountain land for three to four hundred dollars and sold it for six thousand per acre. Although the state legislature passed a land-use bill, the real estate lobby rendered it toothless.

Similar "rip-offs" are taking place throughout the arid West whereby desert land is being sold at exorbitant prices, yet as of the end of 1974, Montana remained the only state that had passed an effective land-use law. Between Albuquerque and Santa Fe, salesmen for Great Western are selling tiny lots on the Cochiti Pueblo Reservation for several thousand dollars each. The company has constructed an artificial lake for eighty-two million dollars and laid out a city on the seamless desert land for an eventual population of forty-four thousand people, or one hundred times more than the number of Indians presently living on the reservation. A few miles northeast of Cochiti at the foothills of the Sangre de Cristo Range, masters of the hard sell are promoting a similar-sized city, one equal to the present population of Santa Fe.

Lots at El Dorado de Santa Fe are selling at from three thousand to five thousand dollars per acre. By the end of 1974 some twenty-five or thirty homes had been constructed on the three-thousand-acre subdivision, or approximately the maximum that the available water supply can support. A few miles north of the New Mexico capital another subdivision, the Colonias de Santa Fe on the Tesuque Reservation, was stopped in 1973 by lawsuits. Whether subdivisions will continue on a smaller scale is questionable, but there are sixteen other New Mexico pueblos equally attractive.

In neighboring Arizona, subdividers are literally butchering desert lands peddling worthless lots to suckers—worthless because there is no water and no prospect of getting any. Fragile arid land broken up by new roads and streets does not heal quickly. To the best of my knowledge, not a single individual in 1974 lived in a new "city" laid out north of Flagstaff more than a decade ago. Enough lots have been sold or are available for a city of fifty thousand people; and this is only one of 182 subdivisions in Arizona with a total population capacity of three and one-half million. Mohave County alone has 46 subdivisions, or enough lots for twenty-two times its present population.

The most famous subdivision in Arizona, thanks to a multi-million-dollar advertising campaign, is Lake Havasu City near Needles, California—one of five desert cities under construction by the McCulloch Corporation. It already claims thirteen thousand residents, but the promoters are planning for an eventual eighty thousand. Lake Havasu City remains Arizona's second greatest tourist attraction, primarily because of the re-assembled London Bridge—about as incongruous to the desert southwest as the bust of Richard Nixon on Mt. Rushmore.

Real estate salesmen are also carting tourists each day from Las Vegas into the Pahrump Valley and pressuring them into buying quarter-acre building sites for $4,500. Preferred Equity, a company forced to refund seventeen million dollars to indi-viduals to whom it once sold worthless Florida swampland, claims that it is building a city for fifty thousand people. Al-though its agents had disposed of 80 per cent of the twelve thousand original acres, only four or five permanent homes had been constructed by mid-1974 in an area that experiences only two inches of rainfall each year. Incidentally, nearby Lake Pahrump is the last spot on earth where the one-inch Pahrump killifish survive. Less than a thousand remain, but as the water is taken from nearby Ash Springs and from the surrounding subsurface by wells, this particular genus is disappearing for-ever.

The people of Wyoming and Montana realize all too well that they too are about to be "Californicated" like their sister states of the region. Thousands of modern Huns and Vandals have already overrun dozens of small communities, and thou-sands more are just over the horizon. Both northern basin states contain scenery of extraordinary beauty and have an appeal almost as great as that of Colorado. Jackson Hole and the Teton area of northwest Wyoming have long been among the major tourist attractions in the nation. Developers in the area are now buying up privately owned land for ski lodges, condominiums, and vacation homes. The potential for similar activity in other parts of the state is not going unnoticed.

Not far from the Tetons and Yellowstone National Park, in the beautiful Spanish Peak Wilderness area of southern Montana, is that state's equivalent to Vail, Colorado—the re-cently opened and controversial Big Sky recreational complex promoted by the late Chet Huntley. The Chrysler Corporation is the chief stockholder in Big Sky's sixteen thousand acres of land and two villages—Mountain and Meadow—which one critic with a sense of history has called "The Second Mountain Meadows Massacre."[4] In its promotional brochures, Big Sky emphasizes its determination to preserve wildlife and prevent pollution of streams. But some conservationists point out that an operation the size of Big Sky destroys the habitat of more than twenty moose alone. "At this rate," an ecologist observed, "a few more Big Skys in the Big Sky Country and moose will soon be confined to road-side zoos."

A major factor related to the rapid changes that the mountain and desert states are experiencing today is the Interstate Highway system. A decade ago when the new roads were approximately one-third completed, they were being praised as one of the greatest engineering feats since the heyday of the Roman Empire. As of May 1974, the system which began eighteen years previously was 84 per cent complete, with construction under way for all but 1 per cent of the projected total of 42,500 miles of surfaced roads. Of this amount, the eight-state region will have 17 per cent, or 7,138 miles.[5] Unquestionably, the new highways are opening up the countryside and providing some esthetic improvement over the old federal roads and ugly billboards, "tourist traps," roadside "museums," run-down filling stations, seedy motels, "greasy-spoon" restaurants, and "ratty-looking" country towns with stoplights every

4The Mountain Meadows Massacre took place near Cedar City, Utah, in September 1857, when a Mormon mob and Indian allies ambushed a wagon train of 140 Missouri emigrants en route to California. They killed all members of the company except seventeen small children. The Mormons claimed that the Missourians had provoked the attack. Twenty years later, on the spot where the massacre took place, John D. Lee was executed for his role in the shocking affair.

5The total cost of the 7,138 miles of Interstates in the eight-state region had not exceeded four billion dollars by the end of 1974. This is a fraction of the cost of similar mileage in other sections of the United States. A minor exception is the five-mile tunnel through the central Rockies between Denver and Grand Junction on IS 70, which represents the most expensive project of its kind in the world.

block to slow down cross-country travelers. At the same time, the new system has made instant millionaires out of thousands of contractors, politicians, and developers. The question naturally arises whether the country has gained more than it has lost in the process. As H. L. Mencken once observed, "Something which everyone accepts as the gospel truth inevitably proves false." One can easily assemble formidable evidence that the Interstates have proved less of a salvation for the West than originally proclaimed by professional boosters, and more of a curse. Consider the following: Thousands of valuable acres of ranch lands, farms, and fragile deserts have given way to ribbons of concrete and asphalt. The new highways have taken a fearful toll in wildlife, contributed greatly to urban sprawl and traffic congestion, polluted the atmosphere, accelerated the energy shortage, and helped transform once attractive cities like Denver, Albuquerque, Phoenix, Tucson, and Salt Lake City into ugly crime-infested megalopolises. Denver now spreads along the Front Range via Interstate 25 as far as northern New Mexico in one direction and southern Wyoming in the other.

The main streets leading from interstate exits to the business districts of cities are lined with garish neon signs, telephone and electric power poles, pizza parlors, Taco Boys, Colonel Sanders' Fried Chicken emporiums, Dairy Queen drive-ins, Holiday Inns, Bonanza Steak Houses, McDonald Hamburgers, and four filling stations at each intersection. John Kenneth Galbraith once called filling stations the ugliest man-made structures to appear in the last two thousand years; but that is not doing justice to the fast-food chains. In fact, pizza parlors and McDonald Hamburger stands—to mention only two out of several dozens—are about as attractively designed and located as scabs on a sow's ear. And there are the condominiums marring valleys, meadows, lake shores, and mountainsides like festered pimples on the face of a beauty queen.

Even parts of the countryside far removed from population centers often are scarred by piles of rubbish, abandoned cars, junk yards and so-called antique shops. This is especially true in the more arid states of the Southwest along both the old federal and new Interstate highways. When Alistair Cooke was working on the highly successful television series "America," he instructed one crew to film anything of interest between Ely and Sparks, Nevada, particularly ghost towns. The men later returned to report that "everything looks like East St. Louis."

The Interstates have been a major factor in attracting more people into the large cities of the arid West at the expense of rural areas and small towns. Each new resident that moves to Colorado today will ultimately cost present residents an estimated twenty-one thousand dollars in additional taxes and services.[6] That is why some Westerners are now talking more and more about zero population growth, and a few state universities already have put an absolute ceiling on future enrollment. Unlike retired farmers from conservative Iowa, Nebraska, and Kansas who migrated in droves to Southern California a generation ago, recent arrivals in the Mountain West, especially in Colorado and Idaho, generally are younger and more liberal. As a consequence, Colorado has suddenly changed from one of the most conservative states in the entire region to one of the most liberal, or progressive. In the November 1974 election, liberal Democrats captured the governorship and a United States Senate seat. Thus, for the first time in a third of a century, the Centennial State does not have at least one Republican senator in Washington or a Republican governor.

In spite of Nixon's landslide victory, the trend toward a less conservative philosophy in the arid and mountain states began long before 1972. Nine of the United States senators from the region are Democrats, while all of the eight governors in 1975 belong to that same party. Along with Colorado, traditionally conservative Montana has also moved more in the

[6]Colorado's growth rate experienced a dramatic decline between July 1973 and July 1974—from 3.9 per cent to 1.1 per cent. At the same time, Nevada and Arizona ranked as the second and third fastest growing states, with a 4 per cent and 3.9 per cent rate per year respectively.

direction of liberalism. It adopted a new constitution in 1973, the first state west of the Mississippi to do so in more than forty years.

Although Wyoming elected a moderate Democratic governor in 1974, its little-known Republican senator, Clifford P. Hansen, has one of the most conservative, or reactionary, voting records on Capitol Hill, including those of Senators Roman Hruska and Carl Curtis of Nebraska, John Tower of Texas, Strom Thurman of South Carolina, Barry Goldwater of Arizona, and William Scott of Virginia. Hansen's Democratic colleague from Wyoming, whom I called a decade ago "one of the most outspoken liberals in Washington" (p. 190), could hardly be classified in the 1970's as a "knee-jerk" liberal. Indeed, Senator Gale McGee reflects the conservative attitude of most Wyoming residents, one that until very recently was not being disturbed by a large influx of outsiders.

Fifty-four per cent of the people of Wyoming in a 1974 poll classified themselves as "very conservative" or "conservative," 36 per cent claimed to be "independent," and only 12 per cent said that they were liberal. Although he still calls himself a liberal—before liberal audiences—Senator McGee represented one of the most "hawkish" members of Congress to the very end of the Vietnam War. As a member of two powerful committees, Appropriations and Defense, he naturally has seen to it that the complex of intercontinental missile bases in Wyoming remains activated. Liberal issues in which McGee scores high, such as school busing, civil rights, and consumer protection, are generally noncontroversial in thinly populated Wyoming.[7]

7In fairness to Senator McGee, it has been extremely difficult in the past for an out-and-out liberal to get elected to a major political office in a majority of the eight states in the arid and mountain region. Exceptions have been Senators Church of Idaho, who won a fourth term in November 1974, and Mansfield and Metcalf of Montana. Church and Mansfield were especially outspoken on the Vietnam War.

Republican Senator Peter Dominick of Colorado accumulated a very conservative, if not reactionary, record during his twelve-year tenure. Gary

The shifting political climate in the arid West to the center has been more of an evolutionary than a revolutionary phenomenon. But other developments are taking place at such a rapid pace that many communities are suffering from "cultural shock." Lifelong residents find themselves total strangers in their own surroundings. The cause of this dramatic explosion is the energy crisis—real or contrived.

It has long been known that immediately beneath the surface of the Great American Desert lay some of the richest coal veins in the world—an estimated 86.1 billion tons worth three hundred billion dollars in gross sales to coal companies. In addition, Wyoming, Utah, and Colorado possess 300 trillion cubic feet of natural gas held in deep sand formations, and an estimated 600 billion barrels of shale oil. Between 1.25 and 1.75 kilowatts of power are needed to process a barrel of shale oil. The estimated water requirement for producing 100,000 barrels of oil per day varies between 5,000 and 20,000 acre feet, depending upon mining techniques used at a particular site.

The tremendous coal and oil shale deposits are located on public, private, and Indian lands. Literally hundreds of articles have appeared recently in magazines and newspapers regarding efforts by federal and state government to regulate strip mining throughout the West, protect surface rights over mineral rights, require coal companies to revegetate the ravaged landscape, and several other related topics. Montana has taken the lead in an effort to regulate strip mining and in advocating strong federal controls. Senate Majority Leader Mike Mansfield believes that his region is being "Appalachianized" and made into the back yard of the nation.

Governor Thomas L. Judge has been even more outspoken and maintains that Montana's responsibility to the rest of the

Hart, Senator McGovern's campaign manager in 1972, defeated Dominick decisively in November 1974 as a moderate liberal Democrat. In the other states of the region where Senate races were held in 1974, Goldwater was a relatively easy winner for re-election in Arizona, while former Republican Governor Laxalt barely won the Senate seat vacated by Alan Bible in Nevada.

nation does not require it to sit idly by and watch its lands
torn up and its water diverted exclusively to energy needs. He
calls it a great "rip-off" by multibillion-dollar conglomerates
such as the Peabody Coal Company, Pacific Power and Light,
Atlantic Richfield, and Exxon. (Ecologists often accuse Exxon
and other great energy corporations of spending more advertising dollars on TV proclaiming their concern for the environment than they actually do in protecting it.)

Montana has also been a pioneer leader among the states
of the Great American Desert in declaring a moratorium on
strip mining leases, but it is like the classic case of shutting
the barn door too late. As early as midsummer 1973, more than
five and one-half million acres of federal and Indian lands
throughout the arid West had been leased to coal companies.
This was in addition to hundreds of thousands of acres let out
by states, railroads, and private individuals. Companies are
still leasing thousands of subsurface rights from cattle ranchers
and farmers, for alleged prices in one case as high as fifteen
million dollars for a three-thousand-acre tract. Some landown-
ers are refusing to sign, but it seems highly doubtful that they
can hold out indefinitely against the unlimited funds and
political power of the great conglomerates.

Westerners realize that they are fighting a losing battle since
they obviously do not have sufficient political power in Washington to offset that of the more heavily populated regions.
When a congressman from Massachusetts is reminded that
Wyoming has less than half the population of Boston, he
wonders if preserving natural beauty is more important than
sufficient heat and electricity for his constituents. Moreover,
the great corporations have invested too much money on ex-
ploiting the natural resources of the west to be stopped permanently by any state or federal regulatory legislation. They are
now looking a few years hence when the cost of natural gas and
electricity will be three or four times what it is today. An
attorney in the Office of the New Mexico State Engineers in an
October 1974 interview observed that the power, gas, and coal

conglomerates will ultimately get the necessary water they want, one way or the other. "The obvious result of course will be less water for irrigation and for the cities."

The West has lived through previous booms, but the upper basin region has not experienced such a great inrush of people in so brief a period since the arrival of the gold miners more than a century ago. The big rush started in Wyoming in 1970 when the Bechtel Power Corporation began construction on the giant Jim Bridger Plant for the Idaho Power and Light Company thirty-five miles north of Rock Springs. At its peak the company was employing three thousand workers, all of whom were living in tents and trailers in what the *New York Times* appropriately described as a desert ghetto. Meanwhile, the population of Sweetwater County more than doubled during the subsequent four years, from 18,391 to over 45,000. Other boom towns suffering from "the Rock Springs syndrome" in late 1974 were Gillette and Kemmerer—with Sheridan, Buffalo, Douglas, and Wheatland destined for dramatic population explosions in the near future.

It is natural that Westerners resent outsiders traditionally coming in and stripping the country of its resources before leaving. And it is not uncommon today to see crude lettering on barns and buildings which read, "Ban Strip Mining," or bumper stickers like the following: "Would You Rather Eat Coal than Food?", "Don't Californicate Idaho," and "Texans Go Home!" Natives are frustrated and divided perhaps as never before. They have good reason to be upset, and they are appalled by the increase in crime, public drunkenness, brawling, X-rated movies, massage parlors, high divorce rates, drugs, skyrocketing wages and rents, shortages of classrooms, and inadequate fire and police protection. They naturally blame somebody else for the quiet life they formerly knew suddenly giving way to traffic jams, polluted air and water, the disappearance of wildlife, more open pit mines, and astronomical increases in taxes.

Colstrip, Montana, has had to double its taxes again and again in recent years. Its school enrollment jumped from four hundred students in 1973 to over one thousand in 1974, with further increases a certainty. Local residents maintained that the nearby coal and power companies which moved in were solely responsible for the flood of students, and therefore they should pay for the construction of a new two-million-dollar school building. When asked at a public gathering early in 1974 how the Colstrip school board could be expected to find money to finance an exploding population brought on by the construction of massive power-generating plants, an official of one of the companies bluntly responded: "That's your problem, gentlemen."

It is not the last time that residents of the arid and mountain states will hear this answer, for their problems are certain to become more complicated and their life styles will change even more drastically. But they are realizing what millions of others in the crowded areas of the East and West Coast long since accepted, namely, that "progress" can be a four-letter word.

Toledo, Ohio   W. Eugene Hollon

January 1975

CONTENTS

THE GREAT AMERICAN DESERT

THEN AND NOW

The Great American Desert

CANADA

WASHINGTON
Columbia R.

Missouri R.
MONTANA
Yellowstone R.
NORTH DAKOTA
MINNESOTA
WISCONSIN

OREGON
IDAHO
Snake R.
WYOMING
SOUTH DAKOTA
IOWA
ILLINOIS

Humboldt R.
GREAT SALT LAKE
Salt Lake City
NEBRASKA
Platte
Missouri R.
St. Louis
MISSOURI

NEVADA
ROCKY MOUNTAINS
UTAH
Denver
COLORADO
KANSAS
Arkansas

San Francisco

CALIFORNIA
ARIZONA
Santa Fe
NEW MEXICO
OKLAHOMA
Red
ARKANSAS
Mississippi R.

Los Angeles
Phoenix
Gila R.
San Diego
El Paso
Rio Grande
TEXAS
LOUISIANA

PACIFIC OCEAN

MEXICO

GULF OF MEXICO

Mexico City

Approximate limit
of Desert influence

Great Basin

INTRODUCTION

In May of 1957 *Harper's* magazine carried a highly controversial article by a prominent western historian, the late Walter Prescott Webb of Texas, entitled "The American West, Perpetual Mirage." Webb stated brusquely that the eight states of the Rocky Mountain region constituted the heartland of an American desert, and he classified the nine that border it as "desert rim" states. The center of this American desert, according to Webb, was to be found in Montana, Wyoming, Idaho, Utah, Colorado, Nevada, Arizona, and New Mexico.

Immediately following the publication of Webb's article there came a howl of protest from western senators, governors, chamber of commerce officials, newspaper publishers, and citizens in general. Some, like Senator Frank Church of Idaho, admitted the impact of desert conditions upon the region but felt that Webb had slighted every Westerner by calling attention to its existence. Senator Barry Goldwater, though he could hardly deny the presence of a desert in his state, objected strongly to Webb's implication that the desert had been a factor in impeding western development. Indeed, he maintained the opposite view and pointed out that the "so-called" desert state of Arizona was leading the country in percentage of population growth, bank deposits, and the expansion of manufacturing.

No western newspaper was more vociferous in denouncing the Texas historian than the *Denver Post*. Its editor, like Senators Church and Goldwater, was righteously indignant and reacted as if the very word "desert" was synonymous with something sinister and foreboding. Perhaps this response was natural, for Americans have been arguing about the desert for more than a century—either denying its presence or else proclaiming that some day it would "bloom like the rose" and become "the garden spot of the world." Emigrants who crossed it in covered wagons and settlers who had their farms and ranches blown away in dust storms have had less kind things to say.

None of these views is unrealistic, for the West has always been a land of extremes, subject to cyclical periods of humid and dry years. But the desert remains, expanding and contracting with the vicissitudes of nature and damages wrought by man. As the Anglo-Saxon pioneers moved westward to settle and farm beyond the 98th meridian, they destroyed the native grass that had held the desert in check like a magic girdle— just as they had destroyed eastern forests. With its protective cover gone, the soil was exposed to the ravages of the sun, wind, and rain. Cactus, sage, and scrub shifted into what had once been lush prairie. The desert literally moved outward from its proper climatic confine into regions far different in character. As the desert expanded, ranchers and farmers were forced to retreat beyond its outer limits. After the cycle ran its course and the rains returned, a ground cover slowly reappeared. The desert drew in its tentacles and frequently divided itself into separate and distinct parts. The settlers came back, a bit wiser and more cautious. But as the new cycle of humid weather continued, they were inclined to forget that the desert was only dormant, never dead. A few years of drought and the desert parts rejoined and advanced in all directions. The process of boom to bust, disaster, and retreat repeated itself. Indeed, millions of Americans who lived through the Dust Bowl of the 1930's and the great thirst of the 1950's have vivid memories of the desert advancing and people retreating from it. The word "desert" has been anathema to Americans, except when applied, with pride, to isolated stretches like the Mojave Desert of southern California, the Painted Desert of northern Arizona, the Red Desert of southwestern Wyoming, the Great Sandy Desert of central Oregon, and some areas of Utah, Nevada, and New Mexico. But others considered the region west of the 98th or 100th meridian to be a desert in name as well as fact long before special interests became involved. Francisco Vasquez de Coronado in 1541 spoke of "these deserts" in reference to the southwestern regions of the present United States, and during the three centuries that followed the Spaniards accepted the desert as a fact of life and made little effort to colonize beyond oasis spots in present Arizona, New Mexico, California, and Texas. In spite of this, the Americans began a campaign to abolish the desert more than a century ago, and for every writer who described the West as a desert, half a dozen promptly denounced him and refuted the charge. Webb is not the first writer to be attacked by editors, politicians, and professional boosters for violating the unwritten code. The desert has been bad for business, and, except for periods of spectacular drought like the late 1880's, 1930's, and 1950's, its existence has often been concealed or minimized.

This ostrich-like attitude is now undergoing a remarkable change. In November 1961, at a White House Conference on natural resources management held in Denver, various speakers stated flatly that "the West is a desert." Even though these remarks came from "outsiders," there was little or no protest from Westerners. The *Denver Post,* which four years earlier had denounced Professor Webb with bitter sarcasm, complimented the Washington officials and observed that it was time for Westerners "to quit kidding themselves. . . . There are signs that state, local groups, and the federal government are today putting a lot more science into their considerations of western resource management than they have in the past. . . . Co-ordination of water efforts and new concepts of what kind of industrial and social development the West can support are growing. In this respect the arid climate of the West—call it a desert climate if you like—can be in some ways a positive advantage to growth. . . . It is almost like having your cake and eating it too."

Several developments have combined to alter the attitude of Westerners and to shift emphasis toward the desert rather than away from it. Population pressures have forced many people into regions formerly shunned as unattractive. Airplanes, automobiles, and superhighways have reduced the time and discomfort of travel, while air-conditioning has made the desert a pleasant place to live for millions of Americans. Industry and agriculture have followed in the wake of the new emigrants, and in turn have attracted more settlers.

The Great American Desert is becoming more and more a place of opportunity and less a place to be scorned. But water is still the key to its future, and it is now the first concern of local, state, and federal officials. At a time when the West is experiencing another cycle of less than normal rainfall, and ground level water is dropping alarmingly in areas around Phoenix, Albuquerque, and other oasis cities, scientists and engineers have many schemes for bringing more water to the arid lands of the West. Several giant reservoirs are under construction, and many new water projects are under consideration. In addition, several plants for the purification of brackish water have been put into operation.

It is improbable that the Great American Desert can ever support a population comparable to that of the humid regions of the United States, even if all the water in the western streams can be utilized. But the region already contains more people and produces more agricultural and industrial goods than anyone a generation ago could have believed possible. The landscape is changing rapidly as great metropolitan centers expand their boundaries in all directions, new plants and military installations appear, and new irrigation projects convert the arid soil into lush fields of alfalfa, cotton, and wheat. There are changes too in the people of the Great American Desert, most of whom are newcomers who see the region as one to be developed rather than disparaged. Like the post-Civil War generation of builders, they believe that all worlds can be conquered.

Spanish, English, French, and Americans first became interested in the continental heartland of North America because they believed it contained an inland water route to the Pacific. The search for this mythical route continued almost to the middle of the nineteenth century. Not until 1821 was the identity of the desert tentatively established. In that year Major Stephen H. Long fixed the name "Great American Desert" to that part of the West between the 98th meridian and the Rocky Mountains. Americans accepted the existence of this desert, but false prophets from time to time aroused hopes that it did not really exist or that its climate could be changed.

Major Long thought of the lands beyond the Rocky Mountains as an extension of the Great American Desert, though he only examined the region that eventually came to be known as the Great Plains. When John C. Frémont explored the western half of the desert in 1844, he named that part of it the Great Basin. The southern reaches of the Great American Desert—New Mexico and Arizona—were considered part of the Chihuahuan and Sonoran deserts of Mexico. The Anglo-Americans tended to confuse the obvious differences in cultural heritage of the areas influenced by the Spanish with the actual geographical and climatic similarities of the whole; as a result, they looked upon the various sections as separate rather than as one unified region. The cyclical changes in rainfall, particularly on the Great Plains, complicated matters even more. But the eight states in what constitutes the heart of the desert have common problems and characteristics, even if they have not always been apparent.

Perhaps the Great American Desert can never be completely

conquered by human effort, but man at last has the resources, the knowledge, and the determination to make it work to his advantage. The long struggle for the conquest of arid America is a mere prologue to the real history of the region. That history is just beginning, for traditionally the desert has been treated largely as a barrier and a wasteland. In time most of it will be used for one purpose or another—farming, manufacturing, grazing, mining, hunting, or recreation. It will have to be, for land is becoming scarce on this crowded continent.

I WHAT IS THE DESERT?

The term "Great American Desert" applies to the Mountain West, an area of 900,000 square miles, or approximately 30 per cent of the conterminous United States. Geographically it is divided into three strips laid side by side on a north-south axis. On the east are the high plains, in the center lie the mountains, and further west the intermountain province, or Great Basin. State boundaries, since they are artificial, cannot be strictly followed; the desert establishes its own irregular pattern.

The problem of establishing boundaries is especially difficult along the eastern edge of the Great American Desert, for there the boundary varies with the cycle of rainfall. There one witnesses an intensive competition between the desert scrub plants and the prairie grasses, each encroaching as far as possible upon the other. The result is that the obvious desert is restricted to the more arid zones where the soil is unable to hold sufficient moisture for any luxuriant type of vegetation. In some places a carpet of grass invades the desert from the prairies of the low plains—the eastern half of the Great Plains—to the slope of the Front Range of the Rockies. Frequently, this carpet penetrates far into the canyons and valleys of the mountains. At other points the desert protrudes into the eastern rim states of Texas, Oklahoma, Kansas, Nebraska, and the Dakotas, and the western rim states of Oregon and California. The drier the climate the more prominent the expansion, although the reverse is true during periods of abundant moisture.

The average American thinks of a desert as a vast expanse of shifting sand, and he associates the word itself almost immediately with the Sahara. But there is more to the desert than sand. Actually, only limited sections of the arid regions of the world offer depressing scenery of this sort. Most desert land is composed of rocky plateaus channeled by dry water courses, basins surrounded by mountains, deep valleys and canyons, cactus, sage, soap weed, yucca, and rolling plains carpeted by a thin cover of grass. We find all of these features in varying degrees in the region between the 100th meridian—the approximate north-south line where the Great Plains divide into the high plains and the low plains—and the Sierra Nevada, roughly the eastern and western boundaries of the modern Great American Desert.

Deserts can be described better than they can be defined. They exist on every great continental land mass, and though they constitute nearly one-fifth of the world's surface, they support no more than one twenty-fifth of the total population. They vary considerably in physical appearance, but generally possess such common characteristics as aridity, low rainfall, high temperature during the day, low temperature during the night, high velocity winds, high rate of evaporation, and sparse, scattered plant and animal life.

These more obvious features make it easy to classify the southern region of the Mountain West and the western slope of the Rockies as a vast and unmistakable desert. No one who has crossed this region in the summer months would refute the fact. Including the Great Plains in the Great American Desert, however, involves several complications: they are semiarid, have considerable ground coverage, and possess greater extremes of temperature between winter and summer. Also, the Rockies seem to divide rather than join this section to the remainder of our Great American Desert. Even modern geography textbooks offer little support for the notion that the plains region along the eastern flank of the Rockies is part of the desert, though this is the area that was originally called the Great American Desert.

It is obvious that the strip east of the Front Range has fewer desert characteristics than the western slope, primarily because it is more humid. During cycles of high rainfall, bountiful crops are produced throughout the eastern strip of our Great American Desert. In the more arid years some crops can be grown by scientific or dry-farming methods, while most lands that have access to irrigation water experience tremendous yields regardless of the natural rainfall. These developments have distorted the traditional concept that once prevailed regarding the high plains. Yet year in and year out this portion of the Great American Desert is in many ways similar to its counterpart, the intermountain region. Though the mountains appear to separate the two north-south strips, it might also be said that they hold them together. During prolonged droughts, such as those experienced in the 1930's and 1950's, similarities in climatic conditions throughout the Mountain West become even more apparent.

The first American geography schoolbook to indicate the existence of the Great American Desert appeared in 1824, and showed it extending from the Mississippi Valley to the eastern slope of the Rockies. As this area became more fully settled and explorers and travelers better acquainted with other parts of the West, the region marked "desert" retreated westwardly. Following the Civil War, American pioneers learned that wheat, corn, and other crops would grow in the Dakotas, Nebraska, and Kansas. They also learned that the brush and grasslands of Colorado, Wyoming, Montana, and New Mexico would support abundant livestock. A humid cycle followed the Civil War, and the pioneers then moving westward altered their concept of the desert. In time the lands that Stephen H. Long had originally labeled the Great American Desert came to be known as the Great Plains. By 1870 the concept that the Trans-Mississippi West constituted a vast and trackless desert had disappeared almost entirely from official maps and school geographies.

The United States Geological Survey maps of the early twentieth century showed the Great American Desert covering a wide triangle, starting at a point near Boise, Idaho, its eastern edge passed through Salt Lake City and Santa Fe southward to the mouth of the Pecos River, and its western boundary extended along the Sierra Nevada to the mouth of the Gila River. A 1925 edition of a standard college geography textbook confined it to that part of the United States which borders the lower Colorado River: western Arizona, the southern tip of Nevada, and southwestern California.

No two books agree upon the boundaries of the modern Great American Desert, even in more recent descriptions. In 1935 the botanist Paul Sears, writing during the height of the Dust Bowl days, confined his classic study, *Deserts on the March,* to a re-examination of the Great Plains. Twenty years later Preston James, in *A Geography of Man,* limited the desert to the large area of inland drainage between the Sierra Nevada on the west and the Wasatch Mountains on the east. And the specialist in desert flora and fauna, Edmund C. Jaeger, practically ignores the mountains and plains region. In his 1957 publication, *The North American Deserts,* he treats the American desert in terms of five or six separate and distinct ones, all lying south and west of the Rocky Mountains.

When Webb's article on the American West was published in *Harper's,* he found that many specialists, as well as the western politicians and chamber of commerce officials, disagreed with his broad definition of the desert. Perhaps the presence of mountains in the heart of this region was a major factor, for snow-covered peaks, great natural forests, bracing cool air, and beautiful green valleys in the summer somehow do not fit the image of a desert. Yet mountains are the chief cause of deserts, since they act as barriers, cutting off the moisture-laden clouds that otherwise would sweep across and deposit rain upon the land. This is true in most arid regions throughout the world, except where cold ocean currents act in similar capacity to rob the rain clouds of moisture. Examples of this kind of desert are found along the west coast of South America and parts of South Africa.

Doubtless there would be no Great American Desert were it not for the Sierra Nevada Range along its western edge and the Rocky Mountains in its center. And since the mountains are the chief factor in creating the Great American Desert they cannot be divorced entirely from their creation. If not climatically and geographically similar, they share a common history, and their people have a common cultural heritage.

A desert has many characteristics, not all of which have to be present simultaneously. Some geographers have arbitrarily set ten inches or less of rain per year as the true desert mark, or the dividing line between arid and semiarid conditions. By this standard large sections of our Great American Desert hardly qualify. Though averages are difficult to determine for the entire region, an estimate of twelve inches would not be far wrong. Yuma, Arizona, at the southwestern corner, rarely records more than three inches per year, while farther east at El Paso the figure is close to ten; the ten-inch mark also holds true for Laramie, Wyoming, and Helena, Montana. Near the center of the rectangle formed by these four points the two important oasis cities of Denver and Salt Lake City receive approximately fourteen to sixteen inches per year.

But not all geographers agree that ten inches of rain each year is the true measure of the desert. Preston James categorically states that deserts cannot be accurately defined this way because so many things combine to determine the effectiveness of rainfall in terms of plant and animal life. Often in the high plains and Great Basin the rains come in a violent cloudburst rather than in a long, continuous drizzle. Much of the water therefore is lost by runoff, particularly where the soil is dry and hard-packed. Thus, it is a curious fact that floods are not unusual in the desert and can cause considerable damage. The rate of evaporation is as important as the amount of rain. Except for the mountainous sections, evaporation is extremely rapid throughout the Great American Desert because of relatively low humidity and high wind velocity. In such places as the Mojave and Death Valley, for example, one frequently witnesses violent rainstorms, but no moisture reaches the surface of the land; and at Yuma the rate of evaporation is thirty-five times greater than its normal rainfall.

Because of its altitude and particular location near the mountains, Denver's average temperature is about 50 degrees. This produces a correspondingly low evaporation rate, so that a continuous grass and plant coverage would exist with no more than ten inches of evenly distributed rainfall. El Paso has a much higher average annual temperature and, at the same time, it is less sheltered from high velocity winds. It therefore would need considerably more rainfall than its normal ten inches to escape the desert environment. Actually, there are regions in northern Mexico that are complete deserts, yet they receive more than twenty inches of rain year in and year out.

The most important sources of moisture are the warm parts of the oceans, where the air is able to pick up large quantities of water. When this warm, moisture-laden air moves onto the land, bountiful rains result. This does not happen along the coast of southern California, where the Great American Desert reaches down to the ocean. Here the off-shore currents are cold, and the winds blowing parallel to the coast prevent the moisture from reaching inland. In northern California the winds blow off warmer waters, but as they continue easterly they have to contend with a series of mountain ranges that strip them of much of their moisture. Thus, inland places along the western slopes of the mountains, such as Salt Lake City, receive more rain than those in the basin and plains area that border the mountains.

Most of the world's deserts possess a supply of ground water, the same as in humid lands. It often lies at great depths below the surface, however, and can only be reached with powerful pumps. Occasionally a deep-lying source of water can be tapped to create an artesian well. Not a few of the oases of the Sahara are dependent on such a natural source of water, as is the region around Carlsbad and Artesia in New Mexico in the Great American Desert.

So-called exotic streams are likewise common to all the world's deserts, except in Australia. An exotic stream is one that has its headwaters in rainy areas and maintains a flow across the dry lands: the Nile in Egypt, the Indus in Pakistan, the Loa in Chile, and the Colorado in the United States. The Colorado rises in southwestern Wyoming and eventually makes its way to the Gulf of California. What the Nile is to Egypt, the Colorado is to a large section of the Great American Desert. It is the fifth largest river in the United States. Today, without the waters of this mighty stream, prosperous cities and fertile farms would wither and be layered over with wind-blown sand.

Like similar desert water courses, the Colorado has the peculiar character of decreasing in volume downstream and of lacking tributaries. Moreover, it constantly drops part of its load of mud and silt, while sand bars split it into separate channels. The Humboldt further north and the Platte, Arkansas, and Canadian rivers that cut across the high plains toward the east possess some of the characteristics of exotic streams. All are wide and crooked and are frequently divided by sand bars into broad areas of shallow lakes. The Humboldt fails to continue uninterruptedly across the desert because of rapid water evaporation, and the flow can only be maintained at times through the subsurface.

Streams that flow down from the mountains and cut across the desert are few in number, and the soil over which they flow often becomes encrusted with alkali and salts. This in turn creates severe problems in certain localities where impounded water for irrigation can do more harm than good.

Also, it is difficult to anchor reservoir dams in many arid regions because of the absence of abrupt river banks, and there is always the danger of established dams becoming great silt traps.

The Great American Desert is also a land of infinite variety, striking contrast, monotonous uniformity, and stunning beauty. Its altitude ranges from 282 feet below sea level in Death Valley to mountain peaks that rise above 14,000 feet. Parts of the desert in midsummer become a veritable furnace, with official recorded temperatures of 130 degrees. On the other hand, temperatures of forty to fifty degrees below zero are not unknown during midwinter in the northern portions of the desert. The high plains of the eastern strip from Montana to New Mexico often appear so flat that one has the feeling of standing in the center of an immense carpet that sags from the sheer weight of his being. Westward from the 100th meridian to the slopes of the mountains these treeless plains rise so gradually that the traveler is often unaware of the fact. In places the landscape is broken by low-lying escarpments or lonely buttes, while in others the desert plains seem to merge instantly with forested slopes that rise into the snow-capped peaks of the Front Range or the Sangre de Cristo Mountains.

The desert seems to leave off temporarily at the mountains, only to reappear west of the Rockies in the form of scattered ranges of barren hills and intermittent basins until it reaches the southern California coast or the Sierra Nevada. Rainwater from the highlands that shelter this area has sculptured it into innumerable ravines and bolsons. Sand and gravel picked up along the way are deposited in the form of alluvial fans that spread out at the mouths of the valleys. Infrequent rains, often hundreds of miles away, create shallow lakes, but rapid evaporation removes the water and leaves an accumulation of dazzling white salt.

A few of the shallow lakes, the most notable being the Great Salt Lake in Utah, receive enough water to maintain a permanent existence. Where the altitude is high and outlets possible, a Utah Lake or Lake Tahoe is found, its waters fresh, pure, and clear. Generally, however, the natural depressions, or playas, become so full of mud, salt, alkali, and other materials that they have only the slightest curvature of bottom. The sun quickly bakes the salty mud into a veritable pavement whose surface is scarred by a jigsaw of cracks caused by the shrinking of the mud as the water evaporates.

Near the common corner of Nevada, Arizona, and Utah the Great American Desert is slashed by canyons and twisting rivers. Further south and west it flattens out and approaches to within a few feet of the waters of the Pacific Ocean. The Gila and Salt rivers cut wide, dry channels across Arizona from east to west, and the Rio Grande meanders down from the north through New Mexico, supporting a number of oasis cities and towns on its way to the Gulf of Mexico.

Among the striking features of the southern portion of the Great American Desert are the great ridges of sand dunes and vast stretches of sagebrush, sotol, cactus, and waste rock. Now and then a mountain rim is visible, as well as steep pinnacles of naked rock and solitary mesas. The landscape offers a wealth of color, with brown and yellow and tawny red predominating. These colors become even more spectacular at sunset and dawn.

Though we have witnessed man's near conquest of the eastern strip of the Great American Desert during the past century, the problems become more difficult in the western and southern regions. It is here, where the mountains and bolsons give way to open stretches of landscape, that the Great American Desert has its most distinctive characteristics. Here the rainfall is especially sparse, the mirage most common, and sandstorms and duststorms most prevalent.

But rainfall and the characteristics of the landscape are not the sole measurements of the desert. Let us look at the amount and kind of plant and animal life found throughout the Great American Desert.

Deserts are not necessarily without life, sparse and bizarre though it may be. And it is the quantity and kind of plants and animals that furnish the eastern strip of the Great American Desert with its outstanding characteristics. Most of the plants indigenous to the high plains and intermountain region are called *xerophytes,* a word derived from the Greek, meaning "dry plants." *Xerophytes* have adjusted themselves to their environment in several remarkable ways. They are able to survive extreme changes in climate. Each plant generally stands at such a distance from its neighbor that it is never shaded and, being equally exposed to the light and air on all sides, it becomes compact and rounded. During rainy seasons these plants sprout forth and flower rapidly, then return to seed stage with the advent of the dry season. When the soil is disturbed, especially during a humid cycle, desert plants will burst forth almost overnight. Gold seekers who followed the Platte River route to California in 1849—a particularly wet year on the plains—accused the Mormons of having sowed sunflowers along their way. The truth was that the sunflower seeds had always been there, but the hoofs and wheels of Mormon trains broke through the sod and caused the sunflowers to spring to life.

Some desert plants have the capacity to store water in their leaves and stems and thus continue to grow throughout the hottest months. They develop long lateral roots that quickly utilize surface moisture or long tap roots that reach deep sources of ground water. This is especially true of the mesquite, whose tap root may extend over thirty feet beneath the surface. The saguaro, prickly pear, and barrel cactus, which grow throughout the southern portion of the Great American Desert, have elaborate lateral root systems. During the rainy season cactus plants appear to be bloated, but as the season gets drier their stored water is gradually used up and the stems shrink and become lean. The grasses may shrivel and die, but the *xerophytes* merely become dormant and temporarily suspend all normal activity.

Ordinary plants lose moisture by evaporation through their leaves, but many desert plants twist and turn their leaves during the warmest part of the day so that only the thin edges are exposed to the sun's direct rays. Leaves that cannot turn may curl or roll up until the cooler hours of evening. Some plants have hairy stems and leaves capable of getting and retaining moisture from the air and also protecting the stem surface from direct sun exposure. Still others have leathery epidermis to prevent rapid loss of moisture or a shiny waxy coating to reflect heat.

Several members of the cactus family have no leaves at all; their stems are modified to take over leaf functions. Usually the stem coating is tough enough to resist the etching action of windblown sand. Most cacti, mesquites, and yuccas also possess a thorny armor that protects them from being eaten, while the sage plants of the northern high plains and the creosote and burro bushes of the intermountain region produce poisonous substances that deter hungry animals. The roots of these plants, both lateral and tap, give firm anchorage against the strong winds. Those with small roots systems hug the ground, and thus are protected from the galelike winds, and tree yucca and desert palm have resilient trunks that will rarely snap or break.

In summary, all plants that survive on the desert are delicately adjusted to excessive heat, sand and dust storms, cool nights, subzero winters, and a host of predatory enemies. They are never roused by any false alarm from nature as are certain introduced plants. Peach trees, for example, can grow in many parts of the arid West, particularly in the more humid and protected valleys and along the margin of the desert. But benign and lovely weather in February or March can entice them into putting forth leaves and flowers, only to be killed by savage spring cold or frost. On the other hand, throughout the Great American Desert those plants that have been adapted by centuries of habitation never bloom prematurely.

Like the native plants, the animals also have adapted themselves to the desert environment, and in fact are more independent because of their ability to move around. To conserve water, most venture forth only in the cool of the night.

Those like the deer and antelope, and earlier the buffalo, that forage over considerable reaches depend upon the few scattered springs or streams and are able to go long periods and travel tremendous distances without water. Desert rabbits, prairie dogs, and kangaroo rats, on the other hand, are capable of manufacturing water from their dry food and thus go through life without taking a drink. Like lizards and snakes they void little or no liquid waste. Practically all desert animals have a protective coloration, which not only helps to conceal them from predatory enemies but also conserves body moisture. Smaller animals spend much of their daytime existence beneath the ground where the rays of the desert sun cannot penetrate. Here they excavate elaborate tunnels. They hibernate during the colder winter months, and the low temperature of the hibernating state keeps their bodies functioning at a very slow rate. Thus they require little or no food during periods of the year when it is most scarce.

As a further protection against the severe character of desert conditions, nature provides many creatures with small ear openings and the added protection of long hairs to keep out the dust. Their eyelashes likewise may be long, eyelids thick, and their nostrils equipped with valves that automatically close tight to shut out the sand and dust carried by the wind.

Just as the desert has forced the plants and animals to conform in order to exist, it has done the same to the peoples who have inhabited it from primitive times to the present. Doubtless the first nomadic Indians who came upon the desert found it as forbidding a region as did the white men who arrived thousands of years later. Both groups gradually learned to survive by persistence and ingenuity.

II THE ORIGINAL OCCUPANTS

Man has inhabited the Americas for a relatively brief period, while evidence indicates that he has roamed the other continents of the world for several hundred thousand years. At some unknown time and place the forebears of the American Indians came to North America from the Old World, perhaps by way of the Bering Strait. The drift of the first population may have followed the Rockies and Andes into the two continents. These people probably moved westward from the eastern flanks of the Rockies through South Pass into the Great Basin and eastward onto the Great Plains and beyond the Mississippi.

Some time later they drifted into the desert regions of the Southwest, thence into Mexico, and finally into South America. All of this probably had its beginning as long as 25,000 years ago; fully half this time may have elapsed before they reached the tip of South America. Spear points have been found in Sandia Cave and elsewhere in the Southwest which indicate that people lived there possibly as early as 20,000 years ago.

Perhaps some 10,000 years later the famous Folsom point came into use. It was first discovered in 1926 on the desert near Folsom, New Mexico. That point was found near the bones of a giant bison that had become extinct at the end of the Ice Age. Discoveries of similar spear points along the eastern edge of the Great American Desert indicate that the ancient inhabitants of North America roamed there extensively, well before the last glacier retreated about 8000 B.C.

For unknown reasons the highest civilizations developed in the arid regions of the New World, especially among the Aztecs of Mexico and the Incas of Peru. These people, along with the Mayas of Yucatán, excelled in architecture, weaving, pottery making, and agriculture. The early inhabitants of Mesa Verde, near the common corner of Utah, Colorado, New Mexico, and Arizona, and those of the desert canyons and river valleys of Arizona and New Mexico, likewise were superior craftsmen and farmers. Their culture, though not as advanced as that of the Aztecs and Incas, nevertheless remained of a higher quality than anything produced by the nomadic tribes scattered throughout the United States.

The first human inhabitants of the Great American Desert faced the same problems as the wild animals did in adapting themselves to the arid climate. Probably they did not come into the desert voluntarily to make it their final home, but rather were pushed into it by stronger and more warlike tribes. In time they learned to build houses that were reasonably comfortable in summer and winter. They diverted water from the streams to irrigate fields of corn, beans, and squash, hunted the small desert deer, and squeezed some sort of use out of nearly every wild plant on their sun-dazzled horizon. Doubtless they learned that the desert offered many advantages, such as a warm, healthful climate, a ready supply of dry wood for their fires, and materials for making clothing, utensils, and shelter.

Like the plants and animals, these primitive inhabitants of the desert faced the problem of water, and so they naturally gathered near lakes, streams, and springs. Some became sedentary, but for the most part they were nomadic hunters who drifted from place to place. Eventually an individual tribe claimed a particular valley, canyon, mesa, or plain as its own until stronger neighbors, droughts, or shortage of game forced it to migrate elsewhere.

Long before the bow and arrow came into use these ancient people hunted and fought with spears, clubs, slings, atlatls or throwing sticks, and bolas—cords weighted at either end with rocks, which were slung around a wild animal's legs to trip it up. Except for scattered fragments of weapons and tools, they left few artifacts. Even though they stayed in the same general areas for centuries, they must have been always moving, following the seasons and animals from hills to valleys and plains and back again. By the sixteenth century, when the first white man arrived among them, the peoples of the Great American Desert had separated into a number of tribes, bands, and family groups. They also had developed distinct cultures and habits and spoke a variety of languages.

Anthropologists are not certain of the origin of all the western Indians, nor of their relationship to one another. According to a prevalent theory, those that came to occupy the southern portion of the Great American Desert had migrated there from the Mesa Verde area. These people are known to us as the Anasazi, a Navajo word for "Ancient Ones." Their early homeland was a high, broken country of red rock canyons, sagebrush flats, juniper ridges, and pine-covered mountains and plateaus. They settled on this plateau at some remote period, and it seems fairly certain that they had completely abandoned their wonderful cities and cliff-houses by the end of the thirteenth century. Tree ring dates indicate that a protracted drought struck the region in 1276; it continued for twenty-four years. Perhaps it was the drought that drove them southward, though it may have been fierce nomadic tribes—ancestors of today's Navajo and Apache—that swept down from the north.

In time the Anasazi people regrouped in northeastern Arizona, along the Rio Grande in central New Mexico, and near the present border between the two states. They located chiefly in oasis-like spots near streams and springs, turned to farming, and built cities across canyon floors, on tops of mesas, or in the vast natural caverns that scarred the sides of the cliffs. Some piled adobe rooms on top of each other to produce compact structures four or five stories high. Because they were town builders, the Spaniards would call these people Pueblo Indians.

Reports from early expeditions indicate that there were more than seventy pueblos, with a population of some 30,000, scattered from the Hopi towns in north-central Arizona eastward to the Pecos River on the western edge of the Great Plains and from the region of Socorro, New Mexico, on the south to Taos on the north. These people spoke a variety of languages and dialects, but their way of life was basically the same. They learned to cope with the arid climate, and their thick-walled houses required no air-conditioning in summer or central heating in winter. They made beautiful pottery and jewelry, irrigated their fields, and obtained food, medicine, and liquid from the plants. Their many kivas and dance courts suggest that they must have had considerable time for their religious ceremonies.

The ancient desert people along the Gila and Salt rivers experienced a parallel development with those of Mesa Verde. They are known as the Hohokam—a Pima word meaning "those who have gone." A century after the cliff houses and canyon cities of Mesa Verde had been abandoned, the Hohokam also vanished. Archeologists believe that the modern Papago and Pima of southern Arizona are their descendants. The Hohokam built miles of irrigation canals, tremendous undertakings comparable to the water systems of the city builders in the Valley of Mexico. Some of their ditches were twenty-five feet wide and fifteen feet deep, with a network along the Salt River, near present-day Phoenix, totaling 150 miles.[1] The first Europeans to see these structures assumed that

---

[1] According to studies by Jesse D. Jennings and others, the disappearance of the Hohokam culture might have been caused by flooding and inundation of farm lands rather than drought.

they had been built to supply water for once great cities, but the Hohokam were farmers, not city dwellers.

Long after the first white man arrived, the Pima and Papago continued to live in the same area in basically the same way as the Hohokam. In comparison with the modern age, their engineering knowledge was simple, but they were more successful than has been realized in managing the available water for farming. By diverting it from the Gila and Salt rivers, or by trapping water behind small terraces of dry stone masonry built across intermittent tributaries, they were able to grow basic food crops. Later they acquired wheat and cotton from the Spaniards. They also obtained livestock and learned the importance of grazing in their desert homeland. Before the Anglo-Americans arrived in the nineteenth century they had become excellent farmers and cattle and sheep raisers.

Late in the eighteenth century, the Spanish explorer Juan Bautista de Anza passed through the country of the Yuma and Cajuenche along the lower Colorado. He saw wheat growing, and stubble fields where maize, beans, calabashes, and muskmelons had been raised "in such abundance that we have marveled." Anza observed that the local people did not need to irrigate the desert soil, but depended upon the wet silt deposit brought down by the melting snows in the distant mountains. Like the Egyptians, they planted their crops in the moist soil when the river receded and harvested them before the earth was baked by the summer heat.

Traces of a third ancient culture, the Mogollon, likewise have been found in the southern portion of the Great American Desert. But at some time before 1000 A.D. the separate cultures and identities of the Mogollon people became blurred by outsiders who moved into west-central New Mexico. During the next three or four centuries all the southwestern Indians seemed to have regrouped.

Not only did the early inhabitants of the desert adapt themselves to their hostile environment; they made the land work for them. They experimented with and found uses for an unusual number of living things. From the mesquite tree many tribes obtained a bean that became a staple food, as did the seeds of small annual sage called chia. The fruit of the prickly pear and sunflower seeds likewise furnished nourishment. The Mescalero Apache made a highly nutritious and much admired dessert, as well as an intoxicant, from the mescal plant. Some Apaches carried on a trade in roasted mescal with the village-dwelling Pueblos, who did not have it to roast.

Dwellers of the desert also knew how to obtain water from the barrel cactus in emergencies. They first cut away a section from the top of the plant, or crushed it with a stone. Then they used a stick to pound the white tissues of the interior to a pulp, forming a cavity capable of holding one or two gallons of water. By squeezing the pulp between their hands they captured a few pints of drinkable liquid. This trick doubtless saved many lives.

In the higher elevations the desert Indians utilized the young shoots of the century plant by roasting them in stone-lined pits. They also harvested nuts of the piñon, and they gathered acorns, which they made edible by crushing them with stones and leaching out the bitter tannic acid with warm water. In addition to wheat, the desert people also obtained from the Spaniards such food crops as watermelons, chilies, onions, and peaches. But even under the best conditions food was not plentiful, and the struggle for it was continuous. Mere survival became a major achievement in itself.

Indians of the high plains region of the Great American Desert experienced a culture that was different in many ways. Basically they remained a desert people, yet they were more nomadic and more warlike than the Pueblo, Pima, and Papago. The Plains Indians depended almost exclusively upon hunting; they did not construct permanent buidings or settle in villages. Unlike the Pueblo they did not alter the environment to make the land work for them, but they adapted themselves admirably to what they found. In many ways they enjoyed a better life than the more sedentary tribes to the south, for while their diet was less varied their food supply was more abundant.

Anthropologists and historians perhaps will never completely untangle the mystery surrounding the origin of the Plains Indians or the relationship of one tribe to another, for they sprang from several different roots. For untold centuries these New World hunters and farmers lived on the plains and slopes of the mountains. Perhaps the first Indians came onto the plains as long as 10,000 years ago to hunt deer and buffalo. Eventually a few of them settled down along the river courses to grow corn. They made pottery and stone knives and spears, and when water became scarce they moved their meager possessions from place to place with the help of dogs. Perhaps their first houses were made of sticks, grass, or skins, but in time some tribes learned to build earth mounds that protected them from the scorching heat of summer and the cold blizzards of winter.

A few hundred years before the Europeans arrived, other peoples pushed onto the plains from the north, south, and east. The inexhaustible buffalo made it unnecessary to grow crops or to make pottery, and eventually the plains people neglected both. In spite of the great diversity of their origins the various plains tribes grew remarkably alike, different only in their style of decorating moccasins, arrow feathering, the manner in which they pitched their tipis, and the ceremonies they regularly observed. The open land lent itself to a restless way of life, to mysticism, and to dreams. Tribes came and went, consolidated to form new ones, or split into smaller groups through feuds and wars. But always they adjusted their lives and actions to the great game herds, which moved across the rolling terrain like dark clouds.

To the Indian the buffalo was a gift from heaven, and it seemed to be endowed with supernatural powers. It was never used as a beast of burden, as the camel and llama were by other desert dwellers of the world, because to the plains tribes the buffalo represented food, clothing, and shelter. Before the arrival of the horse, introduced to them by the Spaniards, the nomads of the Great American Desert stalked the gregarious buffalo on foot, often creeping upon them disguised in animal skins or stampeding them into canyons or over cliffs. Sometimes they set the dry prairie grass on fire to frighten a herd into motion. But once they were mounted and equipped with guns, the Indians suddenly found hunting much richer. The horse enabled them to find the buffalo more easily and thus in a few hours obtain enough meat to feed a whole tribe for weeks or even months.

All parts of the buffalo were utilized: the horns, hoofs, bones, skin, hair, entrails, blood, and muscles. The Indians learned that parts of the buffalo—which white hunters later discarded—prevented scurvy or other diseases resulting from an unbalanced diet. The dried meat, especially when pounded up with suet, marrow, and wild cherries for pemmican, would last indefinitely and could be moved in large quantities. Eighteen or twenty dressed hides sewed together made a room fifteen feet across, capable of accommodating a large family. The sides of the tipi could be raised in summer for ventilation, while a small fire in winter would keep the interior comfortably warm. After the Indians acquired the horse they used the lodge poles as travois to transport tipis and other possessions.

Next to the buffalo the horse was the Plains Indian's most valuable possession. This animal had been native to prehistoric America, but had become extinct in the New World long before the Spaniards arrived near the close of the fifteenth century. Twenty-five years after Cortés landed in Mexico in 1519 with ten stallions, five mares, and a foal, wild horses were roaming the plains and deserts of the American West. Exactly when the first Indian domesticated wild horses or stole them from the Spaniards remains unknown; but the horse frontier moved in from the south, and by 1700 the Crow, Cheyenne, Arapaho, Kiowa, Comanche, and Apache of the high plains were mounted, as were some tribes of the prairies further east. The horse furnished the ultimate weapon for wars and hunts. Eventually the gun and the horse met on the frontier to create the archetype of the American Indian—"the feather streaming, buffalo-chasing, wild-riding, reckless fighting Indians of the plains."

As the great Indian cultures in other parts of the Western Hemisphere all but disappeared, the Plains Indian came into his own. He was less "Indian" than any of his predecessors down through the ages of native history, but he was certainly the most picturesque, and the most free and independent. He also was the most ferocious and cruel, and the most difficult to subdue. The foot people of the plains were no match for mounted tribesmen who could dash upon them with the speed of the wind. And those who failed to obtain horses were either exterminated or driven further into the mountains and desert country.

By the seventeeth century the high plains region of the Great American Desert was the undisputed possession of seven or eight tribes, all mounted and armed with guns. Each warrior counted his fortune in terms of horses, and his status depended not only upon his skill as a rider but also on his ability to capture an enemy's best stock by stealth. Separate tribes had their individual hunting grounds, which they jealously protected from intruders, red or white. The Crow claimed most of eastern Montana and a corner of Wyoming. Below them were the Northern Cheyenne of Wyoming and further south in Colorado the Arapaho, Southern Cheyenne, and Kiowa. Various bands of Comanches, Kiowas, and plains Apaches roamed through the Texas Panhandle and northeastern New Mexico. Altogether the tribes of the high plains probably never totaled more than 10,000, they controlled an area several times larger than New England. By 1800 their culture and that of their eastern neighbors, the Sioux, Pawnee, and Kansa, resembled each other closely. By then these prairie tribes were also mounted and subsisted principally upon the buffalo.

West of the Rockies and east of the great wall of the Sierra Nevada roamed numerous bands of primitive Indians whose ancestors we know even less about than those of the people of the high plains or of Arizona and New Mexico. Except for the Ute and Shoshoni, who ranged up and down Utah and Wyoming and eastward into the Colorado Rockies, the Indians of this area had neither horses to ride nor buffalo to chase. The sun-cracked wastes of Utah and Nevada and southern Idaho were too poor in grass and water to support large animals, and it is not surprising that the Basin people were on the edge of starvation most of the time. Indians who possessed horses and lived in more habitable regions looked down upon these impoverished tribes and treated them with contempt. White traders of the nineteenth century often considered them so worthless that they shot them in their desert hiding places merely for sport.

The various bands of the intermountain region must have had a common origin, for they had short legs and dark skin and spoke a Shoshoni dialect. Whites called them "Digger Indians" because they dug for roots, lizards, and rodents, very much as the primitive tribes of the Kalahari Desert of South Africa do to this day. Anthropologists have separated the Digger Indians into distinct tribes. The Bannock occupied southern Idaho in the early nineteenth century; the Gosiute roamed east of the Great Salt Lake; and the desert Shoshoni, Paiute, and Washo were scattered over the vast basin country of Utah. To the south in Arizona and California lived the Mojave and Yuma, equally poor, primitive, and miserable.

Apparently all of the Basin tribes lived very much the same way in the nineteenth century as their ancestors who occupied the sagebrush, red rock canyons, and scorched wastelands had centuries earlier. Their ceremonies were fewer and their culture less developed than those of any other inhabitants of the Great American Desert, primarily because they were so occupied with finding something to eat. One of the first Americans to discover them was Jedediah Smith, who crossed the Great Basin in 1827 en route from the Great Salt Lake to southern California. His comment that they were "the most miserable objects in creation" was typical of the observations that came later. Practically no one had a kind word for them, and Mark Twain called them "the wretchedist type of mankind I have ever seen."

Father De Smet, the Jesuit missionary from St. Louis, spent a few weeks among the Great Basin people in 1841 and observed that probably no inhabitants of the world lived in a deeper state of corruption.

> Their lands are uncultivated heaths, their habitations are holes in rock or the natural crevices of the ground, and their only arms, arrows and sharp-pointed sticks. Two, three, or at most four of them may be seen in company, roving over the sterile plains in quest of ants and grasshoppers, on which they feed. When they find some insipid root, or a few nauseous seeds, they make, as they imagine, a delicious repast. They are so timid, that it is difficult to get near them; the appearance of a stranger alarms them; and conversational signs quickly spread the news amongst them. Every one, thereupon hides himself in a hole; and in an instant the miserable people disappear and vanish like a shadow. Sometimes, however, they venture out of their hiding places, and offer their newly born infants to the whites in exchange for some trifling article.

Most of the Great Basin people lived in brush wickiups that did not even afford room for standing. They seem to have had few skills other than basket making, and certainly their greatest accomplishment was survival in a land that no one else wanted. Because of the sparseness of natural resources, population density naturally was low. Indian groups larger than a family were never more than temporary, seasonal gatherings, brought together by the annual harvest of pine nuts. During the remainder of the year most families moved systematically over a poorly defined territory; and anthropologists estimate that before the white man arrived in the Great Basin, one native needed the natural products of twenty-five square miles for subsistence. The Paiute later became adept at stealing horses from California ranches and caused minor concern to Pony Express riders and drivers on the Overland Stage. But for the most part the Basin people were too weak to cause much trouble, and in the end they attached themselves to towns and settlements as laborers or beggars.

Millions of primitive people lived out their lives on the Great American Desert without ever knowing the existence of any other environment. Perhaps most died from natural causes, but the eternal struggle for survival involved more than a continuous battle with nature. For most of the four centuries since the Spaniards arrived, the desert has witnessed warfare between two societies—Indian and white. Inevitably the weak had to give way to the strong.

III THE WHITE MAN'S ARRIVAL

Though the Spaniards altered the landscape only slightly during their three centuries of occupation, they left the indubitable stamp of their culture upon the southern half of the inland province. From Texas to southern California their influence is still evident in place names, architecture, land laws, and ranching and irrigation techniques. The voluminous records and documents that they left, and the legends and myths that followed in their wake, have furnished theme and color for a myriad of writers.

In whatever enterprise the Spanish Empire might have been deficient, it was not lacking in the fields of exploration and conquest. For sheer boldness, imagination, and fortitude the Spaniards had few equals. And it was natural and inevitable that they would be the first Europeans to discover and occupy the great desert of North America. There they did not find what they were looking for, but in many ways its climate and landscape resembled their native homeland. Even so, the

Spanish Explorations, 16th Century

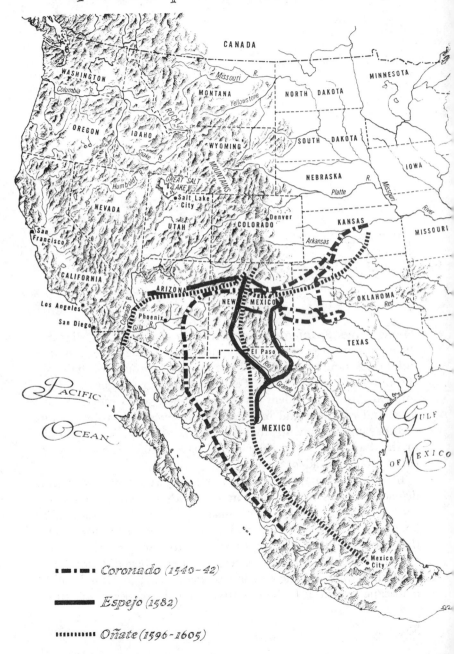

■ ─ ■ ─ ■ Coronado (1540-42)

━━━━ Espejo (1582)

▪▪▪▪▪▪▪ Oñate (1596-1605)

Spanish Explorations, 18th Century

— — — — — — — *Anza (1775-76)*

▪▪▪▪▪▪▪▪▪▪▪▪▪▪▪ *Garcés (1776)*

━━━━━━━ *Domínguez-Escalante (1776-77)*

process of adjusting to the arid environment was long and difficult.

The Spaniards had several motives in coming to the Great American Desert. Primarily they hoped to find gold and other precious metals, as had Cortés in the Valley of Mexico and Pizarro in Peru. They also wanted to solve the great geographical mystery north of Mexico; they believed that it would yield a direct water passage to India. Somewhere within the North American continent must lie a water course that flowed directly into the Pacific: a Northwest Passage, Strait of Anián, or Buenaventura River. The nation that discovered it first would control the North American continent. Adventure, a desire for land, and propagation of the Catholic faith were among the other motivating forces that lured the Spaniards northward from Mexico.

Preparation for the first extensive exploration of the northern frontier of New Spain began in 1536. In that year Álvar Nuñez Cabeza de Vaca wandered into the frontier outpost of Culiacán, on the far Pacific shore of Mexico, with three other survivors of the ill-fated Narváez expedition, which six years earlier had made its way from Florida to the Texas coast. Cabeza de Vaca relayed tales from the Indians that the country to the far north contained seven great cities which were said to contain much gold. The Spaniards eventually launched several expeditions in search of the so-called Cities of Cíbola, both by sea and by land. The sea voyages accomplished very little, but the expeditions by land ultimately resulted in a systematic exploration of the Great American Desert as far north as present Utah and Colorado and from the Colorado River on the west to well beyond the Pecos River on the east.

The most extensive of the four land expeditions was led by the young nobleman Francisco Vásquez de Coronado, who left Culiacán in 1540 with a force of 225 cavalrymen, 60 footmen, 5 friars, 1000 Indians, and approximately 1500 horses, mules, and cattle. So much has been written about this great expedition and the disappointment and disgrace it brought to its leader that a catalogue of details might seem unnecessary. Yet to omit Coronado from the history of the Great American Desert would be comparable to ignoring Columbus's voyage in 1492 in a comprehensive history of the Western Hemisphere.

Before Coronado reached the present border of Arizona he met a party of returning scouts led by Marcos de Niza, who reported that the land ahead was an arid desert with little to offer. In spite of this report, an advance party pushed on and eventually reached the first of the fabled "seven cities," Háwikuh, a Zuñi village of stone and adobe houses near the present New Mexico-Arizona line. While waiting for the main army to come forward, Coronado sent out expeditions in various directions. One of the parties explored as far west as southern California, where its commander, Melchior Díaz, received a severe injury in a hunting accident. His men carried him back toward Coronado's base, but he succumbed after twenty days of intense pain. Díaz was buried somewhere in the desert in southwestern Arizona. Had fortune been with him, he might have discovered that California contained more hidden gold than the Spaniards ever found in Mexico or Peru.

As other small parties wandered about the desert they learned from the Indians of a great river many leagues[1] to the north. Twelve mounted soldiers under Captain López de Cárdenas went forward to search for it. At the Moqui (Hopi) villages in present northeastern Arizona, Cárdenas obtained guides and provisions before renewing the journey to the northwest. Indians were sent ahead of the main party with jugs of water, which they buried in the sand. Even so there was much suffering during the twelve-day journey beyond the villages. The party reached the Colorado River near the Utah-Arizona line. Its banks were so high there that the Spaniards believed themselves to be three or four leagues above the river bed. From the south rim of the Grand Canyon the stream below looked no more than a few feet wide, but the Indians assured them that its width exceeded half a league.

[1] A Spanish league in the sixteenth century was approximately three miles.

According to a Spanish chronicler who was a member of the party, they spent three days searching for a place to descend. An officer and two soldiers finally made the attempt and were out of sight within two or three hours. They returned late in the afternoon of the same day to report that it was impossible to reach the bottom, and that some rocks, which seen from above had appeared no higher than a man, were taller than the Cathedral of Seville. Though the river remained in view during the several days that the Spaniards continued along the rim of the canyon, the party suffered severely from lack of water. Finally, no alternative remained but to return to Coronado's headquarters.

Meanwhile, the main army had arrived from northern Mexico to assist in the conquest of the "seven cities." But one disappointment followed another, for the cities yielded no gold and precious little food. Coronado now turned toward the east, to the valley of another river, which flowed from north to south—the Rio Grande. The move was carried out in stages, with various parties pursuing different routes so as to learn as much about the country as possible. The written narratives of the expedition record very little about it except that the river was eight days' journey from the Zuñi settlements of Arizona and that the travelers suffered from heat and thirst during the day and from the cold at night.

One group came upon a town built upon a rock some three hundred feet above the desert plains. This was the sky city of Ácoma, accessible only by a narrow stairway. The inhabitants proved hostile at first, but the noise made by Spanish muskets—which could barely fire a ball to the top of the rock—frightened the natives into submission. After obtaining food and water, the white travelers and their strange animals moved on toward the river. Gradually the various Spanish parties assembled at Tiguex, a province of approximately twelve occupied towns and half a dozen more that had been abandoned and destroyed by the wild tribes of the desert plains. According to the Spaniards, the nearby provinces contained dozens of towns scattered up and down and on both sides of the river for several leagues. The largest of these they called Braba (Taos) and estimated its population at 15,000.

From Tiguex [2] the Spaniards continued to send out exploring parties to "pacify" the natives at the numerous pueblos. Many Indians were killed, women violated, food confiscated, and clothes frequently taken from the backs of the natives. Rather than submit to Spanish cruelty, they often abandoned their villages and escaped into the desert or nearby mountains, leaving the enemy to live on whatever could be scraped from the barren country. Heavy snows and meager provisions during the winter of 1541 brought great suffering to the army. As spring approached, Coronado prepared once again to move eastward. Meanwhile, two Indians had been found in New Mexico who claimed to be natives of Quivira, a city on the far edge of the buffalo plains that allegedly contained untold quantities of gold and precious stones. They promised to lead the Spaniards there, but evidently their real purpose was to lead them out of New Mexico in the hope that they would perish on the plains.

The long trek from the Rio Grande to southern Kansas added to the growing list of Coronado's disappointments. The main Spanish force turned back somewhere in the Texas Panhandle, while the commander and a small party moved on across western Oklahoma and eventually discovered the collection of straw huts called Quivira. The location was somewhere in southeastern Kansas, perhaps near present Wichita. Coronado's men might have obtained some small satisfaction from the execution of the Indian guides who had betrayed them with false promises, but otherwise the trip was fruitless. The barren country left them no choice but to return to the Rio Grande and ultimately to Mexico.

By the end of 1542 the physically and spiritually depleted commander appeared before the viceroy to report upon his

2 Bancroft puts the principal Tiguex pueblo, which Coronado made his permanent headquarters, in the vicinity of present Bernalillo, between Albuquerque and Sante Fe.

failures. Approximately a hundred men had survived the ordeal of two years in the arid country and were able to return to Mexico; more than one hundred and seventy Spaniards had died of hunger and thirst, became lost, or were killed by the Indians. Two soldiers remained in Kansas to experience an unknown fate, while three friars and six laymen stayed on in New Mexico. The missionaries eventually became martyrs to their faith. In 1547 one of the laymen, Andrés de Campo, staggered into Mexico City to relate a tale of miraculous escape from the Indians and aimless wandering over mountains, plains, and deserts.

Coronado had accomplished more than his superiors appreciated at the time. He laid the foundation for future missionary work and exploration, gathered valuable information about the southern half of the Great American Desert, and provided the first written description of it. The chief historian of the expedition, Pedro Castañeda, thought of the buffalo plains east of the Rio Grande as "deserts" and was baffled by their flatness. "This country," he wrote, "is like a bowl, so that when a man sits down, the horizon surrounds him all around at the distance of a musket shot." He also observed that the travelers learned to mark their route with occasional piles of bones and cow dung so that the rear guard could follow the advance party. Though the buffalo supplied them with an abundance of meat, the intense heat and shortage of water caused constant suffering. It is remarkable that the Spaniards who came later made such small use of the narratives produced by the Coronado expedition. These writings contained little exaggeration and mystery, and from them it is possible to trace with reasonable accuracy the route taken across Arizona, New Mexico, Texas, and Oklahoma. Yet within a generation Coronado's geographic discoveries were well-nigh forgotten.

The Spaniards meanwhile pushed their settlements northward to within a few hundred miles of the Rio Grande and the Gila River. In 1581 a Franciscan missionary named Agustín Rodríguez heard rumors of a superior people who dressed in cotton and whose home was in the north. The good friar obtained permission from the viceroy to visit the mysterious region with a party not to exceed twenty men. Two other Franciscans, eight soldiers, and ten Indians were quickly recruited for the journey. The party set out from Santa Bárbara on the Conchos River in Nueva Viscaya (Chihuahua) on June 6, 1581. It followed the Conchos northward to its confluence with the Rio Grande, veered with this stream toward the northwest and continued to the vicinity of Coronado's Tiguex. According to meager details furnished by a member of the expedition, the last nineteen days of the journey was "through a desert, uninhabited country." While the soldiers explored the region on both sides of the Rio Grande, the friars carried out missionary work among the natives in the Tiguex province.

There is considerable confusion regarding the fate of the Rodríguez party, especially the circumstances that led to the murder of the missionaries. The soldiers returned to Mexico within a relatively brief time, while the friars remained behind with three servants to work among the natives. Ultimately the servants fled south to Santa Bárbara, where they reported that one of the three friars had been killed for certain and perhaps the other two as well. The Franciscan fathers in Mexico, and the viceroy, were much troubled by this news. It was felt that another expedition should be sent north to determine the fate of the missionaries and to investigate reports brought by the returning soldiers of rich silver mines in the province along the upper Rio Grande.

Fortunately a rich citizen of Mexico, Don Antonio de Espejo, chanced to be in Nueva Viscaya at the time, and he volunteered to outfit and command a rescue expedition into present New Mexico. Permission was granted, and on November 10, 1582, Espejo and a small party of soldiers, 115 horses and mules, and a number of native servants departed by the same route taken by Father Rodríguez two years earlier. They reached the Rio Grande fifteen days later and continued in the direction of present El Paso. Espejo discovered that the

Indians along the river were progressively superior to those further south. Their villages were flat roofed and built of stone and adobe, and at one settlement he observed that the natives had a smattering of Christianity, which they claimed to have obtained from "three Christians and a Negro" many years before. These could have been no other than Cabeza de Vaca and his companions, who had wandered through the region half a century earlier.

Espejo eventually crossed into present New Mexico and continued up the Rio Grande, coming upon numerous pueblos that had been visited previously by Coronado and Rodríguez. In the Tiguex province he discovered the natives who had killed two of the missionaries, Rodríguez and López. Fearing punishment at the hands of the Spaniards, the natives fled to the mountains, leaving "a plentiful store of foods." At another village on the buffalo plains, two days east of the Rio Grande, Esepejo learned of the murder of the third missionary, Father Santa María. The Indians were probably surprised that he delivered no retribution to the culprits, but Espejo wanted them to remain friendly in the event that the country contained precious metals.

Before retiring to Nueva Viscaya, Espejo visited more than a dozen pueblos in the northern part of the region. He then made a tour of several leagues across the desert to Ácoma and later reported that some 6000 Indians lived in the village on the mesa top. Nearby the Acomans had cultivated fields which they irrigated from a dammed stream. At Zuñi, some seventy-five miles westward, the Spaniards found several crosses and three Christian Indians still living who had come with Coronado forty years previously. They told the travelers that a great lake with many settlements along its shore existed sixty days' journey to the west. Naturally the people there had an abundance of wealth and valuable metals. This legendary lake, incidentally, would crop up again and again. By the eighteenth century the Spanish geographers were showing it on maps in the approximate location and size of all of Utah and Idaho, with two large outlets flowing directly west to the Pacific.

Extensive explorations of present Arizona failed to locate the lake, but Espejo did discover evidence of silver near present Prescott. From other Indians he met at various desert and mountain settlements he received similar accounts of a rich people living along the shores of a lake, the location of which remained vague. For the most part the natives encountered were friendly, and more impressed with the strange animals than the men who rode them. They cultivated maize, wove cloth, and gathered wild grapes, walnuts, and Indian figs. Espejo eventually turned back to the Rio Grande and continued eastward to the Pecos River to blaze a new trail southward into Nueva Viscaya. In all he visited seventy-four pueblos, encountered less difficulty than Coronado had experienced, and achieved a small degree of success in locating evidence of silver deposits in Arizona.

For the next fifteen years the Spaniards made numerous attempts to colonize the northern province. Their objective was not only precious metals; they also wanted land, which meant almost as much in power and prestige as did gold and silver. Although a few colonies were planted on the upper Rio Grande and the Pecos River during this period, none remained permanent and few of the settlers escaped the hostility of the natives. Finally in April 1598, Juan de Oñate took formal possession of New Mexico and "all the adjoining provinces" for God, the king, and himself.

The preparations for Oñate's *entrada* into New Mexico took three years and considerable money. His contract called for a company of 200 men, though some accounts place his total party at approximately 400. Included among the participants were ten Franciscans, 130 soldier colonists, and several servants and Indians. In addition, there were several thousand head of cattle, sheep and goats, and enough grain seed, supplies, ammunition, and tools to fill 83 wagons. Instead of following the Conchos River, as earlier explorers had done, the Oñate company took a direct route from Santa Bárbara to the Rio Grande, striking the river a few leagues below present El Paso. They encountered no trouble from the various natives along the upper Rio Grande, who by this time must have become reconciled to the sight of one Spanish party after another trekking through their land.

The procession of *caballeros,* women, children, wagons, and animals eventually stopped on the east bank of the Rio Grande some distance above present Santa Fe at a site which Oñate christened San Juan de los Caballeros. Almost immediately the colonists set to work digging irrigation ditches and constructing a church, while the missionaries visited the nearby pueblos. Meanwhile, Oñate sent sixty men eastward to hunt buffalo while he headed westward with another company. At Ácoma, Zuñi, and the Hopi villages of Arizona the natives were forced to submit to Spanish rule. The commander then felt free to continue his explorations, with the idea of examining the mines discovered by. Espejo and then continuing on to the Pacific Coast.

Before departing from San Juan on the Rio Grande, Oñate had left orders for thirty members of the buffalo-hunting party to join him in the west as soon as they returned. These reinforcements, under the command of Juan Zaldívar, followed Oñate's trail across the desert to Ácoma. There they stopped temporarily for supplies, and were surprised by the friendly reception. The natives came down from the mesa and generously offered them all the food they could carry, but as some members of the company ascended the stairway to obtain the gifts they fell into a well-laid trap. After a desperate hand-to-hand fight, Zaldívar and twelve of his companions were slain. The survivors escaped across the desert and eventually overtook Oñate to relate the story of Indian treachery. The combined parties returned eastward to San Juan with the sad news of the massacre.

There was no recourse left to the Spaniards but to avenge the death of their comrades, to discourage other pueblos from similar action. Seventy men under Captain Vicente Zaldívar, brother of the slain officer, left the New Mexico capital early in 1599. As they approached Ácoma they could see the crowds of natives on top of the flat roofed houses above—men, women, and children dancing stark naked in an orgy of celebration as they hurled rocks and insults upon the Spaniards below. Captain Zaldívar ordered his men to pitch camp on the nearby plains and get some rest before launching an attack against the summit of the plateau. The assault began on January 22 and lasted three days. When the Spaniards reached the heights, they put torches to the houses and slaughtered the natives at a fearful rate.

Estimates of the number of Acomans killed vary from three to six thousand,[3] but even the minimum figure would make this the bloodiest battle ever fought in any part of the Great American Desert, if not the entire West. A few Indians somehow managed to escape, and their descendants ultimately returned to the mesa to occupy it permanently. But most of the handful of survivors were taken back to San Juan. Here the women and children were enslaved, and the men over twenty-five had one foot cut off, while the younger ones were sentenced to twenty years of hard labor. The thoroughness with which the Acomans were defeated and the severity of their punishment proved an object lesson to all of the natives of New Mexico. Not for eighty more years would there be another Pueblo uprising against white authority.

From the fall of Ácoma to 1821, when Mexico won its independence from Spain, the history of the southern half of the Great American Desert is largely one of exploration, colonization, zealous missionization and Indian wars. Oñate remained as governor of the province until 1607, during which time he undertook a series of remarkable journeys. In June 1601 he left San Juan with eighty men for the buffalo plains to the east. His route, at least in part, was similar to Coronado's sixty years previously. It is not clear whether he reached Quivira, but he claimed to have visited many large villages in the east and to have seen utensils of gold in the possession of some of the natives. In general, his expedition accomplished nothing except to observe the country and its inhabitants. Meanwhile, disease and starvation had befallen

[3] The mesa upon which Ácoma is built hardly seems large enough to have accommodated such a dense population.

the colony, and most of the settlers and missionaries were in
retreat to the Conchos settlement in Nueva Viscaya.

Oñate acted quickly by sending troops to overtake the fleeing settlers. Some were caught and forced to return to the
upper Rio Grande, where the leaders were tried for sedition
and executed. The deserters later charged Oñate with unjust
cruelty to the natives and neglect of the white settlers. "I pray
that God may grant him the grace to do penance for all his
deeds," one of the missionaries wrote of the governor.

Realizing that the charges against him and the severe financial drain his ventures had brought upon the Spanish treasury
might lead to dismissal, Oñate made one last desperate effort
to get back into the good graces of the viceroy. Early in 1604
the governor started westward with a party of thirty men in
hopes of reaching the Pacific. This last expedition generally
paralleled that of Espejo's journey two decades earlier. Along
the way Oñate picked up rumors of a giant tribe of Amazons
who lived on a silver island further to the west, but he found
nothing resembling either. Eventually he reached the Colorado River and followed it south to the Gulf of California.
Somehow he got the impression that Baja California was an
island, and he fully expected that this information, coupled
with glowing reports of silver and gold, would restore him to
power. His hopes were vain, for when he got back to the Rio
Grande he learned that his removal from office was only a
matter of time. He therefore resigned in August 1607 and
prepared to face the inevitable charge of misconduct that had
befallen most of his predecessors.

Oñate was the last of the great Spanish adventurer-explor-
ers of the desert region of North America. For more than a
century the desert was left unexplored. Meanwhile, Spain concentrated her efforts in the missionary field and discouraged
further search for rich mines or a transcontinental water passage. A trickle of colonists continued from northern Mexico,
and the whites and Indians gradually learned to live together
and to adopt each others' customs. By 1680 the Spanish population approximated 3000 and lived chiefly in the upper Rio

Grande valley, between Taos and Isleta. The largest concentration was at Santa Fe, which became the capital of the province in 1610. A sizable settlement had also grown up at El Paso del Norte, two hundred miles to the south.

But considerable unrest stirred beneath the tranquil surface of the oasis towns. Supplies were always slow in arriving, and the Indians were becoming increasingly irritated with their Spanish overlords. They were required to pay heavy tribute in produce and services. Worse yet was the iron control held over their spiritual lives by the priests, who handed out severe sentences to unbelievers or those who practiced witchcraft. Floggings, imprisonment, slavery, and executions were all too common. Such actions naturally caused the converts to question the advantages of Christianity and to turn more and more to their own priests—sorcerers, the Spaniards called them.

Popé, a native priest or medicine man from the San Juan pueblo, came to obtain considerable influence among the Indians. He had been imprisoned for practicing witchcraft; upon his release he claimed an alliance with the Great Spirit. He then took most of the members of the northern pueblos into a bold scheme to murder the Spanish priests, officers, and white colonists. The plan was elaborately laid, with various attacks to begin simultaneously on August 13, 1680. The Spaniards learned of the revolt, but not in time to warn all of the intended victims. Popé meanwhile ordered attacks on the missions, garrison towns, and farms to begin at once. Some 400 were slaughtered, including twenty-one missionaries, but over 2000 Spaniards managed to escape and flee southward to the El Paso district.

For the first time in a century New Mexico was free of Spanish rule, and the natives were determined to destroy all vestiges of the hated white man's civilization. Noisy demonstrations, processions, and dances characterized the insane excitement of victory and freedom from restraint. Popé assumed complete power and traveled from pueblo to pueblo to supervise the tearing down of churches and burning of crosses and records. Use of the Spanish language was forbidden, men were allowed to put away their wives and take others to their liking, and none but native crops could be raised. The most beautiful women were reserved for Popé himself, as his authority went unchallenged.

For one reason or another the Spaniards were unable to mount an effective military expedition into the upper Rio Grand country during the next decade. In 1691 Don Diego de Vargas, scion of a distinguished Spanish family, was appointed governor of New Mexico, and one year later he set out on a reconnaissance of the northern province with sixty hand-picked soldiers, 150 Indians, and three priests. The time was opportune, for the pueblo people had fared rather poorly under Popé's autocratic rule. Not only had he become a tyrant, but periodic droughts and raids by the Apache and Navajo had made life even more miserable than ever. Vargas therefore found the task of reconquest easier than he had anticipated. Most of the pueblos surrendered without a fight, after which the inhabitants were subjected to lectures and absolved from their apostasy. On October 15, 1692, Vargas could write to the viceroy from Santa Fe announcing that he had conquered all the pueblos for thirty-six leagues up and down the Rio Grande and that the priests had baptized nearly a thousand children born in rebellion.

The Spaniards now turned their attention to the pueblos scattered beyond the Rio Grande. At Pecos on the east, and at the Ácoma, Zuñi, and the Hopi settlements in the desert region to the west, they encountered little opposition. Another 1200 children were baptized, and, except for a minor clash or two with the Apache, no blood was shed. This alone must have established some sort of record for the Spaniards. The next step was to bring in colonists and additional priests so that the farms could be reoccupied and churches rebuilt. Vargas therefore returned to northern Mexico satisfied with his accomplishments.

But the ease with which he reconquered the province soon proved an illusion. Upon his return late in 1693 with 800 settlers, soldiers, and priests, rumors had already spread among the natives that this time the Spaniards planned to kill all of the leaders of the revolt. At Santa Fe they refused to allow Vargas to enter the *villa*. The commander hoped to avoid conflict and decided to camp nearby and use persuasion with the natives. It was mid-December and snow covered the ground; twenty-two of the Spanish children died within a few days. On December 29 Vargas decided to attack. Fighting continued into the next day, and one soldier and several Indians were killed. The chief of the *villa* hanged himself at the moment of surrender, while seventy surviving Indian warriors were lined up and shot as an object lesson to the other pueblos. Approximately 400 women and children were enslaved and distributed among the Spanish officers and soldier colonists.

The fighting did not end with Santa Fe, for most of the natives of the nearby pueblos had to be subdued in much the same fashion. Some evacuated their towns when the Spanish troops approached, and they had to be hunted down. Frequently they took refuge on top of steep-walled mesas and superhuman efforts were required to dislodge them. Again and again Spanish soldiers overcame terrific odds in what seemed a never-ending slaughter on both sides. But the steady arrival of additional troops from Mexico, plus the attrition by war, starvation, and smallpox, finally destroyed the Indians' will to fight. Gradually they returned to their villages and settled down as subservient neighbors to the whites. Throughout the next century and a quarter the peoples of New Mexico merged into a heterogeneous mixture of Spanish and Indian blood.

In time the colonists achieved a degree of self-sufficiency and conformity. The great landholders, or *encomenderos*, divided the fields surrounding the Indian villages into plots for irrigated farming and ranching. Settlers received titles to individual strips of land, in exchange for which they labored for the master. The *encomendero* had the responsibility of protecting and "educating" his charges, building a church, and providing a priest. Sometimes he laid out a town around a small plaza, distributed lots for homes, and set aside community lands for wood and grazing.

In the self-sufficient economy of Spanish New Mexico there was need for little commercial intercourse other than the supplies brought up by caravan from Mexico. Settlers stayed close to the pueblos, but wealthy landholders and government officials made frequent journeys across the desert to distant settlements. They always traveled with armed guards and dozens of pack animals and spare mounts.

Spanish governors came and went, but few were able to enjoy a peaceful term of office. Though the pueblo people no longer gave the Spaniards trouble, the nomadic tribes that lived beyond the oasis settlements of the river valley presented a different story. Pressure from the north and east pushed the Apache, Comanche, Navajo, and Ute closer to the Pueblo, and these wild tribes made murderous attacks and raids on the settlements. By the middle of the eighteenth century all of the wild tribes were mounted and most of them were armed with muskets, which they had acquired from French traders from the Louisiana and Illinois country. Spain failed to bring the wild tribes completely under control, but her subjects in New Mexico did experience intervals of peace.

Most of the settlers of Spanish blood were concentrated at Albuquerque, Santa Fe, and Santa Cruz on the upper Rio Grande. The remainder lived on haciendas of the *encomenderos,* on *ranchos* of the smaller land holders, or in rural villages. Each of the larger pueblos had a Franciscan church run by one or more priests who exercised considerable control over the Indians. Also, there was an *alcalde,* usually a mestizo, whose powers resembled those of a feudal baron. The natives were required to till and harvest his crops on the hacienda and weave cotton and woolen cloth for his family. In addition, the women were forced to do housework and not infrequently perform other "services" for the personal gratification of the master.

The rich soil of the valley was extremely productive, and most of the farms were irrigated by the Rio Grande or its tributaries. The principal crops were wheat, cotton, maize, beans, and squash. Further south grapes were raised from which a superior wine was manufactured. But the main source of wealth and items of trade came from the livestock produced in great quantities on the haciendas: horses, sheep, goats, mules, turkeys, chickens, and ducks. Annual fairs were held at Taos, at which time Indians came from great distances from both sides of the Rio Grande. Here ensued a lively trade in items varying from livestock, fabrics, buffalo skins, hatchets, and captive children brought in by the Plains Indians. Occasionally French traders from Louisiana were admitted to the fairs, and their trade goods of knives, scissors, needles, mirrors, jew's-harps and other trinkets brought astronomical prices.

Spanish officials controlled all trade and sometimes permitted local citizens to conduct expeditions to the Indian country among the various tribes in Arizona, Utah, and Colorado, and as far east as Texas and Oklahoma. Caravans eventually reached California and extended south to Chihuahua, laying the foundation for the great Santa Fe trade, which was begun by the Anglo-Americans in the nineteenth century.

With Spanish power firmly entrenched and the Pueblo Indians too few and too weak to cause serious trouble, New Mexico settled down into the inertia that sooner or later befell all the Spanish provinces in the Western Hemisphere. Now and then there were feeble attempts by the Indians to revive the mysteries of their old religion, and petty quarrels among the *alcaldes*, priests, and military officials were chronic. Though the land did not reveal its hidden mineral wealth, the Spaniards were able to exploit the religious opportunities with courage and determination. Spanish soldiers and missionaries learned most of the geographic secrets of the Great American Desert from California to Texas, including parts of Colorado and Utah, and laid out most of the principal trails that are still used today. And Spanish settlers mastered the technique of survival in an arid climate. They learned to channel the water on to the land, how much watering the various crops needed, and which soils to irrigate and which ones to set aside for grazing. They learned to conserve their strength in the heat of the day, how to ventilate their homes for comfort, and how much and what type of clothing to wear. The settlers also discovered that they had to protect their mounts and livestock against the scorching heat of the desert, and learned to gauge how far animals could travel between watering places, and how much work both man and beast could endure.

The pueblos along the Rio Grande from El Paso to Taos represented the sole Spanish penetration into the Great American Desert for a hundred years following Oñate's *entrada* in 1598. Eventually Spain drove a small wedge of settlements from Sonora to the Gila River in southern Arizona, and later established others in Texas and up the California coast. But these outposts did not provide the permanent American empire for which Spain had hoped, and she remained content to nibble at the edges of the Great American Desert. Finally, internal dissension, Indian warfare, and pressure from Anglo-Americans in the nineteenth century collapsed her control completely.

IV THE NORTHERN MYSTERY

Bernard De Voto observed in *The Course of Empire* that "the dawn of knowledge is usually the false dawn." Perhaps in no realm of knowledge does this observation more aptly apply than in the field of geography—especially the geography of the northern half of the Great American Desert. The Spaniards called this region "the northern mystery," and with good reason. For almost three centuries they retained the hope that it contained great mineral wealth, and also that through it flowed an inland waterway offering a passage to the Pacific and a direct route to India. Their quest for the waterway was continued by the English, French, and Americans before the myth was finally laid to rest in the mid-nineteenth century.

Soon after Columbus returned to Spain from his initial voyage to America, European navigators began probing the coast lines of North and South America. Their desire for a passage through the great land mass was so urgent that they promptly invented one. The Spaniards called it the Strait of Anían, and the English referred to it as the Northwest Passage.

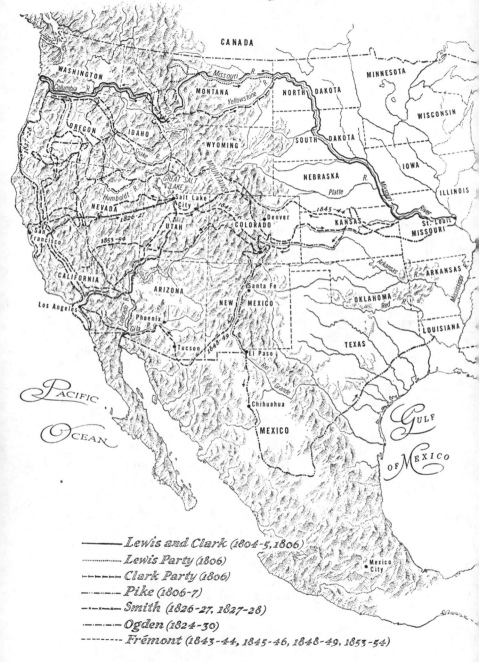

American Explorations

———— Lewis and Clark (1804-5, 1806)
·············· Lewis Party (1806)
– – – – – Clark Party (1806)
—··—··— Pike (1806-7)
—·—·— Smith (1826-27, 1827-28)
—···—···— Ogden (1824-30)
- - - - - - - - Frémont (1843-44, 1845-46, 1848-49, 1853-54)

The search finally narrowed to the interior of North America, and by the eighteenth century it was confined still further to the "northern mystery," the area between the Colorado and Columbia rivers. Gradually the notion of a strait gave way to the idea that there was a series of rivers flowing directly from the Rocky Mountains to the Pacific.

Serious attempts to solve the "northern mystery" began at about the time of the American Revolution. The man who led the way was one of the most heroic figures of American history—Eusebio Francisco Kino. This hardy Jesuit began his explorations into the southwestern corner of the Great American Desert in 1691, and for the next dozen years he and his fellow Jesuits pushed the Spanish frontier to the Gila and Colorado rivers in Arizona. They constructed several resident missions, the most famous being San Xavier del Bac, near Tucson, which is still in use today. To support these desert missions, Father Kino laid the foundation for modern farming and ranching in Arizona. He brought in cattle and sheep and grain and fruit seeds. And he supervised the rebuilding of ancient canals and the construction of new ones to divert the waters of the Gila to the thirsty land along its banks.

After Father Kino's death in 1711, the Arizona missions suffered periodically from neglect by the Spanish government and from Indian raids. Eventually Spain built *presidios,* or military garrisons, near the missions to ensure their permanency. She pushed a line of forts and missions across Texas to stop the advance of the French from Louisiana and another line up the California coast to check the English and Russians. By the end of the American Revolution her settlements formed a giant crescent, extending from San Francisco to Natchitoches, with the bottom rim of the crescent cutting an irregular pattern across the southern part of the Great American Desert.

Supplying these far-flung settlements was difficult. There was urgent need for more direct routes, especially between California and Mexico. During the years 1771–76, Juan Bautista de Anza and Father Francisco Hermenegildo Garcés thoroughly explored the region beyond San Xavier del Bac. Their various journeys carried them from present Tucson to the mouth of the Gila, up the Colorado to the vicinity of modern Needles, thence across the Mojave Desert to present San Bernardino, Los Angeles, and Bakersfield.

Beyond the Colorado, Anza's party encountered a belt of sand whose waterless expanse constituted the worst feature of any of the routes across the desert, even during the great migration of the Gold Rush. After six fruitless days and acute suffering from thirst, the company turned back from the shifting sand dunes. In the end they retreated to a lagoon near the Colorado, rested for two weeks, and finally turned the southern flank of the great barrier of sand. Though they proved that it was possible to take an overland route from northern Mexico to the Pacific Coast, they found that the extreme scarcity of water and pasturage and the vast sand dunes and scorching heat made it far from desirable.

Anza's second expedition (1775–76) was nevertheless a notable one. The march of 240 men, women, and children over 1600 miles from Culiacán to Monterey, with slender resources and equipment, was comparable to Lewis and Clark's great feat thirty years later. Only one death occurred in the long trek across the desert between the Arizona outpost and the California coast, but this was offset by the birth of three infants along the way. The journey was made amid varying conditions of drought, cold, snow, and rain, with the company at times going three days without water. Women and children had priority on the water, so that nearly a hundred head of stock succumbed to thirst.

During the course of their travels Father Garcés discovered the Kern River in southern California, which he called Río de San Felipe. According to the local Indians this stream was part of a larger system that originated far east of the Sierra Nevada Mountains in "Yuta" (Ute) country. The friar deduced from this misinformation that the interior country contained an inland sea and perhaps was drained by a number of rivers that were navigable all the way to the Pacific.

If this were true, then the headwaters of the streams could not be far from the settlements along the upper Rio Grande. Garcés' geographic speculation quickly found expression in a crude map drawn by one of his colleagues, Father Pedro Font, which showed much of present Utah and Nevada covered by water. Other geographers soon copied the idea and added elaborate river courses which connected the inland sea with the Pacific. Meanwhile, a Spanish expedition of major importance, led by Father Francisco Atanasio Domínguez and Father Francisco Silverstre Vélez de Escalante, entered the "northern mystery."

Domínguez and Escalante were the first white men to examine a considerable portion of the Great Basin and to contribute any firsthand information about it. Their party left Santa Fe in the same month and year that the Declaration of Independence was proclaimed by the thirteen English colonies. In addition to establishing a practical overland route to Monterey, the Spanish fathers planned to locate sites for future posts and missions. They traveled in a northwest direction until they reached the Colorado River a few leagues above present Grand Junction, Colorado. Domínguez and Escalante crossed the stream and continued in the same general direction, giving names to the various escarpments, canyons, and plateaus.

Eventually the Domínguez-Escalante party reached the Green River in the northeastern corner of present Utah at a latitude where it follows a southwestern course. This is the stream they called the San Buenaventura, in honor of a thirteenth-century theologian and minister-general of the Order of Friars Minor. It remained a prominent watercourse on most maps of the American West for the next seven decades. A few miles below the point of crossing, the Green River takes a sharp turn southward and eventually empties into the Colorado. Without suspecting this, the party proceeded westward into the Utah Valley, where it made the first entrance into the heart of the Great Basin. Several days later the Spaniards arrived upon the shores of Utah Lake and learned from the Indians of a larger body of water to the north. "The other lake with which this one communicates," Escalante wrote in his diary, "covers many leagues, and its waters are noxious and extremely salty . . . a person who moistens any part of his body with the water of the lake immediately feels much itching in the part that is wet." The lake in question, of course, was the Great Salt Lake, but the Spaniards did not determine its true location and size. Undoubtedly it was the fabled "lake of silver" which earlier explorers had heard about from the Indians, who easily could have confused the Spaniards' description of silver with salt.

Fathers Domínguez and Escalante turned south from Utah Lake to present Mills, Utah, on the Sevier River. The latitude and course of this stream gave every indication that it was the lower extension of the San Buenaventura (Green) River, which is exactly what the explorers assumed. Had they pursued either stream along its course, the error would have been discovered easily, for their headwaters are many miles apart. Nevertheless, Miera y Pacheco, the map maker who accompanied the expedition, joined the two bodies of water in an east-west course, conveniently cutting off the western limits at the map's edge. Others not only copied Miera's error, they extended the San Buenaventura to the Pacific. It took a long time to dispel the belief in its existence, and in the process the Great American Desert grudgingly yielded many of its geographic secrets.

As they renewed their circuitous route, the Spaniards began to suffer from the harsh conditions of the Great Basin. Cold weather was soon upon them, water and firewood became increasingly scarce, and they reluctantly abandoned the idea of reaching the Pacific. Instead, they turned back in the direction of Santa Fe. Near present Cedar City, Utah, they came upon a party of Indian women gathering grass seed. The sight of the Europeans so frightened the natives that they found it difficult to talk. "These Indian women were so poorly dressed that they wore only some pieces of buckskin hanging from their waists, which hardly covered what could be looked at without peril," Father Escalante wrote. "We bade them goodbye. . . ."

A few days later the travelers learned from another group along the trail that the Colorado River was a short distance away, and they quickened their pace to reach it. They were then on the last leg of their journey, and soon they were passing through country familiar to earlier Spanish adventurers—the land of the Zuñi and Hopi people of Arizona. On January 2, 1777, they arrived back at their base after a journey of almost six months and more than 1500 miles over some of the most difficult terrain in North America.

Perhaps it was just as well that the Spaniards did not follow through with the discovery of the San Buenaventura River, for they would only have known disappointment. Besides, they were destined shortly to lose all their empire in the Western Hemisphere, except for a few islands, to enemies from within and without. The warnings were ominous long before the close of the eighteenth century. From Louisiana, Missouri, and the Illinois country French traders were wandering into the frontier outposts of Taos and Santa Fe. Such visitors did not always receive a hearty welcome, even though their goods were much desired by the local inhabitants.

The French threat was removed in 1763, when Spain acquired the Louisiana Territory and extended its boundaries as far east as the Mississippi River. In the same year the British acquired Canada and soon pushed westward to the Pacific. The two powers eventually quarreled over control of the Columbia River country. By the Treaty of Nootka Sound in 1790 the Spaniards in effect pulled back to northern California. Ten years later Spain sold Louisiana to France, and in 1803 it became part of the United States. The international picture changed almost overnight as the young giant created by the thirteen states became a continental power. Spain's sudden alarm came too late, for she had been apathetic about mid-continent America for too long.

The aggressive Americans wasted no time in exploring their new possession west of the Mississippi and in frightening both Spain and England in the process. In fact, Thomas Jefferson had been making plans to explore the Far West since 1783, but for one reason or another his various schemes failed to materialize. When he became President the enterprise stood a better chance of success. Shortly after his inauguration in 1801 he selected Meriwether Lewis, his private secretary, and William Clark, the younger brother of George Rogers Clark, to organize and lead an expedition across what he described as "the immense trackless desert of the West." "The object of your mission is single," the President instructed Lewis, "the direct communication from sea to sea formed by the bed of the Missouri and perhaps the Oregon. . . ." But the venture did not get under way until after the transfer of Louisiana to its new owner.

A few Americans believed that Lewis and Clark would find the mammoth Welsh Indians and the "Lost Tribes of Israel." They also believed that somewhere up the Missouri there was a salt mountain 1000 miles long and 45 miles wide. The explorers found none of these, but they did establish land communication between the Missouri and the Columbia. Also, they described much of the country through which they passed as "desert and barren," a generalization which seemed to substantiate Jefferson's image of it.

Ascending the Missouri was a back-breaking job, and often the party found that every ounce of strength available was required to inch the fifty-five-foot keel boat against the swift current. The 1600-mile journey from St. Louis to the Mandan Village in North Dakota consumed most of the summer and fall of 1804. At newly constructed Fort Mandan the party received protection from the Indians and the weather throughout the winter months. In April 1805 the keel boat and part of the crew returned to St. Louis with furs and scientific collections of flora and fauna. At the same time the thirty-two remaining members, including the famous Sacajawea and her new-born baby, prepared to strike out on a straight westward course.

While en route from Fort Mandan to the Pacific, Lewis and Clark passed through country never before seen by white men. They reached Great Falls, Montana, by mid-June, followed it southward to Three Forks, thence by a winding route through Lemhi Pass and Lolo Pass across the Rockies to the Clearwater River in Idaho. On they went until the Clearwater joined the Columbia, and by mid-November they caught their first view of the Pacific. There they rested until the following spring.

The return trip began in March 1806, but the Americans were not safely through the Rockies until June. Back at Great Falls they divided into two parties. Clark took one group southward to Three Forks before turning eastward through Bozeman Pass to the Yellowstone, thence down this stream to its juncture with the Missouri near the present North Dakota-Montana line. Meanwhile, Lewis and nine companions journeyed northward from Great Falls to the source of the Marias River, doubled back to its confluence with the Missouri, and finally retraced the outward route to the mouth of the Yellowstone, where they rejoined Clark's party. By September 23, 1806, the travelers had returned to St. Louis, having completed one of the most epic journeys in history.

Lewis committed suicide in 1809, and most of the work of completing the journals of the expedition fell to Clark. Publication was delayed until 1814, mostly because of the painstaking work required for a detailed map of the Far West. Clark accurately portrayed the Columbia River, and he assumed that there were one or more rivers further south that likewise cut a path through the Sierra Nevada Mountains en route to the ocean. Thus he kept alive the vain hope of a transcontinental water passage. In plotting its course he borrowed heavily from Humboldt's map of North America published in 1804. Humboldt in turn had copied faithfully the Miera map based upon the "discoveries" of the Domínguez-Escalante expedition into the Great Basin country a quarter of a century earlier. The Clark map showed a great river which the explorer called the Multnomah. It began in the general vicinity of Miera's legendary San Buenaventura and ran westward parallel to the Snake before turning northward to join the Columbia near the Pacific Coast. Actually, Clark had discovered the Willamette River, named it the Multnomah, and simply extended it back to the Continental Divide where he thought it belonged.

Even before Lewis and Clark returned to the United States the Spaniards feared that they had discovered the secret of a transcontinental water course. They talked of intercepting the party led by "the American Captain Merry Weather" but had not the vaguest idea where to find it. Another expedition into what Spain considered its own territory soon caused them even more alarm. It was led by Lieutenant Zebulon Montgomery Pike, whose destination the Spaniards believed to be New Mexico. If so, there was a good chance that he could be turned back before reaching the Rio Grande settlements. But this time they acted too hastily, and Pike slipped into the upper Rio Grande country in the wake of the military expedition sent out to find him.

Lieutenant Pike was twenty-seven years old when he left St. Louis in early 1806 in command of a party of twenty-three men, mostly military personnel. According to written instructions from his commanding officer, General James Wilkinson, he was to follow the Arkansas River to its source, turn south to the Red River, and descend this stream to the Mississippi. Pike also was ordered to collect and preserve mineral and botanical specimens, to regulate his course by the compass, calculate distances by the watch, ascertain the latitudes and variations of the needle, and observe the eclipses of Jupiter's satellites. "In regards to your approximation to the Spanish settlements, should your route lead you near them, or should you fall in with any of their parties your conduct must be marked by circumspection and direction as may prevent alarm or conflict, as you will be held responsible for consequence. On this subject I refer you to your orders," Wilkinson warned.

The last statement has given the critics of Pike considerable ammunition. Some claim that the real purpose of the expedition was to obtain information regarding Spanish military strength in the Southwest for General Wilkinson's personal use. This was the period of the Aaron Burr conspiracy, and evidence later came to light that linked the general with

Burr's dream of carving out a private empire from Spanish and American territories. "It is well understood that Pike had secret instructions from the traitor, General Wilkinson," said Elliot Coues in his 1895 edition of Pike's Arkansas journal, "over and above those which were ostensible; and no doubt the main purpose of his expedition was to open the way to Santa Fe, with reference to such military operation as then seemed probable."

The Pike expedition ascended the Missouri by keel boat to the mouth of the Osage River, thence up this stream until it was no longer navigable. From eastern Kansas the Americans journeyed overland by horseback in a northwesterly direction to the Republican River in southern Nebraska. Here the company turned almost due south until it reached the great bend of the Arkansas in Kansas. A small party then followed the Arkansas through Kansas and Oklahoma to Louisiana, where it joined the Mississippi River. Meanwhile, the main force continued across the plains toward the mountains.

Eventually the American explorer came within sight of the peak in Colorado that now bears his name. A few weeks later Pike's presence near the west bank of the upper Rio Grande became known to Spanish officials in Santa Fe. Ultimately he was discovered, escorted to Santa Fe, and later taken to Chihuahua to confer with the governor of that province. The governor believed Pike to be a spy but did not wish to take the responsibility for shooting him. The lieutenant insisted all the while that he was searching for the Red River, had lost his way, and inadvertently had wandered into Spanish territory. To avoid a possible war between the two countries, the Spaniards returned Pike to the United States in 1807.

The importance of the first American expedition into the southwestern corner of the Great American Desert was temporarily overshadowed by the suspicion at home that the young lieutenant was involved in the Wilkinson-Burr affair. His capture by the Spaniards and his subsequent actions and statements lent circumstantial evidence to the charge. But the real significance of Pike's journey lies in the fact that he was the first American to enter the Southwest and return to the United States to publish his observations. His journal appeared in print in 1810 and contained many oft-quoted passages that contributed greatly to the idea of a Great American Desert. "This vast plains of the Western Hemisphere," he wrote, "may become as celebrated as the sandy deserts of Africa; for I saw in my route, in various places, tracts of many leagues where the wind had thrown up the sand in all the fanciful forms of the ocean's rolling wave, and on which not a speck of vegetable matter existed." Pike reported to his commanding officer that one national advantage might rise from this immense desert region of the West: "It would be a means of restricting the population to some certain limits and thereby insure the permanency of the union." Most of the arid lands, he argued, were incapable of cultivation, the line of white settlement must halt near the borders of the Missouri and Mississippi, and the desert left to the "wandering and uncivilized aborigines of the country." Thus the idea of a desert was firmly fixed in the American mind.

A decade and a half passed before another official expedition came into the region. In 1819 Major Stephen H. Long reached the Front Range of the Rockies via the Platte and South Platte rivers. He and his party of twenty-one soldiers and seven civilian scientists descended the eastern slope of the mountains to the point where the Arkansas River breaks through the Royal Gorge in its descent to the plains. Half of the party went down the Arkansas, while Long and the others continued southward to the headwaters of the Canadian River near Raton Pass in New Mexico. Thinking he was on the Red River, the commander followed this stream across the Texas Panhandle and through Oklahoma. At Belle Point, a few miles west of Fort Smith, Arkansas, the two parties were joined. To his great disappointment Long learned that he had mistaken the Canadian for the Red, which had been the principal objective of his expedition.

The journal and notes of the Long expedition were published in 1823 in two volumes.[1] The editor relied heavily upon the published works of Lewis and Clark and Pike to round out the description and observations of the vast eastern slope of the Rockies. This strip, Long declared, was five to six hundred miles wide; it extended from the Canadian border to the sources of the rivers of Texas and "bears a manifest resemblance to the deserts of Siberia." Its saline, sandy soil, he continued, supported a thin carpet of grass and scattered plants upon which incalculable multitudes of buffalo and other wild game fed, while trees and forests were almost unknown.

Long was influenced by others in predicting that "this region is calculated to serve as a barrier to prevent too great an extension of our population westward, and secure us against the machinations or incursion of an enemy, that might otherwise be disposed to annoy us in that quarter." He was the first explorer, however, to use the specific term "Great American Desert," believing that it was more appropriate than previously used phrases such as the "Great Sandy Desert" or the "Mexican Desert."

In designating the western portion of the continent as the Great American Desert, he explained that the name acknowledged the relationship of the Rocky Mountains to the regions that bordered them on both the east and west. He also pointed out that he believed the western slope of the mountains was an extension of the vast desert region over which he had passed. It must be remembered that the boundaries of the United States in the 1820's extended only to the mountains, and that Long had not gone beyond that line. Thus, the map of the desert that accompanied his published journals showed only the portion of it that lay within United States territory.

Time and the pressure of the frontier provided new knowledge about the Great American Desert, as well as new geographic dimensions. They destroyed old myths, created new

[1] Some of the documents relating to the expedition were lost, but Dr. Edwin James, a botanist and geologist who accompanied the expedition, did a creditable job with the remaining materials.

ones, and shifted the central focus of the desert from one geographic center to another. Among the host of travelers who visited the Far West soon after Major Long were Thomas Nuttall (the English naturalist), Thomas Farnham, Father De Smet, Josiah Gregg, Washington Irving, and Francis Parkman. Most of these travelers confined their excursions to the eastern slope of the Rockies, or to the region which today is known as the Great Plains. Their subsequent reports were "full of deserts" and often contained whole passages from the published journals of other writers. Invariably they compared the region to Siberia or the Sahara Desert, but their designations of its eastern boundary varied from the 96th to the 100th meridian.

The absence of trees in large areas of the Great Plains indicated to each traveler that the soil was sterile and incapable of growing crops even with sufficient water. Thus, some concluded that it would make an excellent home for the Indians. This idea was supported by Secretary of War John C. Calhoun in 1827, and three years later, with the passage of the Indian Removal Act, it became an official government policy. Others, however, did not believe that confining the Indians to the desert would be wise. Among these was Washington Irving, who warned that a "new mongrel race" might spring up here, "like new formations of geology, the amalgamation of the debris and abrasion of former civilized and savage people." He recalled the words of Edmund Burke in the House of Commons in 1775, that the inhabitants of the western portions of the North American continent would some day become the "English Tartars" who would eventually conquer the whole of the American continent.

Meanwhile, the mysteries and myths of the portion of the Great American Desert west of the Rockies were gradually fading. Between 1820 and 1840 British and American traders explored the region thoroughly in search of furs. They discovered that it had no drainage to the Pacific and they confirmed Long's theory that it was a desert. Among these were Peter Skene Ogden, an employee of the Hudson's Bay Company, and Jedediah Smith, who organized the Rocky Mountain Fur Company in 1826 with David Jackson and William Sublette. Even though Ogden and Smith solved the geographical riddle of the Great Basin, they could not dispel the belief that somewhere between the Columbia and Colorado rivers there existed a transcontinental water passage that connected the interior of North America with the Pacific Ocean.

In 1844 this hoary myth was finally laid to rest by one of the most famous explorers in American history, the thirty-year-old "pathmarker," John Charles Frémont. By this time he had already accompanied one expedition to the West and had commanded another, a company of Topographical Engineers, to determine the exact location of South Pass. Although not greatly significant for its contribution to science and geography, the South Pass adventure brought fame to the commander and demonstrated a practical overland route to the Pacific via the Platte River and South Pass.

The second and most important of several western expeditions led by Frémont left Kansas City on May 23, 1843. Among the thirty-nine hardy and able men who had joined up were Charles Preuss, a superb draftsman, Alexis Godey, and Thomas Fitzpatrick. The remainder of the party consisted of French adventurers, experienced mountain men, and a few frontier farmers. Frémont's primary objective was to connect his 1842 survey from St. Louis to South Pass with the Pacific Coast. In addition he hoped to locate once and for all the San Buenaventura River and chart its course from beginning to end.

From South Pass the Frémont party continued westward to the Green River, the stream that Domínguez and Escalante had discovered sixty-seven years earlier and named the San Buenaventura. Their next landmark was the Bear River. From thence they traveled southward to the Great Salt Lake, in an attempt to determine whether it had an outlet, but their findings were inconclusive. Frémont then retraced part of his route northward to the Hudson's Bay station of Fort Hall on the Snake River. The remainder of the journey along the Oregon

Trail to the American mission currently operated by Marcus Whitman at Walla Walla extended through "a melancholy and strange looking country—one of fracture and violence and fire." Frémont established a base camp near the Dalles before paying a visit to Dr. John McLoughlin's Hudson's Bay headquarters at Fort Vancouver. He also sought information about the country from numerous American settlers who had already arrived in Oregon, and he noted the tremendous agricultural potential of the territory that would soon come into full possession of the United. States. Once the official objective of the expedition was completed—mapping the entire course of the Oregon Trail—the pathmarker again turned his attention to the San Buenaventura. In early December he broke camp and moved due south along the eastern slope of the Sierra Nevada.

This leg of the journey was most grueling, and the party suffered unbelievable hardships. By mid-January of 1844 no sign of the San Buenaventura had been sighted, and Frémont decided to cross the Sierras into California to escape the harsh conditions of the Great Basin. Almost immediately the Americans plunged into deep snows and temperatures that hovered near zero. In a fantastic test of endurance, which lasted almost five weeks, they got through Carson Pass and arrived safely at John Sutter's ranch on the American River. There they rested for several days, replenished their supplies and equipment, and then renewed their journey southward down the Sacramento and San Joaquin valleys.

Near present Bakersfield Frémont turned once again toward the mountains and crossed over into the Mojave Desert via Tehachapi and Cajon passes before eventually re-entering the Great Basin. By then Frémont was thoroughly convinced that "no river from the interior does, or can, cross the Sierra Nevada—itself more lofty than the Rockies." Jedediah Smith had reached the same conclusion almost two decades previously, but all reasonable doubt vanished with the subsequent publication of Frémont's remarks.

Eight months after he had left the Great Salt Lake Frémont

was back on its eastern shores. He had traveled approximately 3500 miles in a tremendous circle along the rim of the Great Basin, the name he gave to the western flank of the Rockies, by which it is still known. Ultimately he returned to Washington in triumph and set to work editing his notes and assisting Preuss in constructing the most significant map of the region heretofore published. The map contained many geographic errors, but it represented the most complete cartographic work on the Far West until the 1870's. It also rescued from history's limbo some important facts regarding the "northern mystery."

Printed across the blank space reserved for most of the area between the Rockies and the Sierra Nevada Mountains was the following observation: "Diameter 11° of latitude, 10° of longitude: elevation above sea between 4 and 5000 feet: surrounded by lofty mountains: contents almost unknown, but believed to be filled with rivers and lakes which have no communication with the sea, deserts and oases which have never been explored, and savage tribes, which no traveller has seen or described." In referring to this flank of the Rockies as "deserts and oases," Frémont was on solid ground. But he was less so when he commented in his journal that "the whole idea of such a desert is a novelty to our country."

How could the pathmarker so cavalierly dismiss the writings of Long and the host of other travelers who, before 1840, had regarded the Great Plains as part of an immense desert? Perhaps it was because the period of Frémont's crossing the western plains corresponded with an abnormally wet cycle, and thus, by comparison, the Great Plains region was not so obviously a desert as was the Great Basin.

More important, however, is the fact that as early as 1842 Frémont had made the first sharp sword thrust at the popular view that an American Sahara lay in the region that is now the granary of the United States.

Trails and Railroads

Emigrant Trails
Old Spanish Trail
Railroads
Cattle Drive Trails

V THE FIRST EXPLOITERS

While official explorers were mapping the fringes of the Great American Desert, the intimate secrets of the interior were being discovered by a different breed of men. These unofficial explorers were the trappers who followed in the wake of Lewis and Clark and Zebulon Montgomery Pike. Their mission was not to collect scientific data or produce more accurate maps, but to exploit the four-legged wealth. They left few records in the form of manuscripts and diaries, but they filled in an immense geographic void by discovering mountain passes and the true courses of western rivers, and by exploring the arid vastness of mid-continent America.

Word reached St. Louis before the return of Lewis and Clark that the Far West was a paradise of beaver, mink, and otter. Hundreds of traders made preparations during the winter of 1806–7 to start up the Missouri as soon as the ice broke. Most of the invaders went in large parties, well armed, and equipped with trade goods that they intended to barter with the Indians for furs. The most famous party that first year consisted of forty-two trappers led by the Spanish trader Manuel Lisa. His trade goods and supplies were pushed and pulled in a heavy keel boat more than a thousand miles, to the mouth of the Big Horn. There Lisa constructed a trading post, which he appropriately named Fort Manuel. Throughout the following winter he sent his men into Yellowstone country and every corner of the northern Rockies. In exchange for a few worthless trinkets and watered-down whiskey, the mountain men obtained a small fortune in beaver "plews." Their return to St. Louis in 1808 created as much excitement as did the cry of "gold" a generation later.

But news of Lisa's success was tempered by his sound advice that large companies and adequate capital were essential to the fur trade. The great distances that had to be covered, the danger of hostile Indians, and the difficulties of transporting supplies and trade goods put such an operation beyond the resources of most individuals. Accordingly, Lisa and other leading St. Louis traders early in 1809 organized the first American fur-trading company and prepared an ambitious invasion of the Far West. For the next forty years the Missouri Fur Trading Company and its successors carried out a systematic exploitation of the Far West. These American companies, together with the British Northwest Fur Trading Company and Hudson's Bay Company, ultimately stripped the mid-continent of most of its beaver and other fur-bearing animals. About the time that the western streams were trapped out, the beaver hat went out of style and the bottom dropped out of fur prices.

The Missouri Fur Trading Company remained active for only six or seven years after it was founded. At first it spread its activities to the northern plains and Rockies, where it operated a series of forts to which the Indians came to barter pelts for whiskey, tobacco, cloth, knives, and guns. But many of the company's traders and trappers lost their lives, killed by the extremes of weather or hostile Indians. The company also suffered from mismanagement and undercapitalization, and by 1811 it was forced to withdraw to the lower Missouri region. Its advance into the Great American Desert and subsequent retreat would be repeated again and again by others.

Among the large American enterprises that deserve significant notice was the Rocky Mountain Fur Trading Company, organized in 1822 by General William H. Ashley and Major Andrew Henry. This company became synonymous with most of the legendary names in the business: Jedediah Smith, Thomas Fitzpatrick, Joe Meek, Jim Bridger, and William Sublette. The greatest of the group, and until recently the least known, was Jedediah Smith, who deserves to be ranked among the established explorers of the West. Had he lived to publish his memoirs and maps, his name perhaps would be better remembered today than that of John C. Frémont or John Wesley Powell. Unlike explorers of subsequent generations, Smith was a pathfinder rather than a pathmarker, and he undoubtedly had more firsthand experience of the Great American Desert than any individual of his day.

In the spring of 1824 the twenty-four-year-old Smith led a party of trappers through a wide gap in the Continental Divide, a gap which later became famous as South Pass. From there he moved to the Green River, and found it rich in beaver. Leaving some of his men in the vicinity of the Green, Smith and six others pushed off toward the northwest. They eventually reached Flathead Post, a Hudson's Bay establishment on the Clark fork of the Columbia in eastern Oregon. Their presence was not appreciated by the British, who had tried to keep the Americans out of the region west of the Divide by the simple expedient of trapping-out all the beaver streams.

By July 1825 Smith had made his way back to the Green River, where he attended the first "rendezvous," a meeting place set up through a new system of trade that eliminated the long trek to St. Louis each year by the mountain men. The company sent out caravans of supplies to meet the trappers at an agreed time and place. Here they exchanged powder, lead, traps, tobacco, liquor, and other goods for the trapper's yearly catch, a transaction that worked to the company's advantage and left the individual trapper with a monumental hangover and in debt. That first rendezvous netted the company more than $50,000 in profits, and some of the stockholders decided that they had earned enough money to sell out and leave the business.

By the summer of 1826 all of the stock in the old Missouri Fur Trading Company belonged to Smith, William Sublette, and David E. Jackson. The new partners now devised another system of trade: Sublette was to handle matters in St. Louis, Jackson was to continue trapping the streams of the central Rockies, and Smith was to seek out the legendary streams farther west. During the next three years Smith made two journeys across the Great Basin to southern California by way of the Sevier, Virgin, and Columbia rivers. It was the first time that an American explorer had crossed the entire breadth of the Great American Desert. By his exploration he also furnished irrefutable proof that the Buenaventura River did not exist. Even so, the legend persisted for another generation.

Smith had fourteen men at his command when he left the Cache Valley near Great Salt Lake in August 1826. He later explained that he started southwest simply to find beaver, but after traveling so far without success he had no alternative but to continue across the desert to the Spanish missions in southern California. He expected to find the Buenaventura River somewhere south of Great Salt Lake and follow it to the Pacific. Thence perhaps he could go up the coast to the Columbia, trap it to the Snake, and then return to the rendezvous in northeastern Utah.

The party started out on horseback and hit the Sevier River a few miles below present Salt Lake City. The course for the next several weeks was due southwest, through a "country of starvation." The few Indians they encountered gave little or no trouble, but the land was arid and destitute of timber, and watering places were often as much as thirty miles, or two days, apart. The dry soil kicked up by the horses and the searing heat of late summer and early fall were unbelievable. Eventually the travelers reached the Virgin River and followed it to its juncture with the Colorado. By the time they arrived on the edge of the Mojave Desert near present Needles, California, their horses had died and they were afoot.

Smith had located neither beaver nor the Buenaventura, and he had no alternative but to continue across the Mojave to the coast of California. It took two weeks to make the journey over land which he described as "complete barrens." Eventually he discovered a stream (the Mojave) and he promptly named it Inconstant River, because it frequently disappeared from sight. Here and there it rose to the surface to support a grove of desert willows and cottonwoods and to furnish shade and water to the parched travelers. Somehow the men survived the wretched conditions of the desert to reach Mission San Gabriel about one hundred miles north of San Diego.

The Spaniards were even more displeased with Smith's visit to California than the British had been in Oregon, and they ordered him to retreat by the same route by which he had entered. He began the return journey early in 1827, and by spring the party had reached the edge of the desert once again. Smith then veered northward into the San Joaquin Valley, still hoping to find the Buenaventura. After 350 miles or more he realized that the river did not exist, and he decided to turn eastward across the Sierra Nevada into the Great Basin. Most of the men were left behind to trap beaver while he and two companions made the historic crossing of the mountains, skirted Walker Lake, and struck out into the desert for the rendezvous near Great Salt Lake. The route across Nevada is not clear. The explorer later described the country as being completely barren, with water holes some two or three days apart. "Some isolated mountains rise from this Plain of Sand," he wrote, "to the region of Perpetual snow, the small streams that flow from these, are soon absorbed in the Sand. It contains a few miserable Indians, and but little Game."

By the time the three travelers had reached the present Utah line they had been forced to kill all of the horses they had purchased in California, drink the blood, and eat the flesh. Eventually one of the men collapsed from fatigue and burning thirst, and Smith feared that all three "might perish in the desert unheard of and unpitied." But he and the other companion pushed on and soon came upon a water hole. After quenching his thirst Smith hurried back over the trail with a kettle of water for the stricken man. "Putting the kettle to his mouth he did not take it away until he had drank all of the water, of which there was at least 4 or 5 quarts and then asked me why I had not brought more." At last they reached the Great Salt Lake, from which they moved on to the rendezvous at Bear Lake near the Utah-Idaho border. "My arrival caused a considerable bustle in camp, for myself and party had been give up as lost," Smith recorded in his journal.

Jedediah Smith not only has the honor of being the first white man to cross the Great Basin portion of the Great American Desert; he made the second journey as well. Ten days after he had rejoined Sublette and Jackson at the rendezvous, he headed back over the same general route of the previous year. Bad luck trailed him all the way. Half of the second party was killed by Indians near the edge of the Mojave Desert, and Smith was imprisoned at Monterey by Spanish officials. After endless wrangling the trappers were released on a $30,000 bond (posted by an American sea captain who happened to be in Monterey at the time), and the Spanish told them to leave California forever. On the Umpaqua River, about half way up the Oregon coast, they were attacked by the Indians, and suffered a devastating defeat. Only Smith and three other men escaped to make their way another hundred miles northward to the Hudson's Bay base at Fort Vancouver on the Columbia.

Dr. John McLoughlin, commander of the British outpost, helped recover part of the furs and equipment that the Smith party had lost. In return the Americans furnished the Hudson's Bay Company officials with a map of their extensive discoveries, undoubtedly the first accurate one of the vast region between the Rocky Mountains and the Sierra Nevada. From Fort Vancouver the small party traveled up the Columbia and across to Montana, where Smith joined his partners in August 1829. He continued his trappings for another year, but by then he was tired of the mountains, and he returned to St. Louis. Later, in 1831, he led a wagon train to Santa Fe.

Smith crossed and recrossed the Great American Desert when much of it was still an unknown land. His untimely death on the Santa Fe Trail near the southeastern corner of the desert, and the unaccountable destruction of many of his letters, maps, and journals, forced others to duplicate much of his work a generation later. He opened a new route to California across the Great Basin, but, surprisingly, he missed the Humboldt River. That was discovered in 1826 by Peter Skene Ogden, then head of a company of Hudson's Bay trappers. The Humboldt River eventually became most necessary to the opening of the West, for it pointed the way for thousands of California-bound emigrants. Because of its foul water, it also became the most hated.

While separating geographic myth from reality, Smith and his partners also proved that wagons could be driven from the Mississippi Valley to the Rocky Mountains. "The ease with which they did it," wrote the editor of the St. Louis *Beacon* on November 4, 1830, "shows the folly and nonsense of those 'scientific' characters who talk of the Rocky Mountains as the barrier which is to stop the westward march of the American people."

Other fur-trading companies carried on the work of despoiling the Great American Desert of its animal wealth. Among these was the American Fur Trading Company, organized by John Jacob Astor in 1808. Astor monopolized the business along the eastern slope of the Rockies after 1830. Meanwhile, Ogden and other Hudson's Bay employees had trapped out the Humboldt, Snake, and Columbia, and eventually they confined their activities to the coastal region.

Several years elapsed before the beaver-pelt industry realized that it was dead. The American Fur Trading Company supported a force of 125 trappers in 1838, compared to three times that number the year before. In 1839 the company held its last mountain rendezvous. Frémont observed four years later that trappers in the Far West "had almost entirely disappeared," and the experienced trader James Clyman reported in 1844 that the beaver hunters in the Northern Rockies were "now reduced to less than thirty men." But a force of undetermined size continued to operate out of Taos and Sante Fe until the decade of the 1850's.

Beaver was the quick wealth of the West. When it was gone, the region lapsed into worthlessness, until just before the Civil War when gold was discovered in the central Rockies. The Great American Desert no longer remained the "northern mystery," but it was still a formidable place to be crossed. The first Americans to follow the explorers and trappers were the missionaries and pioneer settlers bound for the green hills of Oregon. They in turn were followed by the gold seekers en route to California.

By 1830 the main trails had already been laid out by the mountain men, while the Santa Fe traders had developed the technique of travel by wagon caravans in semi-military fashion. But the way west was long and dangerous and the desert plains and mountains swarmed with hostile Indians. Nevertheless, there were always men and women willing to gamble on the odds of getting through. Tales of fertile valleys beyond the mountains, of streams teeming with fish, forests of wild game, and grasslands where cattle could be fattened quickened the pulse of thousands of western frontiersmen and Yankee farmers. And the missionaries thought they heard distant voices crying for salvation.

A small group of New Englanders led the way. They were commanded by Nathaniel J. Wyeth, a successful Cambridge businessman who enlisted thirty-one men in the Joint Stock Trading Company and set out from Boston in March 1832. At Independence, Missouri, his party joined the caravan of the Rocky Mountain Fur Company headed for its annual rendezvous in the central Rockies. The combined parties traveled along the North Platte to South Pass and from there to Pierre's Hole, the site of the rendezvous. The remainder of the journey had to be made without the protection of the caravan, and all but eleven of Wyeth's men decided to turn back. The rest continued through Blackfoot country under the guidance of Milton G. Sublette, a mountain man. They eventually reached the Snake River, followed it to Walla Walla, then a Hudson's Bay outpost on the Columbia, and thence to Fort Vancouver near the coast.

Though Wyeth had been successful in trapping furs en route, he temporarily abandoned his trading plans in Oregon when he learned that cargo sent by sea had been lost en route. He started his return trip overland in February 1833. Two years later he set out on a second overland journey to Oregon, accompanied by two Methodist missionaries, Jason and Daniel Lee. Near present Pocatello, Idaho, Wyeth stopped to construct Fort Hall, which later became an important station for Oregon- and California-bound emigrants. Also, it became the nucleus of the first permanent settlement in the heart of the Great American Desert. Near Fort Vancouver Wyeth erected still another post, but his far-flung commercial enterprise soon failed because of competition from the Hudson's Bay Company.

The missionaries did better. They not only recognized the great potential that Oregon offered for farming and cattle-raising, but also the unlimited opportunities for conversion of the Indians. In 1836 they were joined by Marcus Whitman and Henry Spalding, who crossed the Great American Desert with the first white women—their wives—and also established another "first" by taking wagons the entire length of the Oregon Trail. By 1843 this trail was a well-marked roadway from Independence to Fort Laramie, through South Pass to Fort Bridger in the southwestern corner of Wyoming, north-west by way of Fort Hall, Fort Boise, and Fort Walla Walla, thence due west down the Columbia to the Willamette Valley.

A flood of emigrants (they were never called "immigrants") followed in the wake of the missionaries. Encouraged by expansionists like Senator Thomas Hart Benton, who realized that Oregon would belong eventually to the nation that populated it, thousands of Americans caught the "fever." In 1843 approximately 900 people made the crossing in prairie schooners, on horesback, and afoot. The journey of approximately 2000 miles took six months, and most of those who started got through—in spite of heat, dust, mud, mosquitoes, cholera, and Indians. Within three years Oregon was part of the United States, and five years later it could claim a population of 12,000. How many turned back or died along the way is not known. Few saw the region through which they passed en route to Oregon as a land of opportunity. Though none stopped off in the Great Plains, they did make note of the possibilities of farming the eastern edge of the desert.

Near the end of the decade the tide shifted to California with the advent of the gold rush, and literally almost overnight tens of thousands of men, women, and children were on their way west. Indeed, throughout the spring of 1849 there was practically a solid procession of covered wagons spread out along the entire breadth of the Great American Desert. New Orleans, Brownsville, Houston, Dallas, and Fort Smith became jumping-off places, while many more took the Santa Fe Trail across the southeastern corner of the desert. Some eventually continued due west from Santa Fe and Albuquerque to southern California, but most of those who took a southern trail preferred the Gila River route across Arizona.

The heaviest traffic of all occurred on the Oregon Trail as far as South Pass. This first leg of the journey presented no undue difficulties or dangers, for the emigrants were particularly alert while crossing the land of the Sioux and other mounted tribes. At first the grass was plentiful on the plains, the animals fresh, and the equipment new. Generally the ground was solid, but judging from the innumerable references to mud in the many diaries that have been published, the decade of the 1840's must have witnessed unusually heavy rainfall. As the emigrants approached western Nebraska the climate became drier and the solid ground gave way to sandy soil. Pulling became more difficult, and the animals tired more easily. Wagon wheels gave trouble because of wood shrinkage, and wedges had to be driven under the iron tires, or the tires taken off, heated red hot, and reset on the wheels. As the ground became rougher, wagon tongues and coupling poles broke more frequently and delays became more common.

In the mountains the going got even tougher, and the average journey of fifteen or twenty miles per day on the plains was sometimes reduced to a matter of rods. Wagons had to be eased down slopes or lowered over cliffs by ropes. And once across the mountains, the emigrants faced the most challenging part of the journey. Most of the California-bound travelers continued north to Fort Hall and then southwest along the Raft River to the Humboldt, while those going to Oregon proceeded past Fort Hall and then followed the Snake River to its confluence with the Columbia. A few took the Hastings Cutoff from Salt Lake City and traveled due west to the Humboldt over one of the most sterile sections of the Great American Desert.

The Humboldt has its beginnings in northeastern Nevada at some swampy green springs called Humboldt Wells. To the emigrants this place bore a remarkable similarity to the bottomless pits of hell. At first the river gives promise of reaching all the way to the Pacific, but it becomes more sluggish as it follows the course of the sun. Its waters also become fouler, until they finally reach a mysterious "sink," and then disappear altogether. Mark Twain wrote of the sink a dozen years after the gold rush started:

> We tried to use the strong alkaline water of the Sink, but it would not answer. It was like drinking lye, and not weak lye, either. It left a taste in the mouth, bitter and execrable, and a burning in the stomach . . . We put molasses in it, but that helped very little; we added a pickle, yet the alkali was the prominent taste, and so it was unfit for drinking. The coffee we made of this water was the meanest compound man has yet invented.

From the Humboldt Sink the emigrants had to make the final drive to the mountains in a single stretch of approximately twenty-four hours, for the country was almost completely lifeless and the searing heat unbearable. They could take one of two routes. They could head for Boiling Spring on the Truckee River, where unappetizing water could be found. To make it drinkable for man and beast they first had to pour it into troughs, allowing it to cool and the minerals —partly—to settle. The alternative was the Carson River route, where there was no water at all, only forty lethal miles of sunbaked land and dizzyingly hot sun. Those who passed this final test of the desert could look forward to the ups and downs of the boulder-strewn canyons of the Sierra Nevada Mountains. But California lay just beyond the summit.

This final lap of the journey was often even more harrowing than anything the desert had to offer. One emigrant train, whose nucleus was the Donner and Reed families of Sangaman County, Illinois, was blocked by winter snows after having taken the unfamiliar Hastings Cutoff. Camping at Truckee Lake in November 1846, the party suffered indescribable hardships. In the end, forty-seven out of eighty-seven survived, and then only by eating the flesh of those who died.

One survivor was thirteen-year-old Elizabeth Reed, who wrote to a cousin in Springfield, Illinois, shortly after being rescued.

> . . . we had to kill littel Cash the dog & eat him. We ate his entrails and feet & hide & every thing about him . . . there was 15 in the cabin we was in and half of us had to lay a bed all the time. Thare was 10 starved to death . . . 3 died and the rest ate them . . . I have not rote you half of the trouble we had but I have rote you enough to let you know that you don't know what trouble is . . . We have left everything but I don't cair for that. We have got through with our lives but Don't let this litter dishearten anybody. Never take no cutoff and hury along as fast as you can.

In comparison to the Great Basin, the Great Plains region, which Stephen H. Long had labeled the Great American Desert, seemed like paradise. The diaries kept by the forty-niners tell the same dreary story of thirst and starvation, the stench of dead animals, and the procession of unmarked graves that lined the road. "I was overcome and tired out," wrote Andrew Orvis in 1849.

> I would travel a little and I would lay down on the sand
> and rest and the sun shining one me. There is no timber thare.
> I thought I would never get through and I laide down to kick
> the bucket; but I thought of home and it give me a litle more
> grit and I would get up and stager along. I was so thirsty my
> tonge and lips cracked and bled but I was able to get to water
> and after drinking a little—I dare not drink much—I felt
> much better. Towards knight, I took some grass and water
> in my canteen back to the horse. He was in the same place I
> had left him. I poered water on the grass and he eat and then
> he went to the river [Humboldt] first rate.

The desert brought out the best and the worst in the men and women who traveled it. Stories of heroism and self-sacrifice are offset by a catalogue of quarrels, fights, and murders. The desert was cruel and exacting; the emigrants expected little from it and gave little in return. Men forced to abandon valuable property were often determined that no one else should use it. The road was strewn with partially burned furniture, wagons deliberately broken, clothing torn to pieces, bacon on which turpentine had been poured, and flour, sugar, and salt mixed with dirt. And large patches of grass were burned over to add to the miseries of those behind.

Disease and death rode the wagons and left little room for sentiment and little time for funerals. Reference to death in the many diaries is almost casual, and each day somebody's oxen or mule collapsed at the yoke or in harness. Men wandered off and were never seen again, a wife or child came down with the fever, a wheel would not keep its rim—all are mentioned with monotonous regularity. And of course there was Indian trouble, especially with the despised Diggers of the Great Basin or the treacherous Apache and Yuma of Arizona.[1] When not crippling the oxen with arrows, driving off

[1] South of Salt Lake City in 1849, twenty-seven wagons of the Jefferson Hunt emigrant party separated from the rest and tried to find a short cut to California. They were attacked by Indians. In Death Valley, the sur-

livestock at night, or stealing everything in sight by day, the Indians often found that they could blackmail the emigrants into giving tobacco and other gifts as tribute.

Even without the troubles that became a part of everyday life on the trail, the audacity of crossing 2000 miles of arid country in covered wagons or on horseback is breathtaking. Yet during the first three years of the gold rush some 35,000 Americans successfully navigated the desert to California over one or the other of the overland trails. And they kept coming in great numbers until 1859. That was the year the news came out of the Comstock Lode, found on the western edge of the desert in present Nevada. The rush started back the other way, as virtually every miner in California dropped what he was doing and headed eastward to the new Eldorado. The year 1859 was also the high tide of the Pikes Peak rush near Denver, when thousands made the relatively short trip across the plains from Missouri. By this time the entire West had become a part of the United States. The horrors of the desert had diminished somewhat, and the new Argonauts, as they were called, would leave behind a partly settled country throughout the Great American Desert.

The discovery of gold and silver in almost every range of the Rockies altered the normal pattern of pioneer development. The prospectors who converged upon the heart of the desert from west and east were not frontiersmen, who had been part of American past tradition. They came from all walks of life, the rich and the poor, the godly and ungodly, merchants and laborers, illiterates and college graduates, criminals and law-abiding citizens. They did not seek out the fertile valleys or rich farm lands, for the desert rarely hid its mineral treasures there. Instead, it concealed them in the most inaccessible places—in the arid highlands and deep canyons, the beds of cascading streams, or beneath layers of sand, rock, and debris. From the Canadian border to Mexico, men

vivors killed their oxen, burned their wagons to cure the meat, and struck out on foot to the west. Thirteen are said to have died of one cause or another before they reached California.

trouped up and down every foot of the mountains, examined each rock and tested each stream. In time they learned far more about the West than even the mountain men had known, and the names they gave to places are still used: Denver, Cripple Creek, Silver City, Butte, Placerville, Bannack, Eureka, Virginia City, Leadville, Creed.

Unlike the trapper a generation earlier, the prospector established settlements all over the West. Instead of a "possibles sack," a rifle, and a half-dozen traps, he carried a canteen, pan, pick, shovel, and perhaps a six-shooter or a bowie knife. Each rumor of a strike touched off a new rush, and if the rumor proved correct a collection of shanties sprang up overnight along some creek or river bed. More often than not the new "diggins" proved disappointing and produced angry cries of "humbug." Some returned home, while others wandered off in search of an undiscovered stream or an unworked gulch. With thousands of prospectors in the field there were bound to be important finds and quick wealth for the lucky ones. Indeed, the desert has always meant quick wealth for the few and disappointment for the many.

From Colorado and Nevada the mining frontier leapfrogged to Montana and Idaho, back to Utah and Wyoming, down to southern Arizona, and finally to the Black Hills of Dakota. News of a discovery traveled fast. Men came in over back trails to stake out a few feet that had not already been taken, or they purchased a claim that showed signs of profit. Some found gold where others had abandoned the effort.

The rush of prospectors forced the new towns to establish some form of government to protect individual claims and provide for a fair division of the remaining lands. Mass meetings were called, officers elected, and simple rules and regulations passed. Claim jumpers were treated to a "neck tie party" or "drummed out of camp." Streets were laid out or simply sprang up along the line of shanties and hastily built cabins. Roads were cut to the nearest supply center, and wagon trains brought flour, sugar, coffee, eggs packed in lard, beans, bacon, lumber, whiskey, and other necessities. As soon as supplies could be unloaded, new stores and saloons were opened. Inevitably, an army of harlots, gamblers, and con men arrived.

In time law and order came to the mining camps, provided they were not abandoned as ghost towns beforehand. Enterprising individuals quickly discovered that there was more profit in supplying the camps and operating businesses than in panning gold. Some learned to irrigate small patches of vegetables and grain near the stream beds and to pasture livestock on the native grasslands. Within a few years the main trails became highways over which wagon trains moved regularly and stagecoaches brought in the mails and carried out the gold dust. Except for the remote areas, the railroads soon put freight wagons and stage lines out of business.

Western society developed, and remained, basically urban rather than rural, for the Indians, scarcity of food, and the climate forced the settlers to remain close together. Also, they desired companionship, for hardships were too much to bear alone. Some settlements, notably Denver, remained as supply centers long after the nearby gold fields were depleted.

Contact with the cities east of the desert depended at first upon the older roads such as the Oregon Trail that followed the Platte and the historic Santa Fe Trail along the Arkansas River to Pueblo and Colorado Springs. Additional roads developed quickly. One was the Smoky Hill route along the Kansas River to eastern Colorado and Denver. Another ran along the Republican River to Big Sandy Creek, thence straight into Denver. The Oregon Trail continued through Idaho, and Montana could be reached after 1863 by the Powder River, or Bozeman, Road, which extended from Fort Laramie to the Yellowstone River and Bozeman. Indians later forced its abandonment, and miners found it safer to enter Idaho and Montana by a road cut north of Salt Lake City by way of Corinne, Utah.

But already the days of the individual prospector were numbered. Within five or six years after the first discovery of pay dirt on Cherry Creek near Denver and the great Comstock bonanza in western Nevada, the industry changed from placer mining to mining by heavy machinery. Most of the gold was locked in quartz below the surface and required a large outlay of capital before it could be refined. Like the petroleum business in future years, corporations soon took over. They introduced stamp mills and hydraulic equipment, and operated on a large scale. Most of the individual miners who stayed in the West at first sought employment with the mining companies, but many turned to small-scale farming and ranching. In a few areas, notably the Comstock, silver was always more important than gold mining. In Montana it was copper.

The permanent settlement of the Great American Desert was inevitable, but unquestionably the discovery of precious metals speeded up the process by at least two generations. It hastened the arrival of the transcontinental railroads, which in turn begot hundreds of new towns and introduced thousands of new emigrants. It made local agriculture and live-stock-raising absolute necessities. And it divided the Great American Desert into half a dozen new territories: Colorado and Nevada, 1861; Idaho and Arizona, 1863; Montana, 1864; and Wyoming, 1868. The other two territories, New Mexico and Utah, were products of the Compromise of 1850. All of these eventually would take their places in the Union as states.

With the decline of mining the people of the Great American Desert were forced to find another basis of existence, for too much had been invested in real estate and transportation for it to be abandoned. This basis was found in the combination of land and water which the Mormons meanwhile had discovered was capable of yielding wealth far more valuable than either gold or silver.

VI THE MORMON CONQUERORS

At least two of the world's great religions, Christianity and the Islamic faith, came out of the desert, inspired there by solitude, mysticism, and desolation. Some of the greatest empires of antiquity arose and flourished in arid lands, such as the Babylonian, Assyrian, Persian, Phoenician, Hittite, Egyptian, Carthaginian, Aztec, and Inca. Each achieved wealth and civilization thousands of years before the first European arrived in North America. As yet the Great American Desert has produced no great religion, nor has it produced a great empire, in the historic sense, and perhaps it never will. But the Mormon Church did find a place for survival there.

Historically, the Great American Desert has been a place to loot and leave. The fur traders sought beaver and the prospectors gold. After them came the cattlemen for free grass and the homesteaders for free land. The weak and the disappointed gave up quickly, while the strong and the fortunate remained no longer than necessary. The Mormons were the outstanding exception, for the desert offered them escape from persecution and violence. They looked upon its remoteness, its barren soil, and arid climate as advantages. And they came to the desert not to exploit its wealth and leave, but to build a permanent Kingdom of God.

The Mormons hardly could have picked a less promising portion of the Great American Desert than the Great Basin itself, but they suffered no illusions about its character. In fact, its very poverty and bareness favored its selection, for the Latter Day Saints wanted complete isolation from the gentile world. To establish an empire in a Godforsaken country, separated by a thousand miles of slow ox-cart communication from all previous American frontiers, took courage and resourcefulness. Fortunately, the Mormons possessed plenty of both.

From the day that Joseph Smith founded the Church of Latter Day Saints in Fayette, New York, in 1830. its followers faced persecution and scorn. Perhaps no religion ever started with less promise, and had it been ignored by the nonbelievers it might have died without a trace. Its founder was an uneducated youth who purportedly received visitations from angels. They revealed to him the "one true religion," inscribed on golden plates. With the aid of magic spectacles, he translated them into a six-hundred-page record of the ancient inhabitants of America, which he called the *Book of Mormon.* (Then he returned the plates to their original hiding place.) A small group of relatives and neighbors accepted the work as divine scripture, and others soon followed. Its emphasis upon militant faith and providential interpretation of history, plus the "chosen people of God" concept, attracted many descendants of New England Puritans who were disenchanted with the precepts of Calvinism.

Mormonism was almost as much an economic as a religious movement. Though individual salvation was essential, one also needed to improve his secular life so as to prepare for the earthly Kingdom of God ("Zion") over which Christ one day would rule. These goals could be achieved only through a union of church and state. Ultimately war, pestilence, and poverty would disappear and heaven and earth would unite. In the meantime church leaders would gather God's chosen people into a single flock and administer to their social, economic, political, and spiritual needs.

Converts to the Church of Latter Day Saints inherited from their Puritan ancestors an unshakable confidence in their own destiny. This belief, along with unlimited optimism, equalitarianism, and the habits and patterns of collective behavior later proved invaluable in the arid West.

Joseph Smith's background, his frequent revelations, prophecies, and talk of a Kingdom of God on earth invited skepticism and ridicule. In 1831 he moved his flock to what he hoped would be more friendly surroundings. It was the first of several migrations. The Mormons settled in Kirtland, Ohio where their new neighbors proved no less tolerant to radical ideas than those of New England. Another move westward began in 1833, this time to the region of Independence, Missouri. Once again they prospered and grew in numbers, but their very success threatened their position. In 1839 they retreated from their town of Far West, Missouri to settle a short time later in Nauvoo, Illinois.

Proselyting activities by missionaries brought a constant flow of new members and soon made Nauvoo the largest city in the state. Joseph Smith received a liberal charter from the Illinois legislature, which allowed his followers to maintain their own militia force and to establish local courts. For a while they functioned as a state within a state, and by voting in a block they held the balance of power between the Illinois Whigs and Democrats. Outsiders grew alarmed over the possibilities that they might soon control the entire state, for many regarded the sect as a gang of renegades who would stop at nothing to promote their objectives. They also whispered charges of lewd and immoral behavior by church officials.

Women seem to have been more easily converted to the new religion than men, and a disparity in number soon existed among the sexes. In January, 1843 Joseph Smith announced a divine revelation, condoning the practice of polygamy. This, coupled with other developments, led to tragedy. Missouri officials charged the prophet with responsibility for an attempted assassination of the former governor of that state. Though they failed to extradite him from Illinois for trial, he nevertheless stood convicted in the court of public opinion. There were charges made against the Mormon community of thievery, counterfeiting, and other misdeeds. Nor did Smith's announced candidacy for the presidency of the United States help matters. Harried on all sides and split by internal dissension, the Mormons faced their most serious crisis on June 17, 1844, when Joseph Smith and his brother Hiram were murdered at Carthage. Obviously, the Saints no longer could remain in Illinois.

Two years before his death Joseph Smith had written in his diary:

> I prophesied that the Saints would continue to suffer much affliction, and would be driven to the Rocky Mountains. Many would apostalize; others would be put to death by our persecutors, or lose their lives in consequence to exposure or disease; and some would live to go and assist in making settlements and building cities, and see the Saints become a mighty people in the midst of the Rocky Mountains.

This prophecy now approached fulfillment.

The Saints turned to Brigham Young, a man of extraordinary ability and courage. Young was forty-four years old in 1845, and stood five feet and ten inches, fairly tall for his day. His deep set, blue-grey eyes, long dark hair and massive shoulders and chest gave him a commanding appearance. Lacking in formal education, he nevertheless possessed a keen intellect and an intuitive faculty of selecting the right man for the right job and delegating full authority. Young was less of the mystic than Smith, more practical, and more thorough in his planning. But once he made up his mind regarding a particular enterprise, it took "a direct act of God" to change it. Fortunately for the Mormons, he was more often right than wrong.

The new leader secured an immediate promise from Illinois state officials that there would be no more violence until his people could dispose of their property and migrate elsewhere. But the governor and local peace officers could not maintain law and order, as Mormons and gentiles committed atrocities against each other. Meanwhile, Brigham Young and the church council considered various moves, to Oregon, Texas, California, and even Vancouver Island. They quickly ruled out Oregon and Texas because so many former Missourians lived there. Vancouver Island belonged to Great Britain, while California languished under Mexican influence and was not sufficiently isolated. The choice finally narrowed to the Great Basin region of the Great American Desert.

Several precedents already existed in favor of the Great Basin. Before his assassination Joseph Smith had planned to dispatch a party of young men to "the mountain country to hunt out a good location for settlement." The Great Basin lay within the boundary of northern Mexico, and no one would envy those who settled there. The recently published maps and journals by Frémont had erased much of the mystery associated with it. Also, primitive Indian tribes in the region would offer little resistance, while its valleys might be cultivated with the aid of irrigation. Perhaps more important, the Bible had said that Zion of the last days would be built on the tops of mountains.

As the Mormons contemplated these things, their position became more precarious. Mobs moved in and burned and looted property or forced the owners to sell at ridiculous prices. One man who obtained $250 for a house and farm worth $3000 considered himself lucky, for many of his neighbors received nothing. A fire destroyed the million-dollar church temple which the Saints hoped to sell for $200,000. Though the temperature hovered below zero and ice covered the western roads and rivers, they could not wait for the scheduled departure in the spring. To avoid further tragedy they began evacuating the holy city of Nauvoo in February 1846. Within a few days approximately 16,000 people had crossed the Mississippi River in ferries with everything they owned, including 3000 wagons and immense herds of cattle, horses, and sheep. Before them stretched a thousand miles of desolate country.

In spite of the pressure of time the Mormon leaders had left few details of the migration to chance. Young believed that the best antidote for discouragement and grumbling was hard work, and he kept a tight hand on all activities. Work parties moved across Iowa in advance of the main body to build roads and bridges, plant gardens and crops, and erect permanent camps for those who followed. Even so, many refugees died before they reached the Missouri crossing near present Omaha, Nebraska. Doubtless the toll would have been greater had there been less discipline.

As the flock gathered at Winter Quarters, on the west bank of the Missouri, church officials continued plans for the final move to Zion. Young selected an exploring party to go forth in the spring of 1846 in search of a permanent location, but the Mexican war intervened. President Polk called upon the Saints to furnish 500 volunteers to accompany General Phil Kearney to California. This development proved a godsend, for each recruit received an advance of forty-two dollars, most of which he turned over to the common church fund. The total donations of $21,000 were later supplemented by monthly payments collected by the church at regular intervals. But the subsequent loss of valuable workers forced a postponement of the Great Basin expedition.

The exploring party finally selected in the spring of 1847 consisted of 143 men, three women, and two children. They left Winter Quarters with 72 wagons and enough tools, seed, and livestock to lay out a city and establish experimental farms. Meanwhile, approximately 16,000 others remained behind on the Missouri, but with customary thoroughness they completed a stockade, constructed temporary homes, several mills, and put in crops.

Brigham Young accompanied the advance group, which laid out a road along the Platte, later known as the Mormon

Trail. "We have gone to find a home where the Saints can live in peace and enjoy the fruits of their labors," wrote the camp clerk. Along the way they met Father De Smet and other travelers, and questioned them extensively regarding the Great Basin. Though they invariably received discouraging news about the country to which they were destined, they nevertheless believed that it was the answer to their prayers. From Fort Laramie they continued through South Pass and on to the Green River to rest before tackling the rugged Uinta and Wasatch Mountains. Jim Bridger urged them to settle in Oregon, but they believed that their destiny lay in the isolation of the desert.

Up to this point travel across the plains had been fairly easy. The company followed strict military routine, with each man assigned specific responsibilities. Where possible the wagons moved in double file so as to form a square or circle during Indian attacks. By starting early and continuing past noon they averaged twenty miles or more each day. But as they reached the mountains their problems multiplied. Many, including the leader himself, became sick with the dreaded spotted fever, and the trail became increasingly difficult. On July 21 a small party somehow emerged on the western rim of the Wasatch Mountains and viewed the great valley below. The next day it descended and immediately began work on a summer crop.

Young and the others followed a rough trail through the mountain canyons to a lookout point on Big Mountain. Too ill to leave his carriage, the leader looked out from his sick bed at the country he said he had seen in a vision. Today an imposing monument marks the spot where the prophet is supposed to have uttered his dramatic phrase "This is the Place."

The Great Basin Kingdom contained almost 210,000 square miles of salty dry lands broken by isolated ranges of undulating plateaus and bolsons. Bounded on the east by the Rocky Mountains and by the watershed of the Columbia River on the north, it extended westward to the Sierra Nevada Mountains and southward to the Colorado River. This vast territory not only included present Utah and Nevada, but parts of Colorado, New Mexico, Arizona, California, Wyoming, Idaho, and Oregon. Originally the Mormons claimed all of it, but the Compromise of 1850 later confined their holdings to the region between the 37th and 42nd parallels. And subsequent boundary adjustments reduced them further to the present 85,000 square miles of the state of Utah.

Ninety-five per cent of the land originally claimed by the Mormons was mountain and desert. The average rainfall varied from three to fifteen inches, and the altitude ranged from below sea level at Death Valley to the snow-capped peaks of the Wasatch, 12,000 feet above sea level. Of its few rivers, only the Colorado reached the sea: the Jordan, Weber, and Bear rivers empty into Great Salt Lake, while the Sevier and Humboldt flow into smaller lakes or sinks. A tremendous amphitheater, enclosing approximately twenty to thirty square miles, lies along the western slope of the Wasatch. Frémont had noted this spot during his 1843 expedition, and observed in his journal that "a civilized settlement would be of great value here." It was well watered by creeks and streams flowing out of the mountains and had excellent mill sites. Though almost devoid of timber, it did support a thick cover of bunch grass and an enormous quantity of jack rabbits, rattlesnakes, and coyotes. Here the Mormons concentrated their first efforts.

Other valleys suitable for farming or grazing dotted the eastern edge of the Great Basin. But further north and south of the Great Salt Lake the wild and broken land offered no immediate promise except for its timber. Twelve hundred miles due east across the Rockies and Great Plains lay the Missouri Valley trading posts. An immense expanse of desert stretched westward to the foothills of the Sierra Nevada Mountains, supporting little plant life other than sagebrush. Certainly, the Mormons had found the isolation that they were seeking. The nearest settlements of importance were on the Pacific Coast, the Columbia River to the northwest, and the Rio Grande to the southeast.

Even before they reached the Salt Lake Valley, the pioneers realized the arid problems they would face. "We have to search for land that can be irrigated," the church leaders declared at Winter Quarters. They studied the Old Testament as well as the histories of great civilizations founded on watercourses. They took succor from the words of the prophet Isaiah: "The wilderness and the dry land shall be glad, the desert shall rejoice and blossom; like the crocus it shall blossom abundantly, and rejoice with joy and singing." In more practical ways, the Saints discussed the crude forms of irrigation they had observed in the East and assembled information on the techniques of "dry farming." In addition, they collected various grains and seeds which they hoped would ripen with minimum moisture.

Irrigation had been practiced in Egypt, India, Spain, Italy, and other arid countries centuries before the Mormons set foot on the parched earth of the Salt Lake Valley. Also, the ancient Americans and their modern successors, the Indians and Spanish, had developed their own methods along the Gila, Salt, Verde, Agua Fria, Little Colorado, Rio Grande, and other desert streams of the Southwest.

There is no reliable estimate of the amount of land originally under irrigation in the southern portion of the Great American Desert, nor when the first work began. Some idea can be obtained from the ancient canals in the vicinity of Tempe and Phoenix, Arizona. In places these ditches were thirty feet wide, and they obviously required considerable co-operation in building and maintenance. Lieutenant Colonel William H. Emory found Pima and Maricopa Indians still irrigating corn, beans, pumpkins, melons, wheat, and cotton in the region as late as 1846. Lateral ditches indicated that the average field approximated five acres.

Regardless of what already had been done elsewhere, the Mormons had to draw upon their experience of trial and error in Utah. Though an American named Miles Goodyear had preceded them in the valley and was irrigating a few acres when they arrived, his methods remained unknown to them until later. Meanwhile, church leaders had suggested to members of the advance party that they "prepare pools, vats, tubs, reservoirs, and ditches at the highest point of land in your field or fields, that may be filled during the night and be drawn off to any point you may find necessary." This suggestion proved impracticable because of the tremendous work involved, but it demonstrates that the Mormons were prepared to experiment with new ideas.

The first reference to actual irrigation is found in Orson Pratt's diary, in the entry of July 23, 1847. Pratt was a member of the small party that preceded Brigham Young into the valley by one day. He and eight others established an advance camp on what is now known as City Creek, and immediately implored divine guidance. "In about two hours after our arrival," he wrote, "we began to plow, and the same afternoon built a dam to irrigate the soil, which at the spot where we were plowing was exceedingly dry." The entry for the following day continued: "This afternoon commenced planting our potatoes; after which we turned the water upon them and gave the ground a good soaking. In the afternoon the other camp arrived, and we found all the sick improving very fast, and were so as to be able to walk around."

They still had a long way to go to develop a practical irrigation system, but their previous experience in collective enterprise at Kirkland and Nauvoo proved invaluable. Indeed, without this experience and the enormous powers exercised by the church leaders, it is doubtful if they could have succeeded at all. Furthermore, the Mormons had sufficient foresight to realize the relationship between an enduring economy and an equitable distribution of water. Ordinarily, men in arid regions will fight for their lives to defend a water right from others. But Brigham Young stated upon his arrival at the advance camp on July 24: "There shall be no private ownership of the streams that come out of the canyons, nor the timber that grows on the hills. These belong to the people; all of the people."

An enormous amount of work confronted the first pioneers

in the desert, for survival during the winter depended largely upon successful preparation. Some thousands of additional emigrants would be arriving from Winter Quarters, buildings had to be constructed, and a city laid out. With the season for planting already well advanced, the Mormons quickly divided into committees. The first group concentrated upon plowing and planting and eventually had an irrigated field of thirty-five acres prepared for corn, potatoes, beans, and turnips. Other parties hauled logs from a nearby mountain slope, erected a sawmill, grist mill, community store house, blacksmith shop, and corrals. And some gathered salt from the lake, hunted wild game, or tried their hand at fishing.

On July 27, Young and the elders present laid out Temple Square, which would become the hub of the city. From there they surveyed north-south streets, intersected by east-west parallels. They made each street 172 feet wide and the city blocks ten square acres. The blocks in turn were divided into eight lots, one and a quarter acres in size. Streets were named or numbered in relation to Temple Square: First East, Second West, and so forth. Sidewalks were to be twenty feet wide and houses set back another twenty feet from the street. One of the blocks near Temple Square was reserved for a fort, around which a stockade of log cabins was built. Choice sites were reserved for church officials, while those that extended beyond the Square were to be distributed by lot. The city was officially named "Great Salt Lake City, Great Basin, North America."

Ditches brought in a water supply and made the stockade self-sufficient in case of Indian attack. Eventually the entire block that contained the stockade was walled off on three sides with adobe brick. Twenty-nine buildings to house the first emigrants had been erected inside the stockade by August 1847. But even this was not adequate to house all who arrived before the end of the year, and many were forced to spend the winter in wagons.

The original survey for Salt Lake City contained 135 blocks and 1080 lots. Each lot was large enough for one family and a small vegetable garden and fruit orchard. Irrigated fields varying from five to twenty acres extended beyond the city, while large common grazing fields surrounded the outskirts. By 1849 the pioneers had dug canals by hand for each of the ten-acre blocks and obtained additional water from Big Cottonwood Creek. Where possible they extended ditches to the larger fields by the aid of specially made plows. These implements were shaped like an inverted capital A, made of planks five to eight feet long, and were pulled through the hard, dry soil by ten or twelve horses.

Surveyors usually ran the lines of the ditches with improvised instruments, such as a bottle of water attached to a square piece of timber. Sometimes they sighted across a pan of water, or plowed a furrow from the stream and determined the fall by merely letting the water run to its terminal point. The early ditches gave the least trouble, for the irrigated lands were selected with great care in regard to the water supply. Later the high-line canals running along the mountain side and traversing deep ravines proved more costly to build and more difficult to maintain. Dams across streams often went out in the turbulence of the spring runoff, while the earthen banks gave way easily. Seepage caused considerable losses, and in some cases water never reached the end of the ditch. Many projects ultimately were abandoned, but little by little and with great toil and patience the Mormons surmounted most of their early difficulties.

As Salt Lake City grew, it was divided into twelve ecclesiastical wards, each with an appointed bishop to oversee the distribution of water. When a city government was established in 1853, the people elected a general watermaster. By this time other settlements established in the surrounding area had adopted the irrigation practices developed for the Mormon capital. Under the direction of the bishops or local watermasters, residents of each town ward constructed the ditches that channeled the water to all the blocks in the ward. Major projects, like the larger ditches from the main stream, were directed by the High Council, who apportioned the labor to the wards. Those owning lands outside the city formed community groups to construct the common canal. They allotted water on the basis of acreage, and the acreage taken by an individual determined the amount of work done on the construction and maintenance of the project. Later settlers earned a share in the ditch by labor performed, or joined others in a new location.

The watermaster often was assisted by several deputies. He saw to it that the dams, headgates, canals, and lateral ditches were kept in good order and that water was equitably divided. Even today many of the irrigation works in Utah are managed in much the same manner, though users more commonly pay for their water in cash rather than in labor.

Brigham Young remained in the valley for one month in the summer of 1847, long enough to help determine the general policies and plans for the settlement. On August 26, 1847, he and Heber C. Kimball started eastward for Winter Quarters. En route they met a party of approximately 1500 men, women, and children who had left the Missouri Valley the previous July. This group reached Salt Lake City in September and was put to work immediately on various projects under construction. Back at Winter Quarters, Young and other officials busied themselves organizing the 1848 migration. This, plus the experience gained during the previous spring, enabled them to work out a more systematic plan.

Parties were organized and sent forth to locate camp sites, build bridges, and improve the road. They in turn were followed by groups of 110 wagons, each commanded by a captain and moved forward in double column. Individual units carried all their household furniture, livestock, and seed. Since the Mormon capital could not immediately absorb the entire population of Winter Quarters, only 2417 Saints took the road to Zion in 1848, arriving there by late September.

In spite of the excellent beginning, many pioneers died of exposure and starvation that first year. This initial period of hardships and misfortune was characteristic of all frontier societies. Had the Mormons not been inured to disappointment nor sustained by deep religious faith, their desert experiment would have collapsed immediately. As it was, everything seemed to go wrong that first winter and following spring. Livestock broke into the gardens and destroyed much of the vegetable crop, mountain lions and wolves killed many of the cattle, and vast armies of desert mice invaded the cabins. Bedbugs made sleep a nightmare of scratching and tossing, while an epidemic of measles devastated whole families.

The arrival of the second company of emigrants in the fall of 1847 placed a severe strain on the already limited food supply. A shortage of flour brought strict price control and rationing of this and other staples. Many turned to roots, bark, crows, wolves, and thistle tops—anything to fill their empty stomachs. Somehow the majority of settlers survived the relatively mild weather, only to see the spring crop damaged by frost and later eaten by swarms of dumpy, black, swollen-headed desert crickets. Every weapon and ounce of energy they could muster proved hopeless against the invaders. Finally sea gulls flew in from islands on the Great Salt Lake and devoured the crickets, but not until they had destroyed two-thirds of the crop. The future looked so bleak that church officials contemplated a move elsewhere, but in the end only a few individuals left for California or returned to the East.

By the second winter livestock and supplies had been brought in from California and more houses erected. Settlers who were planning to emigrate were advised to bring enough food to last until their first harvest, but even so the suffering continued and another strict rationing program followed. But shortages and cold weather did not halt work on the streets, public buildings, and canals. An additional 11,000 acres of irrigated land was opened up, mostly in five-acre plots. This area, called the "Big Field," was enclosed by a common fence, and produced a good crop. But population increase soon created new demands. By the third year Utah had 926 improved farms and 16,330 irrigated acres. They increased to 3636 and 77,219 respectively by 1860, and doubled again by the end of the Civil War. The network of canals was increased to more than a thousand miles. By this time some 65,000 people lived in reasonable comfort in the heart of the Great American Desert.

Meanwhile, as early as 1849, Salt Lake City had taken on a permanent look. A bower-like structure 100 feet long and 60 feet wide had been constructed that could accommodate 3000 people. In addition, the Mormons had built a council house, a small church office building, an armory, a public bathhouse, a tannery, a glass factory, a leather factory, and hundreds of log and adobe residential houses. But nothing insured the survival of the settlement so much as the California gold rush, which brought an estimated 10,000 Argonauts through Salt Lake City in 1849 and again in 1850.

The California emigrants gave the local economy an enormous boost. Most of the west-bound travelers, by the time they reached the Mormon capital, found their supplies depleted, their animals worn out, and their wagons badly in need of repair. They eagerly sold their equipment and purchased new outfits and supplies that would carry them through to California. Sales prices rarely exceeded one-fifth the actual value, but the emigrants were forced to pay $200 for fresh horses and mules that were ordinarily worth $25 or $30. On the other hand the Mormons could buy cheaply and sell at inflated prices. Blacksmiths, wheelwrights, harness makers, teamsters, millers, and other workmen naturally took full advantage of the emigrants' need of their skills. Ferry operators on the North Platte, Green, and Bear rivers also profited from the overland trains. Others organized companies to salvage the articles discarded along the way, especially iron stoves, axes, plows, drills, augers, spades, and hundreds of similar items.

Leonard J. Arrington, who has written extensively on the economic history of the Mormons, estimates that the Utah settlers recognized more than $250,000 profit from the gold rush by 1854. "This sum appears to have represented precisely the margin needed to catapult a struggling valley economy, in three short years, into a burgeoning, confident, regional commonwealth. . . . The overland trade not only cured the California fever, but enabled the brethren to furnish themselves with . . . every (almost) variety of necessary needful thing for the Saints to make use of."

Doubtless the desert experiment by the Mormons would have survived even without the California gold rush, but the event enabled them to obtain in a few years what ordinarily would have taken a decade or more. To exist in such an inhospitable climate required strict discipline and community effort. This could be provided best by a "theo-democratic" government, similar to that of the original settlers of New England. Like their Puritan ancestors, the Mormons settled in a region that allowed them to practice their peculiar religion in isolation.

In the humid East the Puritans had adopted a system of individual competition; in the Great American Desert the Mormons tried almost complete co-operation. In both instances the church provided necessary controls for the social benefits of the group. It made decisions regarding marriage, entertainment, doctrine, and tithing, but the Mormon officials went beyond these to include job assignments, relocation to other communities, military service, and distribution of land. Such extraordinary civil and religious powers provided a unity of purpose especially needed for successful irrigation, the basis for Mormon survival.

Later, when Utah became part of the United States and church and state were theoretically separated, the civil government continued the practices relating to irrigation. The territorial legislature in 1852 gave control of all water for "irrigation and other purposes" to the local country courts. Subsequent legislation protected the community's interest above the individual's; this later became the pattern for other states and the federal government to follow.

When all of the Great American Desert was brought within the boundaries of the United States by the Treaty of Guadalupe Hidalgo, the Mormons realized the threat to their new Kingdom of Zion. Brigham Young believed that his people could only be protected from the wrath of their fellow Americans by immediate statehood. Accordingly, he issued a call for a state convention to assemble in Salt Lake City in March 1849. It forthwith named the new state "Deseret," and adopted a plan of government similar to that of the other members of the Union. Its ambitious boundaries took in the present state of Utah, all of Arizona, most of Nevada, all of southern California, and parts of Wyoming, Colorado, and Idaho. Brigham Young became the first elected governor, while the other officials came from the group of church elders and bishops.

Preparations began immediately to establish new settlements between Salt Lake City and the port of San Diego, along what was called the "Mormon Corridor." Already the towns of Bountiful, Centerville, and Ogden had been planted near the capital on streams flowing into Great Salt Lake. To the southwest, Lehi, Provo, and Fort Utah took form by the end of 1849. Three years later a half dozen small outposts extended on down to San Bernardino near Cajon Pass and thence to San Diego. By 1854 another line reached across Nevada to present Carson City. By this time, however, the federal government had refused to recognize the state of Deseret, creating instead the Territory of Utah as part of the Compromise of 1850.

A glance at a Utah map shows a familiar and rather consistent pattern of ecological factors determining new Mormon settlements. Each was located at the base of a mountain front, at an altitude conducive to raising farm crops, or in a valley plain of rich soil. The nearby mountains provided a perpetual flow of life-giving water, timber for building, wood for fuel, and forage for summer grazing. Most villages likewise supported various industries, in keeping with Young's determination for self-sufficiency.

These new settlements not only opened additional irrigated lands for the hordes of emigrants from the East and from

Europe, but they strengthened the Mormon's claim to the Great Basin. Within a decade after the settlement of Salt Lake City some ninety-six communities had been established. The process followed a careful plan of action. First, the church appointed and equipped a committee to undertake a preliminary exploration. After a new site had been thoroughly explored and selected, calls for volunteers were issued from the pulpit. Leaders usually were specified by name, and to refuse the challenge meant censure by the whole community. Also, particular attention was given to individual skills of the colonizers, since each group would largely depend upon its own resources.

As soon as the company had been "recruited," the First President called it together for instructions and questions. After further preparation for the final move the members organized themselves in traditional military fashion and adopted rules and regulations. The colonizers then disposed of their property and assembled tools, seed, and supplies for the new venture. Sometimes the church made loans or gifts, especially to aid the poorer emigrants who had just arrived in the desert kingdom.

Upon reaching their destination the colonizers dedicated their new home to the glory of God. They then erected a fort or stockade, built temporary shelters, and assigned each member to a specific work group. Engineers laid out streets, blocks, and fields along the pattern previously worked out at Salt Lake City. Others dug canals, erected fences, planted crops, built roads, mills, and public buildings. As in Salt Lake City, the timber, grasslands, minerals, and water became community property and the leaders invoked religious sanction to prevent their use for private advantage.

The limited amount of irrigable land was made to support as many people as possible. Operations necessarily were confined to comparatively easy projects which involved the diversion of water from accessible streams. In the absence of major water storage, the capacity of each irrigation project rested on the capacity of the nearest stream during the low flow period of the summer. By hard experience the pioneers soon learned that the only way they could expand their crop land was to build large reservoirs to capture the abundant supply of water in the spring and early summer. Otherwise, their community could support a limited population at best. They made heroic efforts in several instances to build community reservoirs, only to have the dam give way during spring floods. The settlers of the small town of Deseret, for example, constructed eight dams on the Sevier River between 1859 and 1890. Each was larger than the other, but only the last one held.

Not all of the early settlements established by the Mormons became permanent. Some were charged with the responsibility of growing cotton, sugar cane, or sugar beets, and other crops that were unsuitable to the climate or the soil. A few never did succeed in constructing a dam that would hold, and eventually they had to abandon the effort. Others depended upon one or two crops. They suffered from inadequate transportation, for often they could not exchange their surplus produce for essential items that could not be produced locally. The Mormon War of 1857–58 likewise proved disastrous to several outlying communities, particularly those in the Carson River Valley of Nevada. This so-called war was precipitated by the sending of a gentile governor to Utah Territory to replace Brigham Young. Settlers abandoned their farms in a fruitless effort to defend Salt Lake City against what they called an invasion by the United States Army, and they did not return to their settlements when peace was restored. Not until 1890 did the church direct all Mormons to "refrain from contracting any marriage forbidden by the law of the land." Six years later Utah was admitted to the Union as a state. Meanwhile, successive adjustments of the territorial boundaries had left many communities outside the kingdom.

That so many of the settlements did survive is a tribute to the wise planning of church officials, especially Brigham Young. At the time of his death in 1877, thirty years after the founding of Salt Lake City, there were more than 360 Mormon towns in the desert. The magnitude of this accomplishment can best be understood by comparing it with Spanish activities. By 1574 these most successful of all European colonizers had planted approximately 200 towns in North and South America. Eighty years after Columbus's initial voyage the Spanish population in the New World approximated 160,000 to 200,000 persons, only a few thousand more than the Mormons claimed after a mere three decades. Furthermore, Spanish colonists probably had no more problems to surmount than did the Mormons, thousands of whom pushed their belongings in handcarts from the Mississippi Valley to their desert home in Utah.

The Mormons accomplished much of their growth by sending missionaries to various parts of the United States as well as to Europe, Canada, Hispanic America, Africa, India, Australia, and the islands of the Pacific. Not only did the Great American Desert absorb this heterogeneous mass of humanity, but Brigham Young and other church officials fused them into a harmonious social unit. Today, membership of the Church of the Latter Day Saints exceeds two million. The larger proportion of these live in Utah, but an additional 4000 congregations are scattered throughout the world.

VII DEATH AND SURVIVAL IN THE DESERT

Trouble between the whites and Indians of the Great American Desert started with the first contact between the two races. The Spaniards rarely ventured into the northern region, but they experienced continual warfare with the southern inhabitants. In 1680 the Pueblo of the upper Rio Grande revolted against their overlords and killed several hundred Spanish settlers and missionaries. The whites who escaped massacre fled to northern Mexico, and a decade elapsed before Juan de Oñate returned with a large army. For the next century or more after the Pueblo uprisings, the Spaniards carried on unremitting war against the Navajo and Apache. The Mexicans in 1821 inherited the problem of subduing them.

Unquestionably the Apache kept the score even, for they knew every rock and canyon of their desert and mountain fastness. Superb horsemen and warriors, with centuries of experience in raiding the Pima, Pueblo, and their kinsmen the Navajo, they continually thwarted Mexican efforts to control them. After 1848, when the Southwest became a part of the

United States, the fighting intensified, and it continued for two generations before the red man's spirit was broken and he was forced onto the reservations.

Meanwhile, in 1805, Lewis and Clark opened the door for Americans into the northern section of the Great American Desert, and one year later Zebulon Montgomery Pike crossed the southeastern corner. Following on the heels of these explorers came an army of trappers, whose knowledge of the Far West eventually exceeded that of the natives. The "mountain men" lived, worked, and often intermarried with the Indians, and some became more Indian than the Indians. Killings on both sides became part of a way of life; but as the fur market collapsed and the streams became exhausted of beaver, the surviving mountain men turned to other pursuits. A few like Jim Bridger, Kit Carson, and Joe Meek later won fame as guides and scouts for the overland emigrant trains, which first made their appearance two decades before the Civil War.

In fact, covered wagons were crossing the plains and deserts of the Southwest between Missouri and New Mexico as early as 1824. The route carried them through the hunting grounds of the Comanche, Kiowa, Southern Cheyenne, and Apache, who frequently swept down upon the caravans or lay in wait to ambush them. The Santa Fe traders learned to travel in large companies in semi-military fashion, and to carry a cannon or two and ample supplies of lead and powder for their long-range rifles. Despite the hazards of surprise attacks by the red warriors, the trade continued unchecked. Eventually it spread far beyond Santa Fe to California and northern Mexico, and prepared the way for more permanent American intrusion.

Further north the trains of Oregon-bound emigrants followed the Platte to Wyoming, crossed South Pass into western Wyoming and continued to the Columbia. As we have seen, the discovery of gold in California in 1848 attracted thousands of overland emigrants, where a few hundred had gone before. Their wagons quickly cut a dozen trails across the Great American Desert, but the emigrants did not tarry there longer than necessary to rest, make repairs, and bury their dead. Land and opportunities were too plentiful elsewhere and the desert too uninviting. Indeed, to them it constituted a major impediment, a long sojourn through hell en route to the promised land.

Even before the emigrant trains appeared from the east, the Indians of the Great American Desert had already felt the influence of the Americans in the form of whiskey, smallpox, syphilis, and intertribal war, all of which took a fearful toll in numbers. Not the least of the losses were caused by the various wars of one tribe against another. The Northern Cheyenne fought the Crow, the Southern Cheyenne and Arapaho took to the warpath against the Comanche, Kiowa, and Ute, while the Apache in the south fought everyone who got in their way.

American troops were sent to the plains several times in the 1830's and 1840's in unsuccessful efforts to keep the desert nomads under control. After the Mexican Cession of 1848 the frontier line of forts soon extended along the edges of the Great American Desert and protruded at a few points into the interior. From time to time the Indians agreed to a general peace among themselves and to refrain from attacks upon emigrants along the various trails. But as the military garrisons were depleted during the Civil War, conflict broke out all over the West. It continued in some areas for more than thirty years. The Navajo and Apache took advantage of the chaos of the war in New Mexico and Arizona. Further north the Ute, Cheyenne, and Arapaho created a reign of terror, destroying wagon trains and taking scalps wherever they could find them. The Sioux and Crow gave trouble to the ranchers and miners of Montana, while the Kiowa and Comanche raided back and forth from Kansas to the Texas frontier.

From 1860 to 1890 the United States Army and state militia troops fought approximately a thousand engagements with the Indians of the Great American Desert. In June 1864 the frontiersman Kit Carson, in command of New Mexico militia, defeated an estimated 10,000 Navajo on their traditional home grounds in Canyon de Chelly. He took the survivors as prisoners to Fort Sumner on the Pecos River, where they remained until 1868. In that year the United States government returned some 7000 tribesmen to their beloved canyons and mesas of northeastern Arizona, and since that time the Navajo have kept their promise to remain at peace. Meanwhile, in southeastern Colorado in 1864 the Southern Cheyenne were surprised in their camp near Fort Lyons by Colorado militia led by the Methodist minister H. M. Chivington. More than 500 members of Black Kettle's band were killed in what has been described as "one of the bloodiest events in the annals of Indian warfare." Eventually the Cheyenne were moved to western Oklahoma, only to suffer another disaster on their reservation at the Battle of the Washita in 1868 against Custer's famous Seventh Cavalry.

Other tribes that gave trouble were the Comanche and Kiowa, who for two centuries controlled the southern plains section of the Great American Desert, or what is presently western Oklahoma and west Texas. The Comanche were an offshoot of the Mountain Shoshoni who came down to the plains after the acquisition of the horse, which enabled them to become superior hunters and warriors. They were regarded by white and red people alike as the greatest horsemen the New World ever produced. Their estimated eighteenth-century population of 5000 made them one of the largest tribes on the plains.

Mystery surrounds the origin of the Kiowa and their relationship to other Indians that lived in or on the edge of the desert. According to tradition, the Kiowas constituted a distinct linguistic stock and are believed to have originated in southwestern Montana near the headwaters of the Missouri River. The Kiowa are generally acknowledged as having developed the sign language, the universal communication of the plains, to its most elaborate form. Situated as they were in the eighteenth century between the French in the Mississippi Valley and the Spaniards in New Mexico, the Kiowa and Comanche became great traders. As emigrants and settlements moved in from the east during the nineteenth century they also became great raiders, but their relative isolation prevented serious trouble until the post-Civil War period. By this time travelers and hunters had depleted their buffalo herds, and the army was taking a dim view of their murderous raids.

Efforts to restrict the Comanche and the Kiowa to reservations in western Texas before the Civil War failed miserably. Finally they were rounded up by the United States Army and confined to a reservation in southwestern Oklahoma. The raids against the settlements of western Texas and the camps of the white buffalo hunters developed into another reign of terror. By 1874 most of the Kiowa chiefs, such as Big Tree, Satanta, and Satank, had been captured or killed. Their people returned to the reservation to remain in peace and poverty as they struggled to "follow the white man's road." The Comanche proved more difficult to subdue, but the last of their great chiefs, Quanah Parker, surrendered in 1876 when the so-called Red River War finally ended.

Of all the tribes of the Great American Desert none was more feared than the Apache. These Athapascan-speaking people drifted down from northwestern Canada a few centuries before the first Europeans arrived. They eventually divided into several bands and settled in an area of the desert that stretched from western Texas to the Colorado River in western Arizona. Their traditional enemies were the Pima and the Pueblo—especially the Zuñi. By the time the Americans reached the Southwest the Apache were well experienced in protecting themselves from Indian, Spanish, and Mexican foes. And some bands remained free of American control until near the end of the nineteenth century.

The Apache carried on unrelenting war against the United States before they submitted to reservation life. Leaders like Cochise and Mangus Coloradas spread terror throughout the Southwest and into northern Mexico. Except for hostile bands of Chiricahua Apache, led by Geronimo, most of the tribes were settled on reservations in New Mexico and Arizona by

1874. Not until 1886 were American troops successful in taking Geronimo as a prisoner, and by this time the wars of the southern portion of the Great American Desert had been brought to a close. The overwhelming number of soldiers and white settlers had made raiding too expensive. The Navajo and Pueblo long since had returned to their dreams and ceremonies, while the Cheyenne, Arapaho, Kiowa, and Comanche were too reduced in number and beaten in spirit to offer further resistance. Meanwhile, small desert tribes like the Pima, Yuma, Papago, Havasupai, and Hopi remained on the land they had always considered theirs, the job of taming their formidable environment leaving little time or inclination for anything else.

Before the last Apache in the south had been killed or "civilized" the army had its problems with the tribes of the north. The Homestead Act of 1862 sent in wave after wave of settlers onto the Great Plains. These pioneers, combined with the ranchers and miners that overran the northern portions of the Great American Desert, paved the ground for a final showdown with the Sioux. In the mid-1860's the whites tried to open the Bozeman Trail through the Indian hunting grounds of Wyoming to the mining fields of western Montana. The great Sioux chief Red Cloud made life so hazardous for the travelers along the road that the army had to build a chain of forts to protect them. But the garrisons were eventually abandoned, and the trail became unusable against the determined efforts of Red Cloud's people.

With the discovery of gold in 1874, the scene of conflict shifted to the Black Hills country on the edge of the desert. Prospectors could not be kept out of the Black Hills, nor would the Indians leave their sacred ground. The Crow and Shoshoni joined the white soldiers in a showdown against their ancient Sioux enemies. In June 1876 General George Crook led a thousand soldiers against an equal number of Sioux in the unsuccessful Battle of the Rosebud in southern Montana. Sioux warriors under Crazy Horse and Sitting Bull then moved further west to the Little Big Horn. Here they combined with other Sioux and Cheyenne war parties (the latter, incidentally, containing some survivors of Sand Creek and Washita), to constitute a force of fifteen or sixteen thousand warriors.

A few days after the Battle of the Rosebud the Seventh Cavalry under Custer stumbled upon a large Indian camp. The results are well known to history. The magnificent unit of more than 260 mounted soldiers, which had been especially organized to destroy the northern tribes, was killed to a man. The desperate fight lasted only a few minutes, but it shocked a nation in the midst of celebrating its first centennial. By winning the most decisive battle in the long struggle between white men and red men, Crazy Horse and Sitting Bull insured ultimate defeat for the Indians. The United States Army kept troops in the field until all the Sioux were killed, driven into Canada, or rounded up on reservations. The fighting lasted intermittently for fifteen years.

The Indians of the desert plains clearly saw the end long before it came. Their food supply was diminishing and their rifles proved ineffective against the Hotchkiss guns and other superior weapons brought in by the whites. The only hope for the Indians was a messiah, and, indeed, one appeared before the close of the century. He was a Paiute named Wovoka from the other side of the Rockies, and he preached that the ghosts of dead Indians would return to help drive out the whites and that the vanished buffalo would reappear. Soon the plains and deserts and mountains would belong to the original owners and the old way of life would be restored.

The army became alarmed as the Ghost Dance religion spread throughout the West, but when the millennium failed to appear the whole movement suddenly collapsed. In South Dakota in December 1890, on Wounded Knee Creek, approximately 150 women, children, and Sioux warriors were shot down with rapid-firing Hotchkiss guns as they resisted arrest. For the army the victory was a significant one, perhaps one of the most important in the history of plains warfare. The Indian's spirit was broken, and all hope that he could live his own life was gone. By now warfare and disease had reduced the entire Indian population of the United States to approximately 250,000—less than one-third its original number three centuries earlier.

One of the basic causes of conflict between the Anglo-Americans and the Indians was the attempt to restrict the tribes to specific reservations. The process of allocating certain lands to individual tribes began before the Civil War and continued throughout the last half of the nineteenth century. For the most part Indians were assigned lands in the desert or plains region that the white man considered useless. But soon the western-bound emigrants were trespassing upon territory that had been promised to the Indians "as long as the grass grows and the water runs." During the 1860's the federal government granted ten to twenty sections of land to various railroad companies for each mile of track laid across the West. These acts ultimately resulted in slicing millions of acres off the Indian reservations, which often made them too small to support a hunting economy. But even the reduced acreages began to look bigger and bigger to the whites as more and more of them crowded into the West near the end of the century and as land prices increased in value.

About the time that the Indian wars were drawing to a close, the federal government inaugurated a new policy, the Dawes Allotment Act of 1887. This measure was designed to break up the tribal governments completely, distribute the reservations in individual allotments, and throw open the surplus to white settlement. In this way more than ninety million acres of land were abstracted from the Indians before the allotment policy was reversed in 1934. Meanwhile, the reservations were reduced to approximately sixty million acres, much of which was in the desert regions of the Mountain West. The remaining lands doubtless would eventually have been taken too, had they been considered worth the effort.

According to the Dawes Act of 1887 lands distributed to the Indians in severalty would be held in trust by the federal government for twenty-five years. At the expiration of this period allottees would receive a fee simple title to their holdings and would thus be free to dispose of them in any manner they wished. Few Indians were able to buy the machinery to work their allotments during the trusteeship period, and they preferred to lease the land to white farmers or to large operators for grazing. As soon as they obtained title, many disposed of their lands rapidly, often selling them outright for a "mess of pottage." During the 1920's the federal government extended indefinitely the period of trusteeship for a few thousand allottees that had not yet obtained title. Much Indian land therefore is still under government control. At the same time those tribes which managed to hold on to their reservations eventually found them too small for an expanding population. Their poverty remained chronic until the 1930's, when the New Deal adopted a more benevolent program toward them.

In recent decades the Indian population of the United States has shown a steady increase, to approximately 500,000. It is estimated that this figure will exceed 700,000 by 1975. Most of the Indians today live in the Great American Desert on lands that are appreciating in value. Perhaps no tribe has staged a more dramatic comeback in less promising surroundings than the Navajo. At the same time no tribe has been the subject of more studies and reports by federal agents and anthropologists. In fact, in parts of New Mexico and Arizona it is said that a typical Navajo family consists of a father, mother, two children, and one anthropologist. The Navajo population approaches 90,000, which represents a tenfold increase during the past century, and they have a trust fund from mineral leases in excess of a hundred million dollars. Since 1870 the federal government consistently has added to the Navajo lands in the northeastern corner of Arizona in concerted efforts to provide more living space. Other desert tribes such as the Laguna, Apache, and the Indians of the Wind River Reservation in Wyoming also have recently come into considerable funds as a result of the discovery of uranium, oil, gas, and other mineral resources on their lands.

These developments, along with a more benevolent federal

policy, have enabled tribe after tribe to bring their living conditions up to a reasonable standard. There are still poor Indians desperately struggling to exist on windswept and sunbaked reservations in the West. But education, health, and employment opportunities have improved considerably since World War II, and college graduates are no longer a rarity among the dispossessed former occupants of the desert. The Indian Claims Act of 1946 permitted tribes to file suit for unpaid claims, the object being to clear up past wrongs and pave the way for the federal government to get out of the Indian business. Almost immediately some 850 suits were filed, and by 1960 around twenty tribes had recovered approximately forty million dollars. Several of the remaining claims doubtless will be settled in favor of the Indians, but the great majority will be disposed of without compensation, partly for lack of sufficient evidence.

The final Indian policy of the United States is yet to be developed, and it is too early to judge the result of the legislation of 1946. Perhaps it will end unfavorably as did the allotment policy, or it may mean a great breakthrough for the Indian. At any rate, it is an important change and indicates a new line of thinking and action in Washington. Another indication of this attitude is seen in a resolution passed in 1953, which states that the aim of Congress is to make the Indian subject to the same laws and entitled to the same privileges and responsibilities as any other citizen of the United States as quickly as possible.

Since the passage of the 1953 resolution the Bureau of Indian Affairs has turned over some of its services to other branches of government or to the states in which the Indians reside. Indian education is in the process of being transferred to state public schools; health and welfare to Indians has been taken over by the United States Public Health Service; and civil and criminal jurisdiction over Indians is gradually being assumed by the states.

Today the Indian is a full-fledged American citizen, free to vote, to go where he chooses, and to buy the same things that any other citizen is entitled to buy. Most are proud of their traditions and determined to preserve them. In many ways they are more closely knit than ever, and groups that were once traditional enemies now work together through intertribal councils to raise their standards of living and to obtain further assistance from the federal government.

More than a hundred reservations, large and small, are scattered throughout the eight states that constitute the heart of the Great American Desert. Reclamation practices, mineral resources, and an expanding American population have made these lands valuable, and the Indian is determined to hold on to them. As he becomes better educated and organized, he is no longer an easy victim of unscrupulous action. Perhaps even more important is the attitude of the American people, who have become more tolerant of the Indians' heritage, more concerned with past wrongs, and less apathetic about their future. Economically, the Indian now lives by the same technique as his white neighbor and perhaps with less hardship than in prehistoric days. Still his position is precarious and his life impoverished in comparison with the surrounding white population.

Even though the initial contact with whites disrupted the Indian's way of life, it did add some useful technology. For example, the Navajo acquired sheep and the Sioux acquired firearms, changes that proved helpful but also led to undesirable effects. Subsequent troubles came, perhaps, more from the displacement of the Indian from his land or the destruction of its resources than from any single result of direct contact with the white man. Pushed aside and defeated, the Indian often found his traditional culture unsuited for his drastically changed circumstances. Though the Navajo, Pueblo, and Papago still live where the white man first encountered them, many relocated tribes found that a more arid environment simply added to their problems of survival.

Another problem for the Indian is the substantial population increase resulting from recently improved health standards. In this respect Indians have much in common with peoples from "underdeveloped" areas of the world, whose birth rate exceeds the expansion of their economy. Thus, in spite of higher income, most reservation resources are inadequate to meet rising expectations. Many Indians, especially the Pueblo, therefore have to seek jobs in nearby or distant towns to maintain a desirable living standard. And as the transformation of the Great American Desert continues, native groups whose cultures have constituted unique and colorful assets are forced by necessity to accept full assimilation into the national population.

At the same time there is much that modern Westerners may yet learn from Indians of the arid regions. Their stone or adobe houses, for example, with thick, earth-covered roofs and small doors and windows, are far better suited to conserve night-time coolness and keep out daytime heat in the desert than are poorly insulated houses with an excess of glass. Indian farmers make full use of limited supplies of water by planting widely dispersed gardens in conjunction with small stone checkdams. Though the Soil Conservation Service has copied and improved upon their contour method of planting, it still has no generally accepted means of capturing small runoff that otherwise is lost through evaporation.

Westerners often maintain that the Indian is lazy, since he avoids the midday and afternoon heat as much as possible. But the white man's habit of concentrating his work in the hottest part of the day, even in the desert areas, is both inefficient and unhealthy. A better-adapted work schedule utilizing the early morning hours of relative coolness would be far more logical. Air-conditioning whole cities—as some have suggested—seems a cumbersome and expensive substitute.

However minor the Indian's contributions in comparison to modern technology, his traditional adaptations to a hot and arid climate should not be ignored. Indeed, his philosophy of working *with* the environment rather than *against* it has made possible a far more efficient use of the desert than his white successors have yet achieved.

VIII THE CATTLEMEN'S INVASION

Far from being the vast wasteland that Jefferson originally had imagined, the Great American Desert abounded in natural resources. Successive invasions throughout the nineteenth century, however, dispelled the notion that they existed in inexhaustible amounts. In the wake of the trappers and miners came the stockmen with their trampling herds of cattle and sheep and by the farmers with barbed wire and steel plows. Each army of invaders experienced temporary success, then disappointment and painful readjustment. Only the Mormons accepted the desert for what it was and practiced from the beginning conservation of the region's most valuable resources —water and land.

To early western travelers the most conspicuous of all resources was grass, especially in the eastern portions of the desert. With rare exception they referred to the vast region that it covered as a "Sea of Grass." Though fascinated by its strange beauty, they never believed that it would serve any purpose other than subsistence for the innumerable herds of buffalo. In their quest for other forms of wealth they passed over the grassland and continued to the mountains or the Pacific Coast. Yet within a few years grass ruled as "king" and men fought and died for possession of it.

Frémont was among the first to observe that the blue stem and grama grass on the desert plains and valleys made excellent winter forage for livestock. California- and Oregon-bound emigrants likewise discovered that their horses, cattle, and oxen thrived upon native western grass, even when the wind and sun burned it dry or it lay dormant under a blanket of snow. The fact should have been obvious, for millions of buffalo and other wild game were subsisting upon it when the first white man crossed the continent. Even so, exploitation of the vast grasslands by American pioneers had to wait for the development of large-scale cattle-ranching.

Though Texans played prominent roles in developing the ranching industry throughout the West, they were not the first to introduce cattle into the Great American Desert. Generations before a cow ever set foot in Texas, Spanish *conquistadores* were driving them into the regions now known as New Mexico and Arizona. Juan de Oñate trailed a small herd in 1598 to the upper Rio Grande Valley, where he located his first permanent settlement of San Juan. Additional stock came in, and the herds multiplied slowly until the Pueblo uprising of 1680. What cattle the Indians did not kill that year in an orgy of destruction, the fleeing settlers drove back to northern Mexico.

Fourteen years later, when Diego de Vargas reconquered the New Mexico province, he brought approximately a thousand Spanish cattle with him. These became the seed herds for local ranches, but production never kept pace with demand. For many years cattle remained less valuable to New Mexicans for beef than for tallow candles and leather clothing, saddles, ropes, and shoes. But the coming of the American armed forces in 1846 created new demands, and local ranchers sought new sources of supply in Texas, where by this time cattle existed in much larger numbers.

Meanwhile, before 1830, the Rocky Mountain Fur Trading Company had introduced a few head of cattle into the central Rockies. Also, the Hudson's Bay Company had imported stock from England for the Oregon and Idaho country. Descendants of these scattered herds could be found in the mountains and plains when the Mormons arrived in 1847. But the Saints depended chiefly upon breeding stock driven from Illinois and Missouri, though Brigham Young did send a company of men in 1847 to purchase a thousand head from the Mexican ranches in California and return with them across the Great Basin to Utah. In spite of this start Mormons remained more interested in sheep. Their range history lacks the wild glamor and romance usually associated with cattle-raising.

Cattle came to America with the first English settlers and steadily moved westward with the frontier. But modern ranching started even earlier in Mexico with the Spanish conquest. As the basic techniques evolved, colonizers and missionaries introduced the industry into New Mexico, Arizona, southern California, and Texas. There it languished for several decades, supplying food and clothing to the scattered settlements and hides to a limited outside market. Manifest Destiny eventually caught up with the Southwest and opened the floodgates to settlers from the United States. These late-comers quickly learned ranching methods from the Spaniards by way of the Mexicans, and soon appropriated their "lingo" and dress.

Cattle-raising grew into a major industry in Texas before the Civil War. Later it spread northward to the semiarid, treeless area of the northern plains, burgeoned into big business, and spilled over into the basin region beyond the mountains. Its founders were daring, durable, and sometimes lawless individuals—not too much unlike the men who built fortunes in mining, oil, steel, and railroads.

The cattlemen, however, were not without virtues. During the three short decades following the Civil War they built the industry into the third or fourth most important in the

United States. They established individual empires larger than some of the New England states, but they paid the price for ruthless exploitation of the public domain. In their greed for quick profit they overgrazed the land and destroyed its protective cover, and they saturated the market with more cattle than it could absorb. They paved the way for droughts, blizzards, and declining prices to complete the catastrophe.

The spectacular rise and decline of the range cattle industry typified the events that shaped the history of the Great American Desert throughout the nineteenth century. Though it required an initial investment in cattle, almost everything else that was needed came free or cheap—land, grass, water, and labor. During the formative years even cattle cost little or nothing, especially in Texas, where they ranged over the brush and prairie country like any other wild animals. Estimates of their numbers north of the Rio Grande and along the Gulf Coast in the 1830's approximated 100,000. The Texas longhorns were tough "critters," but settlers soon learned how to round them up and burn a brand into their hides. Yet, there was little incentive to do so without an adequate market.

In the 1840's and 1850's a few enterprising Texans collected herds of wild cattle and drove them to Missouri. Others made drives to Galveston and from time to time shipped a few hundred head to New Orleans and Cuba. In 1846 Edward Piper drove a thousand steers from south Texas all the way to Cincinnati. But the problems and dangers of trail-driving, plus the meager profit at the end, discouraged a second attempt. A short time later the gold fields of California opened a new market, and a few Texas drovers managed to drive small herds across the southern edge of the desert to the Pacific Coast. Some later stopped off in New Mexico and Arizona, staked out claims, fought off the Indians, and raised cattle for the California market or supplied emigrant trains with fresh beef and livestock. Others drove cattle to the Colorado gold fields just before the Civil War, and eventually moved as far north as Montana. Thus, by the time the great conflict started in

1861, Texans had mastered the art of driving beef cattle long distances with minimum losses. More important, American eating habits had changed and the demand for beef had increased.

The war depleted most of the herds east of the Mississippi, but in Texas the number of cattle increased to half a million. Locally, they sold for as little as five dollars a head, while northern buyers were offering twenty to thirty dollars for average steers. Only a few enterprising veterans returned home early enough in 1865 to take advantage of the new market, but the following spring witnessed dozens of trail herds on the move northward. Each drive required careful planning, for the financial risks were high and dangers and misfortunes were commonplace.

Most trail herds got started in early spring to take advantage of the green grass all the way. During the first few days the cowboys pushed the animals at a fast pace until they adjusted to the routine of the trail. Later they followed a schedule of ten or twelve miles per day. Aside from sudden Indian attacks, which were indeed rare, the cowboys lived in fear of a possible stampede. When they did occur, they usually were touched off by an electrical storm or a cloudburst. Not uncommonly the men remained in the saddle for thirty-six hours or more at a stretch, or until they brought the herd under control. Other problems included swollen streams, dry marches, and outlaw bands of cattle rustlers. Rarely did a herd escape at least one or two such adventures, but the cowboys were loyal, and they faced dangers and hardships at every turn without deserting their outfits.

A typical trail-driving outfit consisted of 2000 to 3000 longhorn steers, a trail boss, eight cowpunchers, a cook, horsewrangler, about sixty-five cows ponies, and a four-horse chuck wagon that carried bedrolls and provisions of corn meal, sorghum molasses, beans, salt, sugar, and coffee. The daily program began at sunrise. After breakfast the cowboys picked their ponies for the morning work, while the cook broke camp and the horsewrangler rounded up the *remuda*. Two "point" men started the herd northward, followed by two on the swing, two on the flank, and two drags, whose job it was to look after the calves and laggards.

As the herd ambled along four or five abreast, it stretched out for half a mile or more across the prairies. During the early hours of the morning the pace continued in leisurely fashion in order to allow the cattle to graze. At noon four of the cowboys rode forward to catch a quick meal at the chuck wagon and change horses. They in turn relieved the other crew members without allowing the herd to stop. In the afternoon the trail boss scouted ahead for a camp site near water. As soon as the chuck wagon arrived, the cook pitched camp and started supper. Finally, the herd came up and settled down to drink and graze until dusk. Once again the cowboys ate in relays, changed horses, brought the cattle into a close circle for the night, and prepared for the watch.

The first of the northern trails out of Texas crossed Red River near Denison and continued through Choctaw Nation to Fort Smith, Arkansas. It eventually terminated at the Missouri River Railroad town of Sedalia, Missouri, from which point the cattle reached the new slaughterhouses in Chicago. Several branches of the eastern trail crossed Indian Territory, all of which generally went by the name of the Texas Trail. Later, the cattlemen designated the branches by various names, such as the Sedalia Trail, East Shawnee Trail, West Shawnee Trail, and so forth.

Regardless of the route beyond Red River, a drover's problems multiplied the closer he approached the Kansas or Missouri border. Indians demanded tribute for passage across their lands, or outlaw gangs tried to steal the entire herd. Worse yet were the irate Missouri and Kansas farmers, who feared that their own stock would be contaminated by Texas fever. They did not hestitate to stampede a herd, slaughter the cattle, or "bushwhack" the cowboys. Less than half the cattle driven from Texas the first year after the Civil War successfully reached a northern market.

But conditions improved in 1867. That year the Kansas

Pacific Railroad pushed west as far as the one-saloon town of Abilene. A Chicago cattle buyer named Joseph McCoy arrived a few weeks later and started constructing loading pens and a hotel. He then dispatched riders southward to spread the word among Texas drovers of the advantages of his new cowtown. To reach it cattlemen continued northward from the frontier settlement of Fort Worth to Red River and on past present Duncan, El Reno, and Enid, Oklahoma. Abilene lay almost two hundred miles north of the Oklahoma border. The route to it from Texas quickly took the name of the Chisholm Trail after the frontier trader Jesse Chisholm, who laid it out as a supply road from Wichita, Kansas, to various military posts in Indian Territory. Most of the level country along the trail was carpeted with prairie grass as high as a horse's belly. Distances between watering places rarely exceeded a day's march, and the Plains Indians in the area offered little interference. Approximately 35,000 cattle followed the new route the first year; the number doubled in 1868 and increased thereafter until 1872.

By then other cowtowns had come into being: Newton, Ellsworth, Wichita, and, of course, Dodge City. Albert Alonzo Robinson, who was in charge of location and construction for the Atchison, Topeka, and Santa Fe Railroad, laid out the "queen of cowtowns" in June, 1872, and enterprising citizens lost little time in advertising its location in southwestern Kansas. To reach it from Texas, cattlemen followed the new Western Trail north from Doan's Crossing on Red River along a line parallel to the 100th meridian.

During its heyday Dodge City became known as the toughest cowtown in the West. It was a drab place of dirty saloons, dusty streets, gambling dens, and bawdy houses—typical of the western boom towns of the mining frontier. Cowboys fresh off the trail found violent entertainment there, and Dodge's reputation was even less enhanced by the presence of buffalo hunters. Both groups eventually met their match in the local peace officers, who succeeded in bringing a fair degree of law and order to the place by 1886. By this time only about 25 per cent of the Texas cattle reaching southwest Kansas were being shipped to eastern stockyards. The rest were held over as "stocker" cattle or driven northward to newer ranges.

Texas continued to be the great reservoir of cattle for two decades after the Civil War. During the years of the long drives cattlemen shifted to other trails in search of fresh grass or because of troublesome Indians and quarantine laws of the advancing settlements. Sometimes northern stockmen came to Texas and selected their own cattle and drove them to their home ranges in New Mexico, Colorado, Wyoming, Montana, Nebraska, or the Dakotas, or they contracted with local drovers for delivery. The transcontinental railroads and the expansion of the industry onto the Great Plains created new cowtowns north of Kansas. Among the more notable were Ogallala, Nebraska; Cheyenne, Wyoming; Bismarck, North Dakota; and Miles City, Montana. Each town passed through a normal period of bawdiness before its citizens grew intolerant of such activities and curtailed them.

In addition to the famous cattle trails through Oklahoma and Kansas, other important ones developed across New Mexico. In 1866 a Texas rancher named Charles Goodnight reasoned that an excellent market for his cattle could be found beyond the Pecos River. Mining was just beginning in the territory, and he felt sure that the miners not only wanted beef but that they had the money to pay for it. Accordingly, he and his partner, Oliver Loving, started west on the Brazos River near Fort Belknap to Horsehead Crossing on the Pecos. Here they turned their combined herds northward and continued by way of Fort Sumner, where the government had corralled some 8500 Indians. Despite their antagonism toward the former Confederates, the military desperately needed cattle, and they bought the entire herd. The venture proved so profitable that the Texans hurried home in time for a second drive that season.

Soon the Goodnight-Loving Trail extended beyond Fort Sumner to the mining camps of northern New Mexico. Other cattlemen quickly followed, one of the best known of whom was John Chisum. This Texan allegedly got his start by driving herds for other people and forgetting to pay the original owners. He eventually extended the Goodnight-Loving Trail north of New Mexico through the Colorado towns of Kit Carson, Deertrail, and Pine Bluffs. His cowboys later pushed on from there to Lark, Wyoming, and Miles City, Montana. Meanwhile, Chisum established his headquarters near Roswell and staked out a ranch 150 miles up and down the Pecos River. Thereafter his army of cowboys put the Chisum brand on every four-legged creature they could find. At one time his herd approximated 60,000 cattle. Not only did the Chisum ranch supply cattle to the Miles City market and various northern stock ranches in between, but also it delivered some to the mining camps around Tucson and Prescott, Arizona, several hundred miles westward.

Throughout the 1850's men trailed cattle from the Mississippi Valley along the Platte and thence by way of the Snake and Humboldt into Oregon and California. Some animals strayed from the trail and somehow managed to survive on their own. When Granville Stuart, one of the future "cattle kings" of Montana, arrived on the northern plains with sixty head in 1858 he observed numerous small herds throughout the region. The next year Horace Greeley made his famous trip across the continent and wrote that he counted "several thousand cattle" in Wyoming. Further west, in present Nevada, cattle grazed along the bottoms of the Walker, Carson, and Truckee rivers. Most of these herds had been brought from California and later sold for beef to the silver miners of the Washoe area.

Cattle-raising became sufficiently important in Montana by 1864 for the first territorial legislature to enact a law regulating brands. The next year Conrad Kohrs bought a few head and opened a butcher shop in Helena. Miners purchased his entire stock as quickly as he could slaughter, and when he could not buy enough to satisfy the demand, he started his own ranch. Soon he joined Granville Stuart and the select company of cattle kings of Montana who counted their livestock in the thousands. Elsewhere throughout the West the cattle industry followed quickly in the wake of the mining developments.

The scattered army posts built along the Oregon, Bozeman, and other trails provided additional local markets, as did the numerous Indian reservations. Later the Union Pacific pushed its tracks across the plains from Omaha at the same time that the Central Pacific was racing eastward across the Great Basin. Their crews, particularly the Irish workers of the Union Pacific, needed beef.

The Union Pacific's demand for beef caused John W. Iliff to leave the mining camps around Denver and set up a store near present Cheyenne, Wyoming. Here he went into the cattle industry, and within a few months he amassed enough capital from the sale of beef to the railroad camps to go into large-scale ranching. Eventually he became one of the largest operators in the West, buying from 10,000 to 15,000 Texas longhorns annually and grazing another 25,000 head in Wyoming and Colorado. Iliff employed forty to fifty cowboys on his various ranches during the busy season. He traveled far and wide to acquire cattle and then drove them to his home ranges in northeastern Colorado and southeastern Wyoming. Charles Goodnight alone supplied him with approximately 30,000 head over a ten-year period. At the same time he imported choice Durham and Hereford bulls from England to improve his herds, and he kept from 6000 to 7000 cows for breeding purposes. His cattle fattened on the dry bunch grass of the northern plains, and he produced such superior beef that they commonly sold for fifty dollars a head. Like other large operators of his time and place, Iliff purchased two-year-old Texas steers for ten to fifteen dollars per head. When left out on the range for a couple of years, they could put on 400 pounds in weight, even without shelter or hay. The expense for caring for a herd of 1000 steers amounted to approximately $1.75 per head, which seems little enough, but even this figure decreased considerably with larger units of livestock.

It is no wonder that many enterprising Westerners took advantage of the free grass, water, and land and prospered so rapidly. By 1880 the cattle industry was firmly established throughout the high plains region of the Great American Desert, as the following census figures show:

	CATTLE IN 1870	CATTLE IN 1880
Colorado	70,736	791,459
Montana	36,738	428,279
Wyoming	11,130	521,213
New Mexico	57,534	347,936

In the remaining four states of the Great American Desert the cattle industry developed more slowly—in spite of its early start there. For one thing Arizona and the Great Basin region were more arid and further from the great population centers in the East. Gradually, however, Montana and Wyoming ranchers discovered that southern Idaho and parts of Nevada contained good livestock country, and they began to drive herds there for pasturage. In 1868 a Mississippi-born Texan drove a sizable herd of longhorns all the way from the Lone Star State to the Humboldt Valley. (His name was John Sparks and he later became governor of Nevada.) The hardy longhorns were excellent foragers and generally took care of themselves. They fattened well on the native grass and brought good prices in the California slaughterhouses and western mining towns.

Within a few years the entire country that had so recently belonged exclusively to the Indians was dotted with cattle herds. But it took much more land per cow west of the Rockies than in the Great Plains, and by 1890 only Arizona compared favorably with any of the cattle states along the eastern slope. According to the Bureau of Census Arizona had slightly more than 5000 head in 1870. This figure increased to 135,757 in 1880, and ten years later to 927,880 range cattle.[1] Estimates for the three other sections are as follows:

1 By 1890 sheep had become more important than cattle in Idaho, Nevada, and Utah. The census lists 273,469 for Nevada, 357,712 for Idaho, and 1,014,176 for Utah. Meanwhile, the number of sheep in Arizona had dropped to 102,427 because of its tremendous increase in cattle.

	CATTLE IN 1870	CATTLE IN 1880	CATTLE IN 1890
Idaho	10,456	191,157	219,431
Nevada	31,516	216,823	210,900
Utah	39,180	132,655	278,313

It was natural that cattle-raising would concentrate where it did—the Great Plains region of the Great American Desert. This area remained the heart of the industry until the late 1880's. It stretched north and west of Texas into the 500,000 square miles of land now forming the states of New Mexico, Colorado, Wyoming, and Montana. It was treeless except for the cottonwoods and willows that grew along the streams, a monotonous country with severe winters and hot summers. For the most part its grass was shorter than the growth on the rolling prairies of Kansas and Nebraska, but it was capable of supporting an enormous livestock population.

Stephen H. Long's description of this arid region in 1821 inadvertently contributed to the growth of the future cattle industry. His label "Great American Desert" held up the advance of the farmers and caused the agricultural frontier to leap the vast heartland of America for the lands along the Pacific Coast. Thus, the cattle industry was left with the necessary space in which to develop. Suddenly, the right conditions fell into place like the tumblers in a combination lock: the Civil War brought an increased demand for beef; a humid cycle brought increased rainfall to the Great Plains; settlers learned that cattle could thrive on the native grass and survive the drastic changes in climate; the transcontinental railroads pushed to the Pacific; and, finally, the great buffalo herds on which the Plains Indians' economy had depended were destroyed and the Indians were confined to specific reservations.

Within two decades the desert had diminished in size and the eastern half possessed a stable though scattered population. The ranges were also stocked with cattle from the east and west, and especially by the great trail herds of Texas longhorns from the south. Beef from the grasslands of the plains provided food for the East and for much of Europe. At the same time the basin area beyond the Rockies appeared ready for a full invasion by the cattlemen, for this region was already supplying beef to the Pacific Coast.

Perhaps nothing contributed to the rapid turn of events as much as the railroads, for no sooner had the Civil War ended than steel rails began edging across the desert. The Kansas Pacific reached Abilene in 1867, and pushed on to Denver three years later. Further south, the Atchison, Topeka, and Santa Fe raced toward La Junta, Colorado. From there one branch went on to Leadville in central Colorado, while the other turned south through Raton Pass, worked its way around the mountains to Santa Fe and Albuquerque, and eventually ran across the southern portion of the desert to California.

In the same year that the Kansas Pacific reached Abilene, the Union Pacific arrived at the small village of Cheyenne, assuring the settlement's position as the cowboy capital of the northern plains. But it did not pause until it reached the mountains of western Wyoming. As the Union Pacific battled through the Central Rockies, the Central Pacific shot eastward across the flat desert lands of Nevada. The two lines met near Ogden, Utah, before the end of 1869. A decade and a half later, the Northern Pacific moved beyond Bismarck, North Dakota, and created a chain of cowtowns across Montana and Idaho. And the Southern Pacific connected the principal markets of Texas with southern California, via El Paso and Yuma, Arizona. By then the Great American Desert was four times spanned by major rail lines. In addition, north-south lines connected Denver to the Union Pacific on the north and to the Atchison, Topeka, and Santa Fe on the south.

Before the end of the century the Great Northern further integrated the Great American Desert with the rest of the nation. By that time Great Britain had entered the picture, not only as a great importer of American beef but as an exporter of capital to invest in the ranching industry. Also, refrigerator freight cars numbering in the thousands were built, and packing houses moved closer to the sources of supply. These factors, combined with barbed wire and the opening of the northern ranges, brought the great cattle drives to an end.

Within a few exciting years the entire West had been settled, and all of the Great American Desert had been organized into territories and states. The rapidity with which it happened, however, could not have been possible without the centralization of private enterprise. But even more important was the helping hand of the federal government. It provided easy credit through the National Banking Act of 1863, so vital to westward expansion. It subsidized the transcontinental railroads in excess of the actual cost of their construction. And its public land policies represented the most generous "give-away" program in the history of the world.

Before 1862 settlers on the public domain could purchase 160 acres of land for the minimum price of $1.25 per acre. Under the Homestead Act, passed during the Lincoln Administration, a 160-acre plot of land sold for less than $10, or the cost of filing a claim. Cattlemen as well as farmers quickly took advantage of this law, and by homesteading a tract that controlled access to water, they secured use of the great ranges without owning them. The Timber Culture Act of 1873 enabled them to acquire title to an additional 160 acres by planting forty acres in trees. Four years later the Desert Land Act offered another 640 acres of land at $1.25 an acre, provided a portion of it was put under irrigation. Finally, the Timber and Stone Act of 1878 assured a further chance to raid the natural resources of the West. This amazing law allowed any citizen or first-paper alien to buy up to 160 acres of land "unfit for cultivation" and "valuable chiefly for timber or stone." The price was $2.50 per acre—about the price of one good log.

Each of these measures was an open invitation to fraud, for the burden of proof rested with the federal government. It has been estimated that 95 per cent of the final proof titles were fraudulent. For a fee, settlers filed, then transferred their holdings to some corporation and moved on. Cattlemen often induced their hired hands to take entry on land and then turn it over to the boss. The evil was compounded by illegal fencing —by enclosing land a cattleman claimed without right, imposing his claim by force or the threat of force. At the root of it all was the need for water, for in the West he who controlled the water controlled the land and everything that went with it.

The availability of public lands and the opportunity for enormous profits led to adventurous plunging. The panic of 1873 brought a temporary slowdown by depressing the price of beef and forcing many small operators out of business. It likewise encouraged centralized control in large companies and cattlemen's associations, which could operate more efficiently and withstand the ups and downs of the market. When the effects of the panic wore off, stock-raising companies expanded more rapidly than ever. By the end of the decade the cattle industry was adding billions of dollars of new wealth annually to the national output and advancing hand-in-hand with agriculture, manufacturing, transportation, communication, lumbering, and mining.

Western steers reached an all-time peak of $9.25 per hundred pounds on the Chicago market in 1882. Newspapers and farm journals carried optimistic accounts of how a steer worth five dollars at birth could run on the public domain for four or five years at scarcely any expense to the owner and be sold on the market for forty-five to sixty dollars. "Fifteen years ago there was not a rich man in the cattle business," the editor of *The Stock Growers,* Las Vegas, New Mexico, wrote on June 26, 1886. "Today a man with $100,000 worth of ranch and cattle property is regarded as being in the business in a small way, while their combined holdings are worth more than $600,000,000, and among the wealthiest may be found men who were driving ox teams across the plains a few years ago at $20 per month."

So great was the demand for cattle on the western ranges that new sources of supply had to be found. Approximately 300,000 longhorns came up the trail from Texas each year between 1880 and 1885. In addition, several thousand were being moved from the Pacific Coast into Idaho, Nevada, and northern Arizona. At the same time steers were shipped in from the farms of Wisconsin, Minnesota, Michigan, Illinois, Iowa, and Missouri. Feeders in these states discovered that it was more profitable to sell their young cattle to western ranchers than to fatten them for market. These eastern cattle were commonly called "pilgrims," and from 1882 to 1884 about as many "pilgrims" moved west as range cattle moved east.

Local newspapers throughout the West were filled with announcements of the arrival of cattle from almost every direction, and thus it is difficult to draw accurate conclusions as to the total numbers. Government census figures before 1890 are not much help either, but it is probable that the total approximated 7,500,000 head. Three-fourths of these were in the Great Plains region alone; Arizona, Nevada, Utah, and Idaho claimed the balance.[2]

Some Westerners feared that the rapid growth of ranching was unhealthy. No longer was it a frontier enterprise; men of limited means were finding it difficult to stay in business. Though the small operator had not completely disappeared, most of the business by 1885 was in the hands of large corporations with home offices elsewhere. A few of these organizations had attempted to establish their business on a sound basis by purchasing lands to serve as grazing grounds and by giving careful attention to their stock. But the scramble for profits caused most ranchers to expand beyond the margin of safety. The industry simply became too large for the range. Furthermore, the government forced the removal of cattle companies that had been utilizing the grasslands of the Cheyenne-Arapaho reservation in Indian Territory. This action resulted in the crowding of an additional 300,000 steers on northern pastures that were already overstocked.

The stage was set for catastrophe. Rains did not fall throughout the West during the spring of 1886, and when the spring and summer winds blew from the south, the soil rose in great clouds of dust. For the next two seasons, and intermittently until 1893, the soil moved back and forth with the shifting

2 By this time (1890) sheep herds, especially in the states and territories west of the Rockies, were putting an additional strain on the available grass.

winds. But if the summer of 1886 was the poorest growing season for grass in thirty years or more, the following winter was even more severe on cattle. Snowstorms arrived on the northern plains a full six weeks earlier than usual. By the first week of November the upper two-thirds of the Great American Desert was caught in a blizzard that plunged temperatures below zero. The bad weather even froze some of the streams of northern New Mexico and west Texas into solid ice. No sooner had the blizzard spent itself than it was followed by another, and then another. They swept down both slopes of the Rockies and continued throughout December, January, February, and March, holding the temperatures to forty below zero for two and three weeks at a time.

With snow and ice four or five feet deep on level ground, the drifts in the coulees and river bottoms often extended twenty to thirty feet in depth. The helpless cattle were unable to dig below the successive layers of snow to reach the grass. Some died within two hours after the first storm struck, but most instinctively "turned tail" and headed south. They moved "like grey ghosts with icicles hanging from their muzzles, eyes, and ears," directly into fences and draws. There they were stalled, unable to go forward or to turn back.

The newer stock from Texas and the "pilgrims" from the East succumbed first. Most of these cattle already were weak and footsore from being driven or shipped in and therefore were less able to withstand the severe weather. They crowded into the coulees and creek beds or stood stacked together against the fences, without food, water, warmth, or shelter. They pressed close to each other in groups of several hundred, but there was not enough heat in their huddled forms to counteract the cold, and within a short time they either smothered or froze in their tracks. The native stock were more acclimated and possessed heavier coats. They avoided the crowded coulees and fences and managed to hang on a little longer. Some fed on sagebrush and cottonwood bark where they could find it, or collected around the corrals and ranch houses. They gnawed on fence posts, barns, and even ate the tar paper on the side of the bunk houses until they dropped in their tracks. One stockman made these observations:

> Snow drifts were like hills. There was a straw stack in the field ten rods away, but the cattle would not leave the creek where they were out of the wind. They got water out of the creek. The ice was more than six inches thick, but later froze to the bottom, two feet deep . . . a deep ravine ran through the pasture and the snow filled it. Cattle made paths across the ravine in the snow, and when the thaw came were lost when they broke through the caked snow and drowned.

By March the snow had begun to melt and ranchers rode out to survey the damage. In some sheltered places and along fence rows they found carcasses stacked two and three deep. Losses of 80 and 90 per cent were not uncommon, and most of the emaciated survivors with frozen ears, tails, and feet often were too weak to stand. Cowboys reported riding all day on the ranch without encountering a single live steer. The depth of the tragedy was even more apparent when the spring rains came and carried thousands of carcasses downstream.

Ironically, the abundance of water from the melting snow produced good range conditions that spring, but grass was no longer king. The summer of 1887 turned hot and dry like the previous one, and the following winter was equally severe. Many of the large operators, particularly the corporations, disposed of the remnants of their herds and declared bankruptcy. Whole sections of the plains and basin region were cleared of cattle. The catastrophe demonstrated the desert's impulsive nature and the dangers of abusing its resources. "The experience from the financial standpoint should teach stockmen to keep smaller herds and care for them well," the Bismarck (Dakota) *Weekly Tribune* editorialized on February 26, 1887.

Even without the droughts and blizzards of the late 1880's and early 1890's, the range-cattle industry was destined to make drastic readjustment. Two post-Civil War inventions and the adaptation of a third had already forewarned the inevitable changes that would come before the end of the century. The first was the chilled steel plow, which James Oliver started manufacturing in South Bend, Indiana, in 1868. It provided the pioneer settler with the first instrument capable of cutting the tough prairie sod of the Great Plains. About the same time Joseph F. Glidden of DeKalb, Illinois, secured the first of many patents on barbed wire, a practical fencing material of two strands of wire twisted together so as to hold the barbs rigid. By 1873 he and his partner, Isaac Eldwood, were turning out barbed wire at less than twenty dollars a hundred pounds, and within a few years the price had dropped steadily to half that amount.

Together with large-scale production of the windmill, the steel plow and barbed wire effected profound changes on the desert's landscape. The steel plow brought the moist subsoil to the surface and enabled Westerners to plant crops. Barbed wire provided a cheap and efficient material to confine cattle to their home range and to protect new fields from predatory animals. And the windmill supplemented natural sources of water. In use in Europe since the twelfth century, it was adopted, adapted, and developed to meet the unusual conditions of the Great American Desert. It was the windmill that made it possible for the land to be fenced in small areas and for stockmen to cut their ranges into small pastures. Moreover, to drought-stricken ranchers and farmers it often was the difference between starvation and livelihood.

Aided by several years of above-normal rains and a barrage of propaganda from the railroads and land speculators, midwestern farmers now had the equipment to challenge the desert. Anxious to participate in what Lewis Mumford has called "the great barbecue," they convincingly argued that they were as entitled to the free land as the cattle ranchers. Sheepmen had already advanced the same argument and were moving in with their flocks of bleating woollies. Possession of public domain formerly considered a desert soon became a contest between the army of farmers and sheepmen and the cattle ranchers who claimed the land by right of sufferance. Sheep clipped the grass to its roots, and steel plows turned under thousands of acres of ancient sod that had held the soil in check for centuries. Ranchers struck back by destroying flocks of sheep or hemming in the farmers with miles of barbed wire fences.

In some regions of the West, killings and destruction of property were commonplace, but the trouble was never as widespread and prolonged as the fiction writers later claimed. In time the three groups learned to live together, for they shared a host of common enemies. Foremost among these was the climate. Another was the railroads, at first welcomed and later despised because of exorbitant freight rates and unethical practices. Also, the economic forces that determined profit, interest rates, and availability of credit forced all Westerners into a political alliance against the so-called vested interest of the East.

Though many farmers retreated from the desert following the change of climate in the late 1880's and the economic depression of 1893, the stockmen were more determined. Unlike the trappers and miners of earlier generations, many ranchers stayed on to make the painful transition that nature and economic necessity dictated. Range boundaries slowly contracted, and large herds were no longer turned loose without shelter to graze and drift where they wished. Ranchers kept their herds under more careful control, built shelters for the weaker animals, and placed more value upon blooded stock.

The large ranching companies were broken up and ownership and management were taken over by individuals or smaller companies. Absentee ownership became the rare exception, and the right to public domain came to be based upon leases rather than prior occupation. Ranchers also constructed a network of interior fences to preserve the grass coverage and to control breeding. They combined cattle-raising with agriculture to produce hay and feed for their animals during the winter months. Many ranchers dropped their prejudice against sheep and started raising them in conjunction with cattle.

Within a period of fifteen years after the Civil War cattlemen spread their vast ranches over an empire of grass in the Great American Desert. They arrived when it was open range and developed an enormous industry in an area once considered wasteland. During that period and the decade that followed, men, cattle, and horses held almost undisputed possession. Changing circumstances, aided by the Industrial Revolution, forced the cattlemen to surrender much of the land to other uses. Yet, in spite of the invasion by agriculture and the host of other industries that now thrive side by side in the Great American Desert, the spirit of the cattle kingdom is still manifest.

IX BLOSSOM LIKE THE ROSE

As the Great American Desert slowly surrendered its geographic secrets, it began to lose its forbidding image of dry sterile soil, shifting sand dunes, and imaginary bands of mongrel outlaws. Two generations after the Lewis and Clark expedition thousands of emigrants had crossed it from east to west and the Mormons had scattered hundreds of settlements throughout its most arid regions. Then came the miners, who laid the basis for dozens of permanent cities on the mountain slopes and in the valleys. By the mid-1870's cattle trails extended across the eastern half of the desert from Texas and New Mexico to the Canadian border, and cowboys were herding cattle where Indians so recently had hunted buffalo. Finally came the farmers. Soon the boundaries of the desert were redrawn, and before the end of the century the western plains became a geographic extension of the Southwest and the midwestern prairies.

In the process of detaching the plains from the desert, Stephen H. Long's original Great American Desert would be transformed into the Great American Garden. Special interests, particularly the railroad promoters and land speculators, were among the most active in proclaiming the new order. For obvious reasons they wanted the agricultural frontier pushed out onto the plains to make room for hundreds of thousands of new settlers. Naturally they lent their support to the idea that pioneer farmers could subsist beyond the 98th meridian on the 160 acres of land provided by the Homestead Act of 1862.

Though the campaign to entice settlers into the region pre-empted by ranchers met bitter resistance, the results were inevitable. Patents already had been granted in the United States for the basic modern farm machines. As a result, thousands of farmers had taken up land in parts of Kansas, Nebraska, and Dakota that formerly had been considered too dry to sustain agriculture. The disc harrow, grain drill, planter, reaper, binder, thresher, and straddle-row cultivator, as well as the chilled steel plow, proved ideal for the prairie country which bordered the desert. Furthermore, the lands were devoid of trees, relatively flat, and sparsely settled.

The increased settlement was also based on the belief that a belt of greater rainfall was moving out beyond the Mississippi Valley in the wake of the new migration. There could be no doubt that annual precipitation along the desert rim had increased noticeably and that crops were being produced, though with varying success. At the same time the population of Kansas, Nebraska, and the Dakotas jumped from half a million in 1870 to a million and a half in 1880. The relationship between increased rainfall and increased population seemed fairly obvious to the unsophisticated plainsmen: it was evident that a change in cosmic law was being effected by the presence and activities of white settlers.

Devoid of accurate knowledge of the climate, and ignorant of scientific matters, the farmers were more than a little pleased that they could alter the forces of nature. Not only could they transform the prairies into the garden spot of America, but they began to feel that they might even conquer the desert as well. The crux of the matter was rainfall, since rainfall remained the distinguishing difference between the fertile farm lands and the bleak uplands that were fit only for grazing. Accordingly, Westerners eagerly accepted the notion that in some fashion civilization itself could increase rainfall sufficiently for the agricultural frontier to continue its advance as far as the Rocky Mountains.

The notion that civilization brings increased rainfall first appeared in Josiah Gregg's *Commerce of the Prairies*. This Santa Fe trader observed in 1844 that "the extreme cultivation of the earth might contribute to the multiplication of showers, as it certainly does to the fountains." Gregg went on to say that "The people of New Mexico also assure us that the rains have much increased in latter years, a phenomenon which the vulgar superstitiously attribute to the arrival of the Missouri traders."

The theory of increasing rainfall by human efforts received added support from the Mormons. Soon after their arrival in Utah, they observed that the level of Great Salt Lake was gradually rising, a change they attributed to the cultivation of the desert lands by their system of irrigation. Though prominent members of the United States Geological Survey promptly denied this hypothesis, the belief persisted among Americans for several decades. It was endorsed by many California and Oregon emigrants, who, judging from comments in innumerable diaries, experienced as much difficulty on the plains from rain and mud as from heat or dust.

By the end of the Civil War two schools of thought relative to the plains had emerged. The first maintained that it was still part of the desert, though rainfall appeared to be increasing. This they attributed to a new climatic cycle rather than to civilization itself. Others stated flatly that the thousands of emigrants en route to California and Oregon, the caravans of the Santa Fe traders, the activities of the Mormons, miners, railroad construction crews, and cattlemen, plus the farmers who had settled along the eastern rim of the desert following the Homestead Act of 1862, had inadvertently brought the increase in rain.

Railroad promoters were especially anxious to accept the

latter theory and to convince the public of its merit. Accordingly, they hired journalists and lecturers and flooded the country with articles and speeches in an effort to prove that the plains should no longer be considered part of the Great American Desert. Increased rainfall in the years immediately after 1865 helped their cause considerably. The *New York Tribune,* among other leading newspapers of the day, carried numerous articles on the subject, and even such prestigious organizations as the American Association for the Advancement of Science and the Smithsonian Institution gave indirect endorsement to the notion that rainfall might be increased further through human efforts.

As the campaign to transform the western plains into the Great American Garden gained momentum, it received a significant boost from Ferdinand V. Hayden, Director of the United States Geological Surveys of the Territories. Hayden was the most famous geologist and scientific explorer of the time, and he believed that he had seen experimental proof that trees would thrive on the plains without artificial watering. He wrote in 1867:

> The settlement of this country and the increase of timber has already changed for the better the climate of that portion of Nebraska lying along the Missouri, so that within the last twelve or fourteen years the rain has gradually increased in quantity and is more equally distributed through the year. I am confident this change will continue to extend across the dry belt to the foot of the Rocky Mountains as the settlements extend and the forest-trees are planted in proper quantities.

About the same time, the Commissioner of Public Lands recommended to Congress that it compel new homesteaders on the plains to forest a high percentage of their land to insure increased rainfall. Congress gave statutory dignity to the idea by the passage of the Timber Culture Act in 1873, which attempted to encourage the growth of timber on the prairies and plains. Unfortunately, it produced more perjury than trees, but the westward migration of rainfall continued to stir the imagination of millions of Americans. The cultivation of the soil and the planting of trees, they argued, had increased moisture at such a rapid rate in the West that eventually crops of all varieties would be grown without irrigation.

The Reverend C. S. Harrison of York, Nebraska, wrote a prize essay on the subject in 1873, in which he expressed the belief that the mythical desert would soon be covered with beautiful groves and fruitful orchards to the base of the Rockies. He further stated that parts of the Great Basin formerly considered rainless had received abundant showers wherever trees had been planted. Even this section of the Great American Desert, he hinted, might eventually become "a land flowing with milk and honey" and one that would "blossom like the rose."

This and similar essays were printed gratuitously by the railroads and community developers and circulated widely throughout the East and even in Europe. The idea of increased rainfall, regardless of its cause, corresponded with the interest of every settler in the Kansas-Nebraska area, for many of the prairie farmers wanted to sell and move on. And one could hardly sell if the reason he was moving was that he could not make a living where he was. Farmers, like the journalists and pseudo-scientists in the pay of the railroads and other western boosters, eagerly embraced Hayden's thesis. One went so far as to claim that every yard of steel rail laid in the desert would draw from the heavens a gallon of water per annum.

Others argued that there always had been a good rainfall in the West, as evidenced by the numerous canyons and creek beds. But the most plausible answer seemed to have been found by Dr. Samuel Aughey, a distinguished Nebraska scientist, who claimed that the prairie sod prevented the rainfall from soaking into the ground. "After the soil is broken," he wrote in 1880, "a rain as it falls is absorbed by the soil like a huge sponge." Aughey further explained that the soil returned a little moisture each day to the atmosphere by evaporation; it then received it back at night in the form of heavy dew.

Thus, by a process of osmosis the climate changed for the better, the humidity increased, and rain came more regularly, less at any one time, but more often.

Aughey's argument appeared in a year of unseasonable rains and attracted considerable scientific support. Thus, it seemed plausible that the absorbent power of the soil, wrought by civilization, had caused and would continue to cause the increase in rainfall—rather than the planting of trees. The hypothesis was soon reduced to a maxim, "Rain Follows the Plow," and as long as the humid cycle continued, the maxim gained wider acceptance. Meanwhile, some alarmists were predicting that plowing up the ancient sod and sparse vegetation of the plains would eventually prove disastrous. Among these were the ranchers, who hoped to keep the agricultural frontier from spreading beyond the 98th meridian.

Obviously, the ranchers opposed the extension of settlements or "nests" of farmers on the plains for selfish reasons, but they were on more solid ground than their opponents. They knew from their experience in the early 1870's, that dry years followed wet ones, and they did not believe that traditional agriculture could be sustained on a permanent basis in regions where the rainfall varied from ten to twenty inches per year. They had powerful support from several prominent figures, among whom was Major John Wesley Powell, geologist in charge of the United States Geographical and Geological Survey of the Rocky Mountain Region. Powell stated in a famous essay submitted as early as 1878, *Report of the Lands of the Arid West,* that except for the Columbia River Valley the entire region between the 100th meridian and the Pacific Coast was arid. "In this area," he wrote, "many droughts will occur; many seasons in a long series will be fruitless, and it may be doubted whether, on the whole, agriculture will prove remunerative."

Powell's main thesis concerned the traditional 160-acre homestead, which he maintained was insufficient to support an average family in the Far West. He recommended, therefore, that the size of each homestead should be increased and that holdings along watersheds, or rather along the divides between them, be divided into districts, each homesteader controlling his own runoff, timber, grazing lands, and irrigation efforts. In this way, and by a combination of grazing and irrigation, farmers could prosper even during the drier years. Powell was convinced that the plains and basin region of the West would prove in the long run to have inadequate rainfall, no matter what some of his fellow scientists claimed. He was right, of course, and in time the desert would have to be settled just as he had predicted—in spite of the disapproval of the current occupants and in the absence of new homestead laws.

The Powell report became the basis for Congressman Abram S. Hewitt's efforts to revise the public land system. That effort ultimately failed. Proponents of western expansion realized that larger homestead units, such as the recommended 2560 acres, meant fewer people, and fewer people meant less business for railroads, western trade centers, and real estate developers. It also meant cheaper land prices for the settler who wished to sell out. "The report is proved false by every one of the 100,000 new occupants who last year [1880] carved his new farm out of these very 'non-farming' lands so greatly coveted by the aristocratic lords of the herds," the argument ran. Also, "the Creator never imposed a perpetual desert upon the earth, but on the contrary, has so endowed it that men by the plow, can transform it, in any country, into farm areas."

The wet years seemed to substantiate all the claims made by the special interests. Never before had the plains been subjected to such praise and flattery. They were depicted as lands meant for the plow, where there were no trees to interfere with cultivation, where the climate was the most healthful in the world, the valleys the most beautiful, and the meadows completely carpeted with flowers throughout most of the year. Here on the western plains the rainfall was increasing at such a rate that settlers eventually would even have to take precautions against mildew. While such propaganda lasted, people flocked onto the plains. Railroads established immigration bureaus and land departments and sent their agents through-out the prairie country, as far east as the Atlantic seaboard and even to Europe. They offered excursion rates, choice farms along their rights-of-way on easy terms, and loans to buy seed and tools. Eastern banks likewise were eager to lend money to prospective settlers, and mortgage companies flour-ished throughout the Midwest. Not only were the lobbyists successful in defeating a revised homestead law, but by 1885 they had practically reduced the Great American Desert to a small area southwest of Salt Lake City.

The illusion vanished quickly. The disastrous winters that followed finished the cattle corporations' paradise on the Great Plains. As we have seen, it never again reached such ebullient proportions. The hot winds and dust storms drove out most farmers along the eastern rim as the drying-out proc-ess spread in all directions. Fortunately, large sections of New Mexico and Arizona were still unsettled and therefore the effect was less disastrous then it might have been.

As crop failure followed crop failure, the retreat from the plains and prairies resembled a rout. Thousands of farmers deserted their much-mortgaged claims in western Kansas and Nebraska and eastern Colorado and Wyoming. Towns that had once boasted of becoming a commercial metropolis or a great railroad center, or both, were abandoned. Banks and loan companies failed, and foreclosures on farms were too numerous for the few remaining newspapers to print all the notices. Receivers of bankrupt properties sold them for as little as 3 per cent of original cost and were glad to get it. Farmers loaded their families into prairie schooners, and, in the current phrase, "went back to the wife's folks." One hun-dred thousand people departed from the western third of Kansas and Nebraska alone. Fortunately, many of them got out in time to participate in the first land rush into Okla-homa in April 1889, their covered wagons still carrying the bitter phrase: "In God we trusted; In Kansas we busted."

The beautiful theory of transforming by the plow the Great American Desert into the Great American Garden became a haunting and mocking memory, and it took the West many years to pay the debt incurred by the settlers' folly. The depression began in 1888 and lasted eight years. It affected the entire nation, and before it ended, Westerners had worked themselves into a mass hysteria and were demanding a major overhaul of the government and the economy. Their grievances went well beyond the sudden change of climate, and ran the whole gamut of charges of dishonesty against the railroads, bankers, politicians, and land speculators. Before the anger subsided, it transformed the people of the prairies and plains into radicals who saw nothing un-American in asking for direct federal relief and in resorting to force if necessary to bring about a new order.

Pioneer farmers had placed too much faith in the quick and easy conquest of the desert, their last great hope for free land into which they could expand. In 1892 they joined western ranching and mining interests to send delegates to a national protest convention at Omaha. There the Populist party officially was born, and a remarkable platform adopted which promised to lift the West from its economic doldrums and usher in a new era of justice, equality, and prosperity. Evangelical speakers, such as sad-faced Mary Lease, who advised farmers "to raise less corn and more hell," "Sockless" Jerry Simpson, and Ignatius Donnelly, enthralled audiences across the country in behalf of James B. Weaver. Even so, the Populists' candidate carried only Kansas, Nevada, Colorado, and Idaho.

Far from discouraged, the Populists looked eagerly toward the presidential election of 1896. Meanwhile, crops continued to wither and prices to fall. By 1893 the whole country was suffering from a money shortage. The Populists won some impressive congressional and state elections the next year, but there was evidence that their movement already had reached its peak as a third-party force. Both the two major parties, who represented conservative philosophies, were still flexible enough to head off the movement, even at the local level where Populists were strong. The zealous leaders soon found themselves in a quandary, for they not only were short of funds but had limited appeal outside of the immediate area of the West.

Richard Hofstadter points out in *The Age of Reform* that when a third party's demands become popular enough, they are appropriated by one or both of the major parties. "Third parties are like bees: once they sting, they die." This is exactly what happened to the Populists when the 1896 Democratic platform embraced reforms in transportation, land, banking, and other matters dear to Westerners. Unfortunately, the major demands quickly got submerged by the cry for "Free and Unlimited Coinage of Silver." The campaign turned into an all-out fight between East and West, of gold against silver, and urban versus rural. William Jennings Bryan proved more than a match on the stump for his Republican opponent William McKinley, but silver was no match for gold. Bryan carried Washington, the six states of the Great American Desert—New Mexico and Arizona were yet to be admitted to statehood—and most of the Great Plains and the South.

Even in defeat, however, western Populism triumphed, for within a generation it won all it demanded in one form or another. Plentiful rains near the end of the decade brought good crops and prosperity; gold discoveries in Alaska, Africa, and Australia brought inflation; and rising prices brought relief from debts. Theodore Roosevelt gave Westerners railroad regulation; William Howard Taft, postal savings banks; and Woodrow Wilson, a flexible currency through the medium of the Federal Reserve System. On the local level most desert states had adopted initiative, referendum, and recall before World War I. Indeed, all of the radical demands of the "Omaha Platform" were so well accepted by the mid-twentieth century that they now appear conservative.

However fanatical or bigoted some of the old Populist leaders may appear in retrospect, their party constituted the first modern political movement of practical importance in the United States to insist that the federal government take responsibility for the common welfare. The Populists were the first to make a serious attack on the problems created by industrialization and the end of the frontier, and they stirred the latent liberalism in many Americans and forced responsible conservatives into a new flexibility.

Many of those who retreated eastward during the turbulent decade at the close of the century resettled in more humid portions of the prairie states of Kansas, Nebraska, Oklahoma, and Iowa. Meanwhile, buffalo grass and cactus contended with alien weeds for repossession of the abandoned farms along the desert's rim. Empty and ruined houses dotted the landscape, and railroads found two or three trains a week ample to handle traffic. The lesson seemed obvious: instead of dense communities of farmers, the plains would forever be doomed to the sparse population of a purely stock-raising country, perhaps with meager lines of irrigated land along the streams. The cattlemen doubtless were not too distressed at the prospect, for once again they had the country to themselves. As they slowly rebuilt their herds, constructed fences, erected windmills, and took over the abandoned farm lands, they were joined by small armies of sheepmen from Texas and New Mexico.

By now the prejudice against sheep had declined somewhat. Cattlemen discovered that by proper management they could run both sheep and cattle on the same range. Furthermore, sheep produced two cash crops per year, lambs and wool, and in many areas of the West they could subsist where cattle could not. By 1910 they outnumbered cattle almost four to one throughout the eight desert states, or twenty-three million to six million.

But the West was not destined to remain a purely stock-raising country. The rains returned by 1897, and except for occasional dry years they continued for more than three decades. Farmers again overran Colorado, Wyoming, and Montana in the belief that the Great American Desert had receded permanently to the Great Basin and parts of New Mexico and

Arizona. With new determination they prepared for another assault upon the desert. This time they would be more cautious, less extravagant, better equipped to make the most of the resources that the desert possessed and less inclined to worry about those it did not. The lessons of the past had been burned deep into their hearts. They knew that the hot winds would return, that grasshoppers would come back to eat their crops, and that the dust would blow again. They also knew that they could not always depend upon the heavens for water, but they came prepared to subsist without it if necessary.

The prairie farmers who ventured forth a second time approached the problems of the desert with something more substantial than oversimplified slogans. Science and invention came to their aid and enabled them to make headway in the prairie regions. They came equipped with barbed wire, windmills, drought-resistant plants, and radically different farm machinery. They hoped to develop a plan of successful operation without irrigation, in spite of the capricious climate and sharp variations in rainfall. They called it "dry farming." As before, optimism would outrun accomplishment, but with the new science of agriculture people did secure a toehold that would be challenged but never permanently relinquished.

The originator of dry farming was Hardy W. Campbell, who for more than a decade before 1900 had successfully grown wheat, corn, and vegetables in the natural habitat of the cactus and other desert plants in western Nebraska. He preached incessantly that the "arid" West is not arid if the farmer but uses properly the ordinary rainfall that its climate yields. By revolutionary farming methods he demonstrated beyond a shadow of a doubt that commercial crops could be produced in areas where the rainfall often fell below fifteen to twenty inches. Thousands of skeptical farmers were soon converted.

Even though in the long run dry farming did not live up to all the claims made for it, it did represent a major advance in man's struggle to survive in an arid climate. It was based on the observation that the months of greatest precipitation in the West are April, May, and June, the season for growing crops. Enough rain fell at this time to produce an entire crop, Campbell argued, only it evaporated too quickly. As early as 1883 he began experimenting with various methods to retain spring and summer moisture in the ground by grasping every suggestion of leaf and blade and observing the effects of wagon tracks and hoofprints in wheat fields. Gradually he worked out an elaborate system of conservation by deep plowing, subsurface packing, and constant shallow cultivation of the surface.

Campbell discovered that deep plowing provided an ample reservoir for water. To prevent moisture from escaping by capillary action, he pulverized the surface with a crude harrow to keep it loose and mellow. Three or four inches of loose soil on top, commonly called a dust blanket, formed an insulator between the moist earth and the dry air above. But it had to be restored every five to seven days during the growing season. "When the hot winds blow," he lectured repeatedly, "cultivate; when the temperatures rise, cultivate; and especially after a shower."

Dry farming began to win wide acceptance in 1893, after Campbell grew 124 bushels of potatoes per acre in competition with a neighbor. His opponent put in the same acreage in seed potatoes, cultivated them in the traditional New England method, and experienced complete failure. The widely publicized contest not only made believers of thousands of farmers, it encouraged railroad and elevator owners to establish model farms for further research and development in dry farming. At the same time Campbell continued to operate experimental farms throughout the prairie and Great Plains region and to produce successful crops of sugar beets, wheat, corn, and fruit in areas of less than fifteen inches of annual rainfall. Within a few years the Campbell method was being hailed as the salvation of the dry belt. Herbert Quick wrote in *The World's Work Magazine* in August 1906: "The new system of agriculture had brought another boom to Montana,

Wyoming, Colorado, and New Mexico." But he warned that unless the newly arrived emigrants practiced it religiously, "we may expect—with a recurrence of dry years—a repetition of the distressful conditions which spread ruin over these communities in the early nineties."

Those who followed Campbell's methods generally made excellent crops, especially during the wetter years. Those who did not suffered ruin and bankruptcy when the rains came at the wrong time. In the face of such tragedy the plains people often became superstitious or religious, and called in the rain-makers with magic, dynamite, and prayers. But, as Professor Webb facetiously remarked, the rain-makers succeeded best during abnormally wet seasons.

Attempts to invoke rain during periods of drought have long been part of the culture of primitive societies. The Iroquois burned tobacco, the Zuñi used medicine sticks, the Muskhogean performed elaborate dances, and the Incas starved sheep. Indeed, in nearly all parts of the world, even comparatively recently, people have resorted to an endless variety of superstitious and pseudo-scientific rain-making devices. The intermittent droughts throughout the West in the late nineteenth century spawned a legion of proposals and experiments by would-be rainmakers. Many of them were charlatans and fakers, but a few were serious men of learning and reputation.

The most popular methods were based upon the widely accepted belief that concussion in the air induced moisture. "Proof" of this idea could be found in the well-worn tradition that rains invariably followed military engagements—a tradition whose origin even preceded the use of gunpowder. So convincing were some of the proponents of the idea that Congress in 1890 appropriated $2000 "for experiments in the production of rainfall," under the supervision of the Department of Agriculture. The individual selected to conduct the experiments was Robert Dyrenforth, a former employee in the United States Patent Office and a man of varied background and experience. Dyrenforth believed that explosives in the atmosphere would create "something in the nature of a vortex or a momentary cavern into which the condensed moisture is drawn from afar, or falls."

Several "cloud compelling" expeditions were carried out in the Southwest during the summers of 1891 and 1892. Dyrenforth fired off explosives from makeshift cannons, balloons, kites, and even from prairie dog holes. The shower of complaints from irate citizens exceeded the showers that fell from the sky. The Chicago *Times* believed that the $20,000 eventually appropriated by Congress for the experiments would have been "less ridiculously employed if it were devoted to the manufacture of whistles out of pig's tails." Dyrenforth, now dubbed "Dryhenceforth" by wags and critics, proclaimed loudly that his efforts had been successful. He soon retired to private life.

Though the federal government tried to forget the "cloud compelling" experiments, many Americans continued to believe that rains could be induced by explosives. During the Dust Bowl days of the 1930's a prominent Southwesterner urged President Roosevelt to declare a national "Explosive Day" at which time each county in the United States would fire explosives to bring rain. Another suggested the assignment and regular use of one hundred pieces of field artillery. Not until after World War II was the theory finally displaced, and then by cloud seeders dropping dry ice, silver iodide, or carbon particles from the air. While they achieved limited success, optimism once again outstripped accomplishment.

As part of the process of learning to dry farm, new tools had to be invented. As early as 1906 Westerners began to experiment with crude rod weeders and with shallow disc plows. The rod weeder, commonly called a "go-devil," consisted of a sharp blade or rod, which went a few inches under the surface to cut the weeds. It was largely ineffective, however, since it dragged the weeds along the surface and piled·them into heaps, thereby robbing the land of moisture. Also, much of the pulverized soil left in its wake was blown away in high winds. Later an improved version with a rotating rod brought the weeds near the surface and distributed them more evenly over the ground. It not only reduced the sheer physical labor for man and beast, but it left a mulch on top of the ground which more effectively reduced evaporation. Farmers were also experimenting with a shallow disc plow. This machine had a series of concave rotating discs, which merely scratched the top of the soil. Instead of plowing under the stubble and weeds and later bringing them back to the surface with a "go-devil," it transformed the vegetation into a dry mulch. At the same time the disc plow left clods of sufficient weight to hold the mulch in place. The combination of vegetation and loosely disturbed soil controlled evaporation and kept blowing dust to a minimum. "When I first tried discing in 1906," one old-timer observed, "my neighbors . . . said I might just as well be dragging a turkey gobbler backwards by the tail and letting him scratch." Nevertheless, it represented a vast improvement over Campbell's original methods, and most of what the Department of Agriculture later published on the subject was learned from the farmers themselves. In fact, these early plains farmers were practicing shallow plowing two generations before Edward Faulkner and Louis Bromfield wrote best-selling books on the subject.

By 1920 discing and the use of the rotating rod weeder to prepare the ground for planting were common practices in the eastern half of the desert. Yet the victory was not final, especially where speed in plowing remained as much a problem as deficient rainfall. Farmers had long been aware of this fact and had observed that the outer edges of a field gave better yield than the center. This obviously resulted from their discing and weeding the outer edges first. By the time they had reached the center with their horse-drawn machines, much of the moisture had evaporated. By the end of the decade, however, the first diesel caterpillar tractor had come into use, and within a few years mechanization on western farms was almost universal. Tractors did not change the technique, but they did supply the element of speed so essential to conserving moisture in the summer fallow.

With the use of tractors and placing workers on a day and night shift, it was possible to cover 120 acres of land per day instead of the traditional fifteen acres. Tractors also cut the need for hired labor, reduced the cost of production by about 35 per cent, and gave the farmers much more leisure. Tractors likewise made it possible for farmers to raise cattle on the pasture formerly used by horses. By proper management a farmer could produce as much beef on 500 acres of pasture as had been realized a generation before from 5000 acres of open range. Furthermore, tractors eventually harvested wheat and other crops in some of the most arid portions of the desert. In parts of Idaho and Nevada, for example, nonirrigated lands with approximately nine inches of rain averaged thirty bushels of wheat per acre in 1946.

Almost equally important, drought-resistant crops were introduced. One of the first such crops was kafir corn, initially grown on the plains around 1890. Within fifteen years the yield of kafir corn was worth ten million dollars. Others were sorghums, Jerusalem corn, millet, and maize. "These crops mean the adoption of a system of agriculture that is permanent," an agricultural specialist wrote in 1906. "They will furnish 'roughness' for the stock and make bread for the family, no matter if the rainfall is below the average."

Congress meanwhile in 1897 had created the Office of Foreign Seed and Plant Introduction as a branch of the Department of Agriculture. Its specialists were sent scouring the world in search of plants adaptable to the arid climate of the West. From Peru they obtained species of alfalfa and cotton, which thrived on the irrigated desert lands of New Mexico and Arizona. From Siberia they brought a crested wheat grass, which adapted well to the colder climates of Idaho, Montana, and Wyoming. Superior varieties of soybeans were brought from Japan, and by 1900 several other forage plants of less importance were proving to be useful acquisitions. Brome grass from Hungary, berseem clover from Egypt, and alfalfa from Turkey also proved successful. In addition, heartier varieties of okra, pumpkin, red pepper, muskmelons, radishes, squash, peas, and cucumbers supplemented the less dependable garden crops. And by 1910 the Egyptian date palm trees had altered much of the desert landscape, especially in the oasis spots of New Mexico, Arizona, and Nevada.

These and dozens of other new exotic plants greatly increased the desert's contribution to the national economy. Yet they required only a small portion of land usage. The West still needed a commercial crop that would command a world market. Because of the flat, treeless character of the plains the ideal solution appeared to be wheat. Special attention, therefore, was given to those wheat-growing regions of the world where the climate and soil resembled the plains sections of the Great American Desert. Already samples of wheat from the arid regions of Algeria and Chile were being grown with varying success in Nebraska and Kansas. But it was in eastern Russia where Mark Alfred Carleton, a cerealist for the Department of Agriculture, discovered a land almost identical to the American West.

On the Kirghiz Steppes of western Siberia Carleton observed a monotonous, unbroken expanse of treeless, arid plains, which received less than ten inches of rain per year— and nearly all of it fell in the growing season. Sages, feather grasses, and salt bushes made up the native vegetation, and the dry heat of midsummer even produced the mirage so familiar to the western traveler. The rich black earth of the Steppes was dry, strongly alkaline, and powdery, like the plains and basin region at home. Even though the ground absorbed the moisture greedily and evaporation went on at a rapid pace, Russian farmers were producing enormous amounts of wheat, without irrigation and with only crude machines and hand tools.

Carleton brought back several samples of hard wheat acquired from both Russia and Hungary, including Kubanka, a drought-resistant spring wheat; Kharkov, a hard red winter wheat; and Kanred, a very hard red winter wheat. The American farmers found that each variety did well in areas with little more than ten inches of rain, but in 1900 few mills in the United States had the equipment to grind such hard

wheat. Furthermore, Americans generally had not yet cultivated a taste for macaroni and spaghetti, the principal food
products of hard wheat. Even so, western farmers welcomed
the new varieties of wheat. The yields exceeded anything that
they had experienced in more humid areas of the East, and
the wheat belt spread quickly from the prairie states of Kansas,
Nebraska, and the Dakotas into the northern portions of the
Great American Desert. "One is forced to believe that there
is before us the possibility of establishing practically a new
wheat industry of great magnitude," Carleton wrote as early
as 1901. He was a better prophet than he thought, for within
a few years wheat had become the main crop in Montana,
Idaho, and Colorado. In addition, millers had installed new
machinery capable of producing a superior flour from the
hard wheat for a vast home market.

Thus, after endless experimentation, the struggle to inte-
grate the Great American Desert with the national economy
began to bear fruit. But the desert dwellers ultimately came
to realize that no innovation could guarantee final success
without more water. The old notions that deep plowing,
more trees, iron rails, or explosives would induce rainfall had
long since been discredited, and Westerners regretfully turned
to other methods of increasing their water supply. If they
could not bring more rain down, they at least could raise more
water up. And they did so, with even deeper wells, pumps,
and increased efficiency.

These individual efforts, however, still did not suffice, and
Westerners began to look for help, as has ever been their
custom, from the federal government. In time the enormous
interstate irrigation projects would help produce the prosperity which their own efforts and inventions could not. It
was from these great projects that the promised "rain" would
follow the plow, and, at least in a metaphorical sense, the
desert would indeed blossom like the rose.

X LESSONS IN CONSEQUENCES

Early explorers of the Great American Desert believed that its soil was sterile and could never support large-scale human habitation. But the Mormons proved that the desert contained extensive areas where all of the soil elements necessary to produce crops were present, save moisture. And even moisture existed in limited amounts, perhaps enough for one acre in twenty. They soon learned how to cut into a river bank and divert the flow through ditches to their thirsty fields. The operation was as old as man, but that first community-irrigated garden in Salt Lake Valley in 1847 was the beginning of an unending struggle to overcome a major environmental handicap.

It took the Mormons many years to learn to use water properly. Knowing that a little water turned upon the dry soil was good, they reasoned that a lot of water was much better. Eventually they discovered that too much water frequently brought alkali and salts to the surface and ruined the crops, and that some lands were not conducive to irrigation at all. Experience likewise taught them that the old doctrine of riparian rights, which Americans had borrowed from England, would not work in a desert environment. The doctrine, designed to protect the stream for mill sites and transportation, required water users to return undiminished in volume that water which they took from the main stream. It likewise gave a disproportionate advantage to people who lived closest to the water's course.

The pioneer period of irrigation among the Mormons depended upon co-operation and a minimum of tools and equipment; the burden of allocating land rested primarily upon the Mormon Church. All a Mormon pioneer needed to do was go to the bishop and ask where he could settle. If he was a member in good standing, he was assigned a tract of twenty acres or less and allowed to "pay" for it by laboring on a co-operative canal or dam. The results were remarkably successful, for the Mormons unhesitatingly set aside traditional American institutions and sacrificed the individual's welfare to the benefit of the community. Later pioneer settlers were not always willing to profit by the experience. This, combined with the rapid expansion of irrigation and reclamation [1] practices, eventually created more problems for the arid West than it solved.

John Wesley Powell was one of the first men to realize that irrigation was not a panacea for the desert unless developed in accordance with careful planning and co-ordination of effort. Powell had foreseen that what happens in one area of an arid region inexorably affects another. He especially recommended the necessity of establishing water districts in relation to watersheds, and protecting the watersheds against logging, overgrazing, and dry farming. Otherwise the consequences were flash floods from the denuded hillsides, which often brought a wall of mud and gravel down upon the irrigated

---

[1] These two terms are often used together and sometimes interchangeably. Technically, reclamation refers to the process of reclaiming desert lands by means of construction and maintenance of storage reservoirs, canals, and other irrigation works necessary to promote irrigated agriculture.

fields and filled the reservoirs with silt. Such wounds do not heal easily. Uplands have to receive complete rest, trees have to be planted on the slopes to hold the soil, ranges re-seeded, and small retainer dams strategically placed across gullies and tributaries.

Among other things, Powell recommended that the lands west of the 100th meridian first be classified into three groups; the irrigable lands, lying along the banks of the streams; the forest lands, lying high on the mountain sides; and the pasture lands, lying between the irrigable valleys and the forested mountains.

> Within the arid region agriculture is dependent upon irrigation. The amount of irrigable land is but a small percentage of the whole area. The chief development of irrigation depends upon the use of the large streams. For the use of large streams, co-operative labor or capital is necessary. The small streams should not be made to serve lands so as to interfere with the use of the large streams. Sites for reservoirs should be set apart, in order that no hindrance may be placed upon the increase of irrigation by the storage of water.
>
> The grasses of the pasturage lands are scant, and the lands are of value only in large quantities. . . . Pasturage farms need small tracts of irrigable land; hence, the small streams of the general drainage system and the lone springs and streams should be reserved for such pasturage farms. The divisions of the land should be controlled by topographic features in such a manner as to give the greatest number of water fronts to pasturage farms. Residences of the pasturage farms should be grouped in order to secure the benefits of local social organization and co-operation in public improvements. The pasturage lands will not usually be fenced, and hence herds must roam in common. As the pasturage lands should have water fronts and irrigable tracts and as the residences should be grouped and as the lands cannot be economically fenced and must be kept in common, local communal regulations or co-operation is necessary.

Congress rejected Powell's proposals, and for a time the nation continued its unadapted land policy for the arid West.

Just as Powell had predicted, subsequent droughts and floods brought recurring crises and failures. After the "Big-Die-up" of 1886–87, Westerners began to pay more attention to the basic principles of land management, and by trial and error new settlers also expanded their knowledge and technique of dry farming.

As more people moved into the arid West, the need for food, feed, and forage crops for livestock increased rapidly. In spite of the promises that dry farming offered, it eventually proved to be effective only under limited conditions inside the periphery of the desert. Obviously the drier areas required more irrigation water and longer ditches than individual farmers could afford. This led to the growth of large, absentee-run commercial enterprises, most of which failed because the financial burdens simply proved too great.

It became apparent before the end of the century that the natural, seasonal flow of the seven or eight largest rivers that watered the desert was inadequate to meet irrigation needs. They carried plenty of water in the spring when the mountain snow was melting, but not enough in the late summer and fall when the crops matured. Only large dams and river-size canals seemed capable of capturing the flow and carrying the necessary water from reservoirs to distant farm lands. The planning and construction of these large-scale water projects ultimately eclipsed the work of the nineteenth-century Mormon pioneers and brought the reasonably dependable water supply that the people of the arid West had to have in order to survive.

As with almost every other major problem faced by Westerners, the federal government sooner or later had to lend massive assistance to water projects. Under the Carey Act of 1894 it attempted to encourage irrigation development on the public domain by providing land grants to individual states for resale to settlers. The desert states in turn were to construct a network of dams in exchange for the grants, something which they neither had the resources nor inclination to do. Consequently, after six years, less than 12,000 acres had been claimed, and Westerners were seeking more and more direct financial aid from Washington.

In 1900 both major parties adopted platform planks calling for federal construction of dams and reservoirs. Shortly thereafter Representative Francis G. Newlands of Nevada introduced legislation in Congress which would become the basis of the Reclamation Act of 1902. Newlands was convinced that his native state, along with all the other arid regions of the West, had already reached the limit of settlement, unless large dams could stabilize the scanty water supply. He further believed that the best hope for desert settlement lay in the small family farm, and thus he advocated that no one should receive water rights to more than eighty acres from a federal project.

Many eastern congressmen opposed the federal government's role in dam construction on the ground that it would require an outright and unconstitutional subsidy to western farmers. Various Westerners likewise objected to the proposed legislation because it did not provide for larger acreage. But with the enthusiastic support of the ebullient Theodore Roosevelt a comprehensive water storage program was inaugurated.

The Reclamation Act of 1902 attempted to follow many of the essentials of John Wesley Powell's *Report of the Lands of the Arid West* published twenty-four years previously. It authorized the creation of an agency to work out the water problems of the West, select the most feasible sites, supervise the construction of dams, and develop a distribution system for irrigation water. It also limited the sale of water from federal irrigation projects to farms of 160 acres or less, though both Powell and Newlands had recommended half that acreage. The Act likewise established a Reclamation Fund with the proceeds from the sale of public lands and mineral leases. The fund was to be supplemented by revenues from water, and it was to be used to defray construction and operation costs.

Though the author of the first reclamation act had no illusions that the entire arid West could ever be made productive, he did believe that through irrigation and reclamation it

Dust storm in eastern Washington before irrigation. This is now a region of rich farms. (Courtesy Bureau of Reclamation)

mpbell Creek Ranch in the shoe Valley of Nevada. The ilding in the foreground was ilt by John Campbell in the ;o's. (Photo by Philip Hyde)

Desert floods in the arid West often do more damage than droughts. This is Beaver Creek on the rampage near Traer, Kansas, May 24, 1965. (Courtesy Bureau of Reclamation)

A bar of drifting sand piled up by the wind, near Comanche Creek, Grand Canyon National Park. The South Rim of the Canyon is visible in the distance. (Photo by Philip Hyde)

Scattered throughout the desert are scenes such as this (Monument Valley, Arizona), where mesas, spires, and buttes rise abruptly from the desert floor. (Photo by Ansel Adams)

Standing Rock Basin in the proposed Canyonlands National Park, Utah. Hatch Wash, a tributary of the Colorado, is in the center. (Photo by Philip Hyde)

Organ Pipe Cactus National Monument, Arizona. The giant saguaro's branches often resemble organ pipes; the convolute form pictured here is rare. (Photo by Ansel Adams)

This rugged, majestic wilderness area in Wyoming's Wind River Mountains was well known to fur traders and mountain men in the 1820's and 1830's. (Photo by Philip Hyde)

Aerial view of Glen Canyon Dam and power plant from downstream during a test of diversion tunnel and outlet tubes. (Courtesy Bureau of Reclamation)

Secretary Udall dedicating the new saline water conversion plant at Roswell, New Mexico, July 1, 1963. (Courtesy Dept. of the Interior)

Lava Creek Canyon in Grand Canyon National Park after a spring storm. Named by John Wesley Powell in 1871, during his Grand Canyon expedition. Lava several hundred feet deep once dammed up the Colorado River at this point.
(Photo by Philip Hyde)

Picturesque abandoned mining towns, such as Brodie, California, are common landmarks throughout the Great American Desert. This ghost town, near the Nevada line, once boasted several thousand inhabitants. In 1960 its total population was two people. (Photo by Philip Hyde)

Death Valley's reputation is overdrawn; only one of the '49ers actually died here. Today it is a place of unique natural history and geological interest. (Photo by Ansel Adams)

Zabriskie Point, Death Valley National Monument. High-wheeled wagons drawn by 20-mule teams once hauled borax over the road, barely visible in the distance. (Photo by Ansel Adams)

could support a population many times greater than it then did. Perhaps no better example can be found than in one of the earliest reclamation projects authorized under the new program, the Roosevelt Reservoir on the Salt River. Indeed, this giant project touched off an economic boom in the Phoenix area that has continued unabated ever since. Within two decades after the passage of the Newlands Act a total of twenty-seven similar reservoirs were completed, nearly all of which were in the most arid desert states: Arizona, Nevada, Colorado, and Utah.

Yet, in spite of an expenditure of more than $140,000,000, the work of the dam builders proved to be another lesson in consequences. For after twenty years of effort, federal projects accounted for only 1,200,000 out of a total of more than 18,000,000 acres of irrigated lands in the seventeen western states. Because they were inexperienced in constructing large dams, the Reclamation Service had underestimated construction costs, allowed settlers into projects too soon, and in some cases tried to reclaim land that proved incapable of growing crops. The failure of the Service to control land speculation made it almost impossible for many new homesteaders to pay for the water they received. Experience also demonstrated that big dams alone could not check floods and erosion unless the upstream watersheds were protected.

Immediate steps had to be taken or the whole federal reclamation experiment would be discredited. It was clear by 1920, moreover, that the cost of reclamation could not be defrayed by the sale of water, especially since it had amounted to less than 10 per cent of total expenditures. And too much had been invested to abandon the program entirely. Accordingly, the Secretary of Interior appointed a Fact Finders Committee in 1924 to take a long and careful look at the situation.

The committee eventually secured enactment of legislation which prohibited additional reclamation projects without expert advice on the water supply, land prices, costs, engineering features, adaptability for settlement, and general feasibility. It required each applicant for reclaimed public land to demonstrate qualifications of experience, industry, character, and capital. It called for a classification of all new project lands, with a view to adjusting construction charges according to productivity. It further provided that the annual construction charge for existing land would be 5 per cent of the average yearly gross income per acre, until total construction costs were paid. But, most important of all, the committee recommended that additional turbines be installed at various dam sites. Not only did the arid West need hydroelectric power for its expanding population and industry, but the income from its sales would help finance future reclamation projects. The users also could obtain irrigation water at more reasonable costs.

Ultimately, the sale of hydroelectric power made possible a tremendous expansion in reclamation work throughout the West. The most spectacular example of this is found on the Colorado River, which flows through the heart of the western half of the Great American Desert. This stream drains one-twelfth the area of the United States, or approximately 244,-000 square miles. It is fed by the melting snows of the Rocky Mountains, and it makes its way through a dry and barren land that can be made fruitful only by irrigation. Along its 1400-mile route to the sea it marks part of the boundaries of Nevada, Arizona, and California and quenches the thirst of millions of Americans.

Though it has not yet been brought completely under control, the Colorado's vast system of dams, turbines, canals, and tunnels provides electricity for homes and industry and keeps millions of acres of farm land green in what used to be wasteland. Still there is far from enough water in the Colorado to irrigate all the land, and an agreement had to be reached on sharing it among the seven states of the river basin. This came as early as 1922 with the signing of the Colorado River Compact, which determined a division of the water between the upper and lower basins at Lee Ferry, Arizona, a few miles below the Utah line. In general terms, the 1922 Compact specified that the lower basin should receive its share of the long-term flow of the Colorado, even in years when it is far below average. Thus, in some years the upper basin would be short of water, and herein lies only one of several major problems associated with the Colorado.

When Congress later authorized the first of several multiple-purpose dams [2] on the river, it settled on the water quotas for the states involved. The upper basin states of Utah, Colorado, New Mexico, and Wyoming would receive 7.5 million acre-feet per year,[3] while the lower basin states of Nevada, California, and Arizona would receive a similar amount. Nevada's share was set at .3 million, compared to California's 4.4 and Arizona's 2.8. The upper basin states did not agree upon a division until 1948, at which time Colorado received more than half of the total share.[4]

Work on the main stem of the Colorado began in 1928 when Congress authorized the Boulder Canyon project, the principal feature of which is the giant Hoover Dam across the Colorado River between Arizona and Nevada. When Hoover Dam was completed in 1935, it was the highest structure of its kind in the world and ushered in a new era of multipurpose water projects. Standing 726 feet above bedrock, it affords flood protection to the fertile valleys along the lower reaches of the river. It also holds back Lake Mead, the largest artificial body of water in the world. The ten trillion gallons of water in the reservoir assures a stable supply for irrigation and domestic uses, and as it is released through the power plant turbines, it generates approximately 1,350,000 kilowatts of electricity.

Three other large dams have been completed below Boulder Canyon: Imperial Dam near Yuma, is primarily for reclama-

---

2 "Multiple-purpose" includes irrigation, reclamation, silt control, hydro-electricity, fish and wildlife preservation, and recreation.

3 An acre-foot is the quantity of water it would take to cover a flat one-acre surface to a depth of one foot—325,851 gallons.

4 Arizona was apportioned 50,000 acre-feet of the upper basin water and the remainder was allocated as follows: Colorado, 51.75 per cent; Utah, 23 per cent; New Mexico, 11.25 per cent; and Wyoming, 14 per cent.

tion; [5] Parker Dam, 97 miles southeast of Needles, California, and Davis Dam, 50 miles north of the same town, assist Hoover in controlling floods along the river and regulating the stream's flow for downstream irrigation. Their giant reservoirs, Lake Mojave at Davis and Lake Havasu at Parker, contribute substantially to the Colorado River hydroelectric energy pool and serve market areas in southern California, Arizona, and southern Nevada. They likewise contribute to silt control, fish and wildlife protection, recreation, and related purposes.

The proposed Bridge Canyon and Marble Canyon Dams will complete the complicated network of dams and artificial lakes on the lower Colorado. Bridge Canyon Dam, north of Peach Spring, Arizona, a thin-arch concrete structure towering 740 feet above bedrock, will be the highest dam in the United States, and it will be capable of backing up the water of the Colorado almost 100 miles into the Grand Canyon. It will produce slightly more kilowatt-hours of electricity a year than Hoover Dam, the sale of which ultimately will pay construction costs and at the same time provide funds for regional development. Marble Canyon Dam, 200 miles upstream, will supply an equal amount of electricity. Though both are multipurpose dams, they are primarily designed for flow control and the manufacture of electricity.

Most of the power generated on the lower Colorado will be needed for municipal and industrial developments throughout the area, but a large part will be diverted to the various pumping stations along the Central Arizona Project. This grandiose scheme will cost United States taxpayers more than a billion dollars. The cost will be paid with interest in project earnings over a fifty-year period—not so much from the sale of water itself as from the power generated to

[5] The All-American Canal—80 miles long, 220 feet wide, and 25 feet deep—leaves the Colorado at Imperial Dam, drops down almost to the international boundary, and closely parallels that line to a point some ten miles west of Calexico. By 1955 this huge man-made river had brought more than half a million acres of southern California desert lands under irrigation.

operate various station, municipal, and irrigation pumps. It will take water from Parker Dam, approximately 150 miles downstream from Hoover. From there it will be pumped to a height of almost a thousand feet and then channeled downhill 219 miles toward Phoenix through a concrete-lined trench fifteen feet deep. A complex of pumping stations, aqueducts, canals, and distribution pipes must be built before the waters of the Colorado can reach the private homes and nearby fields and industrial plants around Phoenix and Tucson.

At the time of this writing the Central Arizona Project is still in the future, though Senators Carl Hayden and Barry Goldwater introduced a bill authorizing the project as early as June 4, 1963. Senator Goldwater's support of the federal aid program was more than a little ironic, since he devoted most of his political career in the United States Senate to opposing federal encroachment on state functions. On the other hand, he represented a prime example of western politicians who always demand and receive special consideration from Washington. Such an attitude has made the arid West permanently dependent upon federal paternalism, a position which its people are not always happy to accept, nor the benefits of which they are willing to acknowledge.

Arizonans realize, nevertheless, that they may some day find themselves in the same predicament as the desert civilizations before them that were forced from the land. Already the situation around Tucson is critical. There, as well as in the Phoenix area, subsurface water is being depleted at a dangerous rate. In some places water levels have dropped ten to twelve feet in a single year, and it is common practice today to drill a thousand feet in places to tap underground supplies. Furthermore, the deeper its source, the more brackish the water often becomes. This means that some lands eventually are ruined and have to be taken out of cultivation altogether.[6]

6 Since World War II more than 320,000 acres of Arizona farm lands have been taken out of cultivation because of salt content in the water, or excessive pumping costs. At the same time, much of the fruit and vegetable land has been diverted to cotton, since this crop is more re-

Thus, the Central Arizona Water Project on the lower Colorado River basin is vital to the survival of thousands of desert dwellers.

Work did not begin on the upper Colorado River basin until 1956, when Congress authorized the construction of four major storage units. All have since been completed, and they make a combined storage capacity of approximately 34 million acre-feet and a manufacturing capacity of 1.3 million kilowatts. Glen Canyon Dam, near the Arizona-Utah line, is the key feature of the upper basin and one of the great dams of the world. Its reservoir, Lake Powell, backs up into Utah almost 200 miles and has a capacity of 28 million acre-feet of water—the second largest man-made lake in the Western Hemisphere. Farther upstream on the Green River tributary is the 502-foot-high Flaming Gorge Dam in the extreme northeast corner of Utah. The Blue Mesa Dam on the Gunnison River in west-central Colorado and the Navajo Dam on the San Juan River in northwestern New Mexico are slightly smaller and are devoted primarily to flood control, reclamation, and irrigation.

Seven other water projects currently are under construction on various tributaries of the upper Colorado. Four more are authorized and thirteen are now in the planning stage. Eventually a total of forty projects will be constructed to catch and hold surface water in years of high runoff. Much of this water is now lost in a few short spring months when the snow melts from the mountains, but in the future it can be released as needed to lower basin water users.

Experience gained from Hoover Dam and other early Colorado River projects gradually was applied to major basin regions elsewhere in the desert. The Missouri River basin, which includes parts of Montana, Wyoming, and Colorado, has been equally complex or even more difficult to bring un-

---

sistant to saline water. A few years ago Arizona exported fruits and vegetables, but now it imports large quantities from California and Mexico.

der control than the Colorado. For years the Corps of Engineers and the Reclamation Bureau on the one hand and the states of the upper basin and lower basin on the other have feuded over various plans and objectives. Because of a lack of proper legislation and forethought, the Montana Power Company at an early date was able to gain control of the major power sites on the upper Missouri and its tributaries. So many other special interests likewise are involved that it virtually has been impossible to devise a basin plan to please everyone.

Already some fifteen major federal irrigation, flood control, and reclamation projects have been completed in Montana, eastern Wyoming, and eastern Colorado, while many other downstream projects have been built or are under construction. Similar developments are under way for the upper Arkansas basin in eastern Colorado, the upper Rio Grande in New Mexico, the Snake River Valley in Idaho, the Humboldt and Truckee valleys in the Great Basin region of Utah and Nevada, and elsewhere throughout the eight desert states. Altogether the federal government has constructed more than a thousand dams of various kinds between the Mississippi Valley and the Pacific Coast during the past sixty years. Twenty-five of these are concrete multi-purpose structures more than 200 feet high. At present the eight desert states have fourteen such dams, the largest number of any region in the United States. Before the end of this century it is very likely that all remaining sites will have been developed and that the total runoff from the Rocky Mountain watershed will be completely harnessed.

Each decade since the Reclamation Act of 1902 the Great American Desert so far has kept pace or exceeded the average population increase for the United States as a whole. In the two decades from 1940 to 1960 the population of the entire region grew relatively much faster—approximately 65 per cent for the region compared to 35 per cent nationally. Even so, the population per square mile is only eight people, compared to fifty for the rest of the country. Meanwhile, the desert has reached the point where its people have to find still more water or else conserve what it has for purposes other than irrigation. When the total runoff is captured, it will be insufficient for the region's expected population by the year 2000.

According to a 1960 report of the United States Senate's Select Committee on National Water Resources, there were then more than 30 million acres of irrigated land in the seventeen western states. Approximately half of this acreage is located in the heart of the Great American Desert, with nonfederal development perhaps accounting for some 75 per cent of the total. This nonfederal development has depended upon the easily divertible natural flow of streams and ground water supply. In recent years the federal government has concentrated less upon irrigation itself and more upon water storage and conservation and upon providing the hydroelectricity that the arid West requires for its growing cities, military installations, industries, and pumping facilities.

The whole operation requires a greater degree of co-operation among individuals, local groups, states, and federal agencies than is practiced anywhere in the world. Unfortunately, co-operation is not always smooth. With approximately half the total area of the eight desert states belonging to the federal government—ranging from 86 per cent of Nevada to 30 per cent of Montana—no immediate alternative to federal subsidy is in sight. And western water projects alone might, conservatively, cost the American taxpayers more than a hundred billion dollars before the end of this century.

Even though irrigation is not a panacea for all the ills of the desert, economic development without exception has followed from its expansion throughout the region. During the period of construction of dams and reservoirs, local employment is high, retail sales boom, whole new towns spring up, and real estate increases in value. New highways are built into the area, large orders are placed with heavy industry throughout the nation, and wholesale trade, plant expansion, and manufacturing are stimulated. After water is made available, many of the dam builders and construction workers remain as permanent settlers. Then follows a period of home construction, new churches, schools, stores, land-leveling, and roadbuilding. In time these communities come to depend upon manufacturing, trade, tourism, or recreation as much or more than they do upon agriculture.

Meanwhile, irrigated farms provide feed for livestock and a feed base for sheep and cattle that are pastured during the summer on range and forest lands. This is especially true in the northern portions of the Great American Desert: most of the irrigation water in Wyoming and Montana is used to grow hay. In fact, throughout the Great Plains, farmers have found that irrigation takes much of the risk out of livestock production. A small irrigated acreage on each farm will provide a dependable feed supply and will permit the addition of livestock production as a complement to grain farming. Perhaps 200 million acres of western rangeland are associated with irrigated land in this manner.

West of the Rocky Mountains in the Snake Valley of Idaho, the Strawberry Valley of central Utah, and the Arkansas Valley of eastern Colorado, a wide range of crops are grown, including sugar beets, potatoes, beans, corn, peas, cantaloupes, melons, and fruits. Farther south in New Mexico, Arizona, and parts of Nevada two crops per year often can be grown on irrigated lands. Here we find everything from citrus fruits, dates, avocados, alfalfa, and vegetables to cotton, wheat, and corn. Impressive as these green fields look, especially from the air, they are only part of the economic benefits that have accompanied irrigation projects. For each individual living on a farm in the arid West, there are two more individuals in a nearby community whose jobs directly or indirectly depend upon irrigation.

John Wesley Powell did not foresee the magnitude of the giant dams of the present era nor their potential for producing hydroelectric power. The manner in which they were constructed, moreover—by the federal government rather than the water users themselves—was alien to most Americans of the late nineteenth century. Nevertheless, our modern system of dams and reservoirs represent a major fulfillment of Powell's recommendations. Just as important as the storage of water for dry years is the control of floods during wet ones. Here again Powell proved correct, for floods can best be prevented or minimized by careful attention to the watersheds.

It took another lesson in consequences before the nation fully realized the necessity of protecting the watersheds of the Great American Desert. It was dust rather than destructive floods in the arid West that finally aroused the country to action. Strangely enough, both dust storms and floods are mainly caused by the same factors, namely the removal of timber and the destruction of grass and plant cover. When these despoilations are combined with abnormal rainfall or drought the results are often disastrous. This happened in 1933, at a time when the country still had not recovered from the Great Depression. One of the most severe and prolonged droughts in modern history set in that year. It began in Arizona and spread eastward and northward across every desert state and beyond the rim of the Great Plains. For four or five years the desert smouldered like a giant fire, and the heat and wind and dust exceeded that of the late 1880's.

During the spring and summer months the wind blew sand and topsoil with enough force to strip the paint from houses and barns. Two or three feet of sand covered whole farms, while highways, outbuildings, cultivators, and fences were completely buried. A farmer was heard to remark that the best place to locate a farm in Colorado was over in eastern Kansas, but the story had endless variations. Even rabbits, which can exist almost without water, died of thirst and starvation, along with thousands of cattle, horses, and sheep. Plants succumbed even more quickly, and Russian thistle, which has great tolerance for arid conditions, was used for hay. Finally, this too died.

Black blizzards rolled back and forth across the eastern slope of the Rockies, sweeping powdery loam from tilled fields and filling the air five miles high with eddying swirls of choking dust. They halted traffic on the highways, converted day into night, and caused untold cases of dust pneumonia. Eventually creeks and tanks turned into dry, hard brick, wells dried up, and springs stopped flowing. Hundreds of men, women, and children died of suffocation, malnutrition, or sheer exhaustion before they could escape the fury of nature's madness.

The exodus from the eastern slope of the desert during the "Dirty Thirties" did not follow the familiar pattern. Instead of fleeing to Missouri, Illinois, or Indian Territory to "live with the wife's kinfolks" or to stake out a new claim, the people headed westward for California in worn-out "jalopies." Once there they found little relief from poverty until the war plants sprang up along the Pacific Coast in the early 1940's. After the drought subsided, few of the refugees had the courage to return to their former homes.

The Dust Bowl demonstrated to a new generation of Americans the awesomeness of the desert when its latent powers of destruction were allowed to go unchecked. It likewise demonstrated, far more than Powell's writing possibly could, that old laws, habits, and folklore would have to be altered. No longer could special interests have their way nor federal programs be carried out in piecemeal fashion. No longer would farmers be allowed to leave their land unprotected by ground cover, stockmen overgraze the public domain, or lumber companies indiscriminately strip the mountain sides of timber.

However much many Westerners later came to despise the New Deal, they could not ignore the fact that it did take prompt and drastic action at this time. Perhaps one of the most important steps, and certainly one of the most needed, in the renewed war against the desert was the passage of the Taylor Grazing Act of June 1934. This measure virtually closed the public domain to further settlement and gave to millions of acres of natural grasslands the same protection that the Forest Service gave to trees and brush lands. Its principal purpose was to prevent overgrazing and soil deterioration. Eventually it placed more than 165 million acres of land under the administration of the Department of Interior. These holdings, together with land previously withdrawn from public entry, made the federal government owner of one-half of the lands of the Great American Desert.

By dividing the public lands of the arid West into grazing districts and issuing permits to cattlemen and sheepmen, the Department of Interior could better control its use. Ranchers had to follow certain rules, and overgrazing, soil erosion, trespassing, and loss of stock by starvation were minimized. Though the Taylor Grazing Act favored the large stockmen over the small ones and virtually eliminated the dry-farming homesteader on the public domain, the country gained by minimizing damages from periodic floods and drought. At the same time, the Civilian Conservation Corps reforested millions of acres of watershed lands, and the National Park Service and Forest Service further protected them from cutting, overgrazing, and fire.

On April 27, 1935, the federal government created the Soil Conservation Service and assigned to it the task of preventing future dust bowls. Every proved measure of controlling soil erosion was utilized, and many new ones were developed through trial and error. The Service also warned against overgrazing, and put millions of acres back in grass. It discouraged particular crops on land not suited to them, planted rows of trees to check the winds and break up dust storms on the Great Plains, and constructed thousands of small tanks and reservoirs to hold future runoff. The Department of Agriculture paid farmers and ranchers to reduce the number of their livestock, to take submarginal lands out of cultivation or grazing, and to plant some sort of ground cover to check dust erosion.

World War II interrupted much of the effort to bring the desert and its semiarid rim states under control. The unprecedented demands for beef, wheat, and other agricultural crops, combined with another wet cycle throughout the 1940's, encouraged Westerners to put millions of acres of grasslands back into production. Within three or four years after the war, for example, 90 per cent of eastern Colorado was in wheat and summer fallow, and not a single acre was going back to grass. Suddenly, in the early part of the next decade, another drought set in. The Great American Desert sprang to life with almost the fury and destruction of the 1930's.

Twice in a single generation the desert had expanded to the outer limits fixed by Stephen H. Long a century earlier. But people did not abandon the area in such wholesale numbers during the "great thirst" of the 1950's. For one thing, numerous windbreaks, or shelter belts, planted by the Soil Conservation Commission helped to check dust storms, as did contour plowing and the practice of keeping some lands in pasturage. Moreover, the desert people had faith that rains ultimately would return. But before they arrived in 1957, almost every city between the 98th meridian and the Sierra Nevada faced a water crisis, and irrigation pumps had to reach deeper and deeper to tap underground supplies. By then Westerners had learned to accept temporary disappointment and setbacks as normal events, and they could appreciate more than ever the hard realities of the threadbare aphorism, "water is life."

The need for more water inevitably begets difficult human problems that sometimes prove equally difficult to solve. Nowhere is this better illustrated than in California's ceaseless struggle to prevent much of its southern region from reverting to the desert, as nature seemingly intended it to do. Los Angeles made the first dramatic attempt to overcome nature's limitations on the city's growth, by tapping a distant watershed. The task involved the construction of 142 separate tunnels aggregating 53 miles in length, 12 miles of inverted steel siphons, 24 miles of open unlined conduit, 39 miles of open cement-lined conduit, 97 miles of covered conduit, and 3 large reservoirs capable of storing more than 20 billion gallons of water. This complicated aqueduct extended 232 miles from the Owen River, on the eastern side of the Sierra Nevada Mountains, through the Mojave Desert and across equally desolate mountain ranges. More than 5000 men labored through blazing desert summers and freezing mountain winters from 1908 to 1913 to complete it. This was the most difficult engineering project ever undertaken by an American city.

Though the aqueduct unquestionably proved the salvation

of Los Angeles, it unfortunately resulted in a long drawn out feud between the city and the Owen Valley residents. As Los Angeles siphoned off their water, the little oases they and their fathers had established became indistinguishable from the waste lands around them. Violence was injected into the controversy between 1924 and 1927 when Owen Valley residents set off a series of dynamite explosions that blew up different sections of the aqueduct. Eventually, Los Angeles won out, and many of the impoverished ranchers and townspeople of the valley had to seek work on the various water projects they had helped to sabotage.

In March 1928 one of the three reservoir dams suddenly gave way, and a sixty-foot wall of water swept through the Santa Clara Valley. Three hundred and eighty-five lives were lost, more than 1000 homes destroyed, and approximately 8000 acres of land ruined. Property damages matched those of the 1906 San Francisco earthquake, and Los Angeles suffered seriously from the unfavorable publicity. An official investigation showed that the structure collapsed because of its weak foundation. As it was being rebuilt, many state newspapers criticized Los Angeles because of its "greed," and even warned Arizona to remember the "ravishing of Owen Valley" in negotiations then taking place over Hoover Dam and the use of the water of the Colorado River.

Arizona remembered. Indeed, she long since had refused to accept the Compact of 1922, which divided the water of the lower Colorado among the three states involved. For one thing, she objected to her smaller quota of water in relation to California's, especially since not a single river in California flows into the Colorado.[7] In 1934 California began work on a dam below Boulder Canyon to divert water to Los Angeles.

[7] The main point of dispute over the 1922 Compact was whether the formula applied only to the main stream of the river, or to the main stream plus its tributaries. If all of Arizona's streams and rivers that feed into the drainage basin were included in the amount to be divided, Arizona would receive a lot less and California would receive a million acre-feet more. On June 3, 1963, the United States Supreme Court settled the matter in Arizona's favor.

The governor of Arizona promptly sent out the state militia, and an interstate war was barely averted. The two states have been at odds ever since. Meanwhile, California has been taking more than her 4.8 million acre-feet quota, and Arizona seems unable to divert water from the main stream without massive federal assistance.

In addition to this prolonged interstate squabble, there is the yet unsettled international controversy between the United States and Mexico. That country is entitled to a share of the water too, inasmuch as the Colorado flows through the northwestern corner of Mexico. What she receives for her irrigation farms immediately south of the California and Arizona borders is often worthless. Mexican farmers complain bitterly about the situation. They maintain that so much water is removed upstream that what is left, or allowed to flow back in, contains too high a concentration of salt, sodium, and other minerals. Consequently, several hundred thousand acres of formerly rich cotton and vegetable lands have been taken out of cultivation in recent years. Mexican complaints finally forced the United States to construct a canal to divert salt-polluted waters from irrigation runoff before they can re-enter the Colorado and ruin more cropland below the international border.

Of an entirely different nature is the long-standing feud of the professional and amateur conservationists versus the Army Corps of Engineers and the Bureau of Reclamation. To bring more water to the desert region often means the destruction of wildlife and the inundation of natural wonders that were millions of years in the making. The conservationists are often vehement and articulate in their denunciation of the engineers. Typical of their expressions is the following quote from a recent article by David Cort in *Pageant Magazine* (July 1965):

> The Army Corps of Engineers is moving ahead on a plan to destroy the beauties of the Grand Canyon. It has made an impressive start with the Glen Canyon Dam; now it proposes the Marble Gorge and Bridge Canyon dams, both economically pointless but maximally blighting to the natural wonder of the

Grand Canyon. Cries of "Outrage!" are never enough to sway the Corps of Engineers.

Even more violent are the cries against the destruction of Dinosaur National Monument in Utah, which is so inaccessible that less than 500 people a year are able to visit it. Building a dam at Hell's Canyon in Idaho and at Sun Butte near Great Falls, Montana, likewise have produced floods of protest letters and petitions. "Nothing appears sacred to the dambuilders except their own special interest, which seldom coincide with enduring human needs for unspoiled resources," wrote Donald Aldrich, vice president of the Montana Wildlife Federation. "What do we want for ourselves and our children—a dead world of mud flats and concrete, or sanctuary from such a world?" Obviously, the conservationists and the engineers cannot both have what they want, and a compromise solution is not always easy to find.

When Americans first settled beyond the 100th meridian, they could not foresee the full consequences of the changes in their modes of life. Coming from a humid environment, they possessed little experience upon which to draw. It is no wonder, therefore, that many of the things they tried in coping with the overriding presence of aridity have failed. For too often their solution to one problem has created other problems equally baffling. John Wesley Powell warned of the consequences of following the traditional patterns of settlement in the arid West. Unfortunately, the lessons of Powell regarding reclamation, irrigation, conservation, and a host of other problems have had to be learned by painfully slow and costly processes.

XI DESERT POLITICS

It is easy to think of the Great American Desert as three distinct geographic sections: the eastern Great Plains, the central Rocky Mountains, and the western Great Basin. Yet, the more one examines the tier of states on both sides of the Rockies, the more they emerge as a region—knitted into a single fabric. Holding them together and giving them the homogeneity of a true region is the great spine of the Rockies. And underlying the giant fabric is the ever-present problem of aridity, which unquestionably has shaped its past and will determine its future. Though no two states in the region are exactly alike, their similarities are more numerous than their differences. This is true of the Great American Desert's cultural and political developments, as well as of its geography and history.

The emergence of the Great American Desert as a distinct cultural and political region has resulted from its slow and painful adaptation to the environment of rugged mountains and arid and semiarid plains. From the beginning this process has led western communities to create social forms appropriate to the situation. The miners in the mining camps of the 1850's and 1860's established orderly societies based on *ad hoc* laws that later became embodied in the legal codes of the territories and states. The Mormons worked out irrigation practices that became the basis of water laws, while the ranchers did the same with the free grass on the public domain. In each instance, survival itself depended upon co-operative effort by all members of a particular group.

This willingness of the people of the Great American Desert to submit to their own brand of collectivism was offset by their professed hatred of regimentation and of the influence of the federal government. At the same time they have never hesitated to turn to the federal government for help. Before 1848 they demanded and obtained dominion to the Pacific. From 1850 to 1890 they expected Washington to underwrite transportation improvements, pacify the Indians, clarify land titles, and admit the territories to statehood. They urged the federal government to inflate the currency, and they organized the most efficient and perhaps the most selfish pressure group in American history to force the rest of the country to subsidize silver mines. They have asked for regulation of the railroads; tariff protection for wool, beef, and agricultural crops; reclamation projects; flood control; hydroelectricity; grazing and timber rights on the public domain; and military installations and defense contracts.

Throughout most of the 1930's the desert states received more in subsidies from the federal government than they paid in taxes. At one time, 25 per cent of the population of Montana was on relief, and the federal grants the states received for each tax dollar paid in 1939 ranged from fifteen dollars in Idaho to two dollars in Colorado. The situation has not changed considerably to this day. Except for Idaho and Nevada, federal expenditures in each of the desert states in 1960 were higher than federal tax revenue by state of origin. But the curious fact is that the more Washington has come to their rescue, the more they have distrusted it. Almost two decades ago, John Gunther pointed out in *Inside U.S.A.* that federal assistance only made Westerners more resentful and suspicious. "They carefully and cagily figured out," he wrote, "that the public works programs must be a prelude to expropriation."

This attitude is all the more interesting in view of the political history of the region. Most of the states originally were recognized as "liberal," "progressive," or "radical"—depending on the observer's own political vantage point. It was in the West that such groups as the Bull Moose party, the Greenbackers, Prohibitionists, Silverites, Populists, and Progressives drew strong support and influenced state constitution and early legislation. The New Deal also was popular for a time, particularly since the region had received double blows from the Depression and the Dust Bowl. Before World War II, Democratic registration often ran as high as eight to one, but the steady gains by Republicans and their capture of many state houses have pretty well canceled out one-party domination.

To categorize all Republicans in the desert states today as conservatives and all Democrats as liberals would be considerably misleading. The two parties are so much alike in many respects that it often is difficult to distinguish one from the other. There are liberals in both parties who believe that the federal government should do for the states what they cannot or will not do for themselves, especially in the fields of reclamation, flood control, civil rights, reapportionment of state legislatures, education, and public power. Conservatives in both parties, on the other hand, generally take the opposite view on each of these subjects, some going as far as to oppose so-called "interference from Washington" on all matters except those economically beneficial to their respective states. Candidates for office capitalize upon the similarities between the two parties by playing down their own affiliation and frequently omitting any reference to labels whatsoever.

In spite of its liberal, or progressive, tradition, a conservative wind has been blowing through the American West with increasing velocity since the mid-1940's. At a time when Westerners have to look more than ever to the federal government to develop their natural resources and to underwrite their

economy, they are giving stronger lip-service to the principles
of rugged individualism and states' rights. The physical environment of the arid West, the nature of its natural resources,
and the need for more integrated, multipurpose water-develop-
ment projects places a severe strain upon this laissez-faire
philosophy. The dilemma is compounded by the effects of technology, sparse population, an inadequate tax base, and the
high cost of long-distance transportation.

I discussed the paradox of the situation with a prominent
lawyer in Phoenix in August 1964. He was formerly a member
of the Yale Law School faculty, author of several books on
jurisprudence, and, like so many residents of the area, had
moved to an arid climate for relief from asthma. His observations were as follows:

"Well, human nature is funny. Part of the Westerner's attitude and political philosophy results from a gradual cohesion
of resentment against the so-called effeminate East. And Washington to the people out here *is* the East. Partly, it is due to
an inferiority complex. We're still frontier country, and until
recently we have been pretty culturally isolated. Some people
find it easy to equate eastern liberalism with socialism and
communism. They accept federal money with somewhat the
same attitude of the underdeveloped countries, and they have
come to expect it as a right rather than a privilege.

"Contrary to what Westerners will tell you, we are not too
well informed, and frankly most people don't give a damn.
Just take a look at the news coverage, or lack of ·it, in the
local press. *The New York Times* hoped to fill the void by
putting out a western edition, and the fact that it was sus-
pended for lack of circulation reflects upon our intellectual
aridity. But to come back to your original question regarding
federal aid and increased conservatism. I would say that the
two ideas offer an excellent example of the remarkable ability
of an individual to embrace simultaneously philosophies that
are completely contradictory to one another. As you know,
the West has never stood on its own feet, even though it likes
to think otherwise. It has been 'bailed out' by the federal gov-

ernment throughout the past century. Some of my western friends don't like the idea, and in self-defense they take out their resentment accordingly."

The northern desert states of Wyoming, Idaho, and Montana, in contrast to the national increase, have gained little population since 1930, and many of their citizens have moved to other states.[1] The outward flow has been especially noticeable among the brighter young people, who have sought better opportunities elsewhere. Meanwhile, universities have found it difficult to keep their better professors, so that the area has become impoverished of intellect, youth, and talent. Thus, it is easier for the older generation to maintain a standpat attitude. Belief in non-interference by government is held with tenacity and defended with a violence not often found in the older, urbanized sections of the United States. "The main thing that the conservative farmers and businessmen want to do around here," an Idaho lawyer explained, "is to get control of the capitol building, lock it up, and do nothing."

Where depopulation has tended to make northern desert communities more conservative, population growth has apparently increased the conservatism of the communities in the southern portions of the desert. Originally the migration to Arizona and New Mexico came from Texas and other southern Democratic states at a time when Populist ideals were firmly rooted there. More recently it has come from conservative Republican ranks in the midwestern and northern states.

Though their legislatures remain nominally Democratic, the voting habits in both Arizona and New Mexico have become extremely conservative, and there is no longer any stigma to registering as a Republican. Nearly all of the newcomers have settled in urban areas, thus making Phoenix and Albuquerque Republican strongholds. Senator Goldwater, for example, car-

[1] Based upon U. S. Census figures for 1950 and 1960, Montana showed a population gain of 16.2 per cent, or slightly less than the national average. Idaho grew only 12.8 per cent and Wyoming 9.9 per cent. Meanwhile, Arizona and Nevada increased by more than 75 per cent.

ried his state three times by rolling up big majorities in the Phoenix area while losing much of the hinterlands. Thus, even though the rural areas remain conservative, population shifts in Arizona have made them appear more liberal in comparison to the new industrial urban communities.

Along with New Mexico and Arizona, conservatism has shown considerable growth since World War II in Nevada, Colorado, and Utah. The most frequently repeated explanation of this phenomenon is the familiar cliché about frontier independence and self-reliance. It is true that, in spite of their dependence upon group action, Westerners did have to be self-reliant. They continue to admire rugged individualism as much as any other human trait, but they still expect the individual to conform to the political status quo.

This status quo attitude often represents a kind of economic, financial, and political conservatism that does not budge an inch for anybody or anything unless pushed. It cuts across all groups, but is especially strong in the middle and upper classes. Though there is relatively little poverty in the arid West— except among the Indians—the average family has few funds for "extras," and both husband and wife have to work. Not only are middle-class people particularly sensitive to tax issues, but recent years have seen an influx of retired people from the outside.[2] Like the natives, these newcomers are cold to federal spending programs and foreign aid, which they believe threaten their savings through inflation or higher taxes. As for the wealthy, most have made their money in a relatively brief period. This is true of the modern millionaires—largely in real estate, oil, and commercialized farming—just as it was of pioneer prospectors and cattlemen. Unlike people who have inherited wealth, self-made men tend to feel insecure, and they are suspicious of reforms and changes.

Political conservatism in the Great American Desert is partially conditioned by the fact that these states are not beset by many of the urgent problems of older and more densely

2 Some wag has observed that Horace Greeley's advice of "Go West, young man" should now read "Go West, old man."

populated regions. For one thing, they have few Negroes; Nevada has the fewest number of any state in the union —approximately one thousand. And, except for the Spanish Americans and Indians of Arizona and New Mexico, non-white minority groups are too small to constitute a political factor at all. Furthermore, the relatively new cities of the desert are not yet overwhelmed with problems of unemployment, mass transportation, and urban redevelopment. Thus, Westerners see little need for large federal grants, loans, or social programs for urban society advocated by the New Frontier and the Great Society.

Another factor that undoubtedly contributes to political conservatism in the desert states is the predominance of Protestantism and religious fundamentalism. Religious conservatives invariably seem to be political conservatives as well. Consequently, they generally show marked concern about public aid to private education and, at times, about the teaching of evolution in the public schools. This religious feeling seems to have abated somewhat in recent years, but there is no doubt that it harmed President Kennedy's candidacy in 1960.

Unquestionably, much of the political conservatism in the desert states results from a steady diet of ultraconservatism served up by the local press. With the exception of the *Denver Post* and the Salt Lake *Tribune,* a good number of the newspapers of the arid region must rank among the most bland, reactionary, and partisan journals in the nation. The *Post* and *Rocky Mountain News,* both published in Denver, are the only newspapers that could be called regional in that they have a wide circulation beyond the state's borders. The *Post* crusades with considerable persistence, and usually with success. Generally Republican, it spoke out strongly against the brand of conservatism that Goldwater represented, and it does not hesitate to attack the John Birch Society, Minutemen, and other extremist groups. It strives to give both Republicans and Democrats an "even break" in its columns, which cannot be said for many of Colorado's other dailies and 124 weeklies.

Five daily newspapers and fifty weeklies are published in

Utah. The Salt Lake *Tribune* is Catholic-owned and operated, whereas the *Deseret News* is published by the Mormon Church. Both newspapers are conservative, business-oriented, and exclusively Republican. But they make no pretense of political independence, as does the Albuquerque *Journal*. Compared to the *Denver Post*, it is a dull and most uninteresting metropolitan newspaper. The *Journal* deplores the control of government by special interests, but it consistently campaigns for more federal grants for New Mexico.

Arizona has even more of a one-party press than New Mexico. Both of the state's leading dailies, the *Arizona Republic* and the *Phoenix Gazette,* are published by Eugene C. Pulliam, a close personal friend and promoter of Barry Goldwater. Pulliam represents the nearest thing to a political boss in Arizona. His newspapers constantly editorialize in their headlines and news columns and carry on campaigns against various Democratic candidates, and they deplore the trend toward socialism and excessive spending in Washington. But it goes without saying that Pulliam supports the billion-dollar federally financed Central Arizona Water Project.[3]

The most influential newspapers in Nevada are the Las Vegas *Review Journal* and the Las Vegas *Sun*. Both are Democratic papers, the *Review Journal* being the more conservative of the two. Back during the McCarthy era, the *Sun* gained nationwide notoriety when one of its editors advocated the assassination of the late Senator from Wisconsin. In Reno, the *Evening Gazette* is outspokenly Republican, while the *Nevada Journal* is oriented toward the Democratic party. Both are owned by the same chain and both strongly oppose federal aid to the states —even to Nevada.

Twelve of the thirteen daily newspapers in Idaho claim to

---

[3] According to a recent article in *Time* Magazine (January 7, 1966), Senator Goldwater and Pulliam are no longer close personal friends. Moreover, the *Arizona Republic* and *Phoenix Gazette* have lost their partisan image and have greatly improved their news coverage. Publisher Pulliam recently received recognition from the University of Arizona for "distinguished service in support of freedom of the press and the people's right to know."

be politically independent, which generally means basically conservative. Of the seventy-three weeklies, less than half a dozen are Democratic. Also, out-of-state papers with wide circulation in the state generally reflect conservative Republican philosophy. The most influential local paper is the Boise *Statesmen,* which carries considerable national and international news. Though it frequently campaigns against federal grants-in-aid, it does not hesitate from time to time to support candidates who favor a high Hell's Canyon Dam and various economic and social reforms at the state and national levels. This is somewhat true of the smaller state papers, particularly in the northern Panhandle, where liberal candidates of both parties are not completely shut out of office.

Due to geographic remoteness and sparsity of population, Montanans are more dependent on radio and television than on the state's sixteen daily newspapers and seventy-five weeklies. Until recently, all of the dailies published in the four or five largest cities were owned and operated by the Anaconda Copper Company. The company press traditionally avoided controversial issues and had a reputation for presenting the blandest diet of editorial comment of all western newspapers. The *Missoulian,* for example, formerly had no "letters to the editor page" and featured far more national and international news in its columns than local and state news. This situation has changed for the better since 1959, when Anaconda disposed of its chain of newspapers and the editors began to take stands on local issues. All Montana newspapers still must be classified as conservative, but they are beginning to give space to moderate or liberal candidates, whom they formerly ignored.

The Montana state legislature and most recent governors are ultraconservatives, but the state traditionally elects liberal United States Senators, who stand a better chance of obtaining federal grants-in-aid. Thus, Montana, like its next door neighbors, Idaho and Wyoming, tries to enjoy the best of two worlds—low taxes at home and special consideration from Washington. The liberal face that these states direct toward Washington seems to be reconciled with the conservative face directed toward their state capitals.

The most influential newspaper in Wyoming is the Casper *Tribune Herald*. This paper, like most of the other eight dailies in the state, does not so much shape public opinion as it supports the existing conservative view. Until recently, six of the state's leading newspapers were controlled by Tracy S. McCracken, who long played an important role in the Wyoming Democratic party. His newspapers, plus the *Denver Post*, have a wide circulation in the southern counties, where the political climate is less conservative than it is in the north.

Forty-five per cent of all estimated revenue in Wyoming comes from federal funds, which is ironic in view of the strong states' rights attitude found there. It traditionally elects conservatives to state office, who traditionally oppose new taxes. In 1959 the legislature even submitted a resolution to Congress recommending the abolition of federal income taxes. Yet Wyoming has sent such liberals to the United States Senate as Joseph C. O'Mahoney, and it is currently represented by Gale McGee, a former history professor and one of the most outspoken liberals in Washington.

Personal contacts still play a heavy role in political campaigning in the arid West; there is less reliance upon television there than in any region in the country. The vast distances in each state are offset by the fact that most of the population lives in only a few towns and cities. This enables a candidate to make flying trips to each community several times during a campaign and personally shake hands with half the population. And in the West a handshake still means a lot.

I interviewed dozens of people in each of the desert states during the summer of 1964, and I encountered only two people out of ten in Arizona who said that they would vote for Goldwater. Most of the others were vehement in their opposition to the Senator's brand of politics. Arizona, incidentally, was the only western state carried by the Republican candidate. These statistics were exactly reversed in Wyoming, the state that a few weeks later voted for President Johnson and re-elected Gale McGee to the Senate.

Granted that the sample opinions I got were circumstantial and unscientific, yet they reflect considerably upon the character of desert politics—they are difficult to predict because of the independence of the individual voter. All over the area one constantly hears the remark: "I never voted a straight ticket in my life"; or, "I always vote for the man and not for the party." This brand of independent or personal voting is encouraged by the "open primaries," whereby a voter does not have to disclose his party identity. Thus, ticket-splitting is a common practice, and the individual has a free choice to vote for any candidate seeking nomination.

Almost every desert state today offers an excellent example of unpredictable politics. Since statehood, Arizona and New Mexico have supported seven Republican candidates and seven Democrats for the presidency. Nevada has supported twelve Republicans, fifteen Democrats, and one Populist. With one exception, all Wyoming Senators in the last eighteen years have been Democrats and all Representatives Republicans. Montana now has two liberal Democratic Senators and a very conservative Republican governor and state legislature. New Mexico and Arizona each had one liberal Democrat and one conservative Republican Senator in 1964. This split personality also is evident in one form or another in Idaho and Colorado, and to a lesser extent in Utah.

The vast distances and sparse population of the Great American Desert seem to offer opportunities for pressure groups to exert unusually great political power, and certain forces in local society—corporate interests, newspapers, and ultraconservatives in business and politics—have elevated the laissez-faire tradition to the status of dogma. The situation is complicated by the fact that there are relatively few state senators and legislators to control. In the Arizona state senate, for example, only fifteen votes constitutes a majority. Whoever controls these fifteen seats controls the type of legislation that will be passed, or, more bluntly, the type of legislation that will be defeated. The numbers vary slightly, but the same situation exists elsewhere throughout the arid West, where a handful of state senators have developed a reputation for power through negative action.

Originally, mining, ranching, and railroads formed the most important pressure groups, and the heavy hand of each of these interests is still evident. Though copper is no longer king, until a few years ago it was said that most legislators in Arizona, Nevada, Utah, and Montana wore "copper collars." In Montana, Anaconda can still rely on its influence on key citizens, banks, legal firms, and business organizations to rally them to its support and block legislation that might in any way restrict company activities. The same is true of the stock growers and railroad companies, who—together with the Montana Power Company and other business and financial interests—make up the power structure in most communities. Since little or no restrictions are placed on lobbying activities, various "associations" of these groups are well represented when the state legislatures are in session.

The degree of influence, and which groups have it, differ slightly from state to state and from time to time. Copper, cattle, and cotton interests clearly retain the upper hand in Arizona. In Nevada, the gambling interests pretty well run the state—they pay about a third of the taxes—but the irrigation farmers and ranchers, though small in number, also have powerful influence. Copper is still important there, and lobbyists for it are most active around Carson City during legislative sessions. In New Mexico the Cattle Growers Association is probably the most powerful pressure group. During the 1957 legislature, some fourteen out of the thirty-two members of the state senate belonged to this association, as did a similar ratio of house members. Although they seldom get what they want, the New Mexico Educational Association probably ranks next to the cattle growers in influence, followed closely by the liquor and trucking industries.

The Mormon Church denies that it is a pressure group in Utah, but evidence to the contrary is overwhelming. The church owns considerable property and "encourages" its members to participate in state and local political affairs. In 1954, more than 95 per cent of all elected public officials were Mormons. J. Bracken Lee, a non-Mormon governor with church support during this period, proved to be very conservative. Next in influence to the church are the Utah Mining Association, Utah Taxpayers Association, Utah Manufacturers Association, Utah Industrial Council, Utah Farmers Bureau Federation, Utah Educational Association, and the Salt Lake City Chamber of Commerce. Few of these organizations have ever been known to support progressive legislation.

Pressure groups in Wyoming are limited, but none exceeds the power of the Wyoming Stock Growers Association. In fact, in an average session of the legislature slightly more than half of the state senators are active and influential members of this association—a situation that has been true since statehood. For many years the Wyoming Stock Growers Association had its headquarters in the Cheyenne Club, one of the most famous restaurants and hotels in the West. More than one Wyoming law was conceived in its various rooms by the cattle barons who controlled the association, and thus the state. The Rocky Mountain Oil and Gas Association and the Wyoming Taxpayers Association work with the stock growers to keep the state government conservative and the income and revenue taxes low. Also, the American Legion and the Veterans of Foreign Wars probably exercise as much influence in Wyoming as in any state in the Union other than Montana.

In Idaho the utility groups have been the most consistent in their efforts to influence policy formation over the years. Since Idaho has little industry, the farmers and wool growers also can and do control the state from time to time. At other periods the liquor and beer interests have shown considerable power, and at least on one occasion the drug people mustered enough strength to stop legislation that would have regulated drugstores. The structure is somewhat the same in Colorado, where pressure groups vary all the way from architecture to insurance and to motel operation. But basically, the stock growers, mine owners, and farmers constitute the most powerful pressure groups. Colorado, once known for its radicalism, has drifted consistently to the right since the 1930's. Now that Senator Goldwater has been retired to private life, Colorado can boast of the two most conservative senators in Washington from any one state—Peter H. Dominick and Gordon L. Allott.

Labor unions are probably weaker as a pressure group in the arid states than in most sections of the country, although, because of the trucking industry, the Teamsters Union is fairly active. The mining, building trades, and grocery clerks unions also have some influence. Yet union members are just as apt to vote for a Republican as a Democrat, and endorsement of a candidate by organized labor often is more of a handicap than an asset. In the three states that had right-to-work laws in 1964—Nevada, Utah, and Arizona—union leaders accused their members of voting *for* the legislation. In the five other desert states, however, farmers and rural voters surprisingly joined with labor groups to defeat similar measures. This inability of labor unions in general to deliver the vote gives the conservatives a fairly free hand in local and state politics.

Traditionally, the western states have not presented a united political front like that of the solid South, and except on silver, hydroelectric power, and the tariff issues, their congressional delegations have not voted as a bloc. They do have enormous power in comparison to their population, however. In 1940, the Great American Desert had less than 4 per cent of the population, yet its sixteen senators had the power equivalent to that of eight large eastern states with 50 per cent of the population. These percentages remain approximately the same today, with the arid West voting more as a region than at any time in history. Eisenhower carried all eight in 1952 and again in 1956. Nixon swept Arizona, Colorado, Wyoming, Montana, and Idaho, and barely dropped New Mexico and Nevada in 1960. Four years later Johnson carried all but Arizona, though his margin of victory in most desert states was close.

The geography and climate of the Great American Desert create social problems that cannot be solved quickly and cheaply. Individual enterprisers would have no way of recovering their money if they invested it in this way. At the same time the states themselves have not done a good job, especially in the critical area of resource development. Generally, they are poorly governed, although no more so than particular states in other regions. The caliber of their legislatures is not high, their state constitutions are outmoded, and better administrative personnel are badly needed. Meanwhile, ultraconservative pressure groups—as has been traditional—exert an influence far out of proportion to their numbers, blocking legislation that would be beneficial to their states and to the entire region.

Even without the handicaps imposed by man and nature, it is doubtful that the desert states could prove adequate to the task. They simply are too restricted in jurisdiction to deal with the complex problems they face. The alternative therefore to so-called "federal regimentation" would seem to lie in the adoption of the administrative devices of a regional authority similar to TVA. But the western attitude toward regional interests is not encouraging, as witnessed by the half-century squabble among the upper and lower basin states and that between Arizona and California over the waters of the Colorado River.

The question then naturally arises: Who is to determine the future of the West? Slowly but surely Westerners are answering that only the federal government can do for them what they cannot or will not do for themselves. As this realization becomes more obvious, Westerners become more resentful of the federal government. And the fact that large sums of federal money already have been spent on water development in the arid West does not weaken their general aversion toward federal spending in other areas.

If Barry Goldwater had not come along when he did, Westerners might very well have invented him. Indeed, he represents the closest thing to a spokesman that the Great American Desert has ever produced. His ability to distinguish between a federal project for Arizona as a sound investment and a job-training program for Appalachia as "socialistic boondoggling" is symbolic of the political schizophrenia that the arid West is presently experiencing. Like the South, it wants—and needs—Washington's aid as much as it hates

Washington's regulations. Yet the role of the federal government is conspicuously evident in each arid state. With few exceptions, employment in government, military and defense installations, and public administration surpasses that in agriculture, manufacturing, mining, or tourism. Moreover, one gets the impression while traveling throughout the West that the people view this as something to be expected. They feel little gratitude to their congressional leaders for such benevolence, and even less to the administration in Washington.

Having grown up in a vast expanse of mountain ranges, high plateaus, and desert plains, with sparse population, the average Westerner finds it difficult to appreciate the complexities of overpopulation, scarcity of land, or grinding poverty. He often fails to understand why most world problems cannot be solved in the unsophisticated manner of the frontier. His reaction to the problems of areas other than his own frequently goes something like this: "The communists should be dealt with like horse thieves." "The only way to reason with them is with a gun." "We should either drop the bomb on Cuba or send the Marines there to take care of Castro." "The people in Appalachia [wherever that is], South America, or India are poor because they are too stupid and too lazy to work."

The very number of remarks of this kind that one hears in the West indicates that Westerners in general tend to oversimplify more than most people—though admittedly oversimplification is a universal trait. But it must be remembered that only two generations separate the native of the Great American Desert from the gun-and-saddle days, when the solutions to most problems were quick and simple. Perhaps this fact, plus the frustration of constant adjustment to an arid environment, automatically makes simple solutions to difficult problems appear more attractive than they are. Perhaps too, the Westerner has witnessed so many failures and delays in the struggle against aridity, that he has come to believe that often the best solution is no solution at all—in politics or otherwise.

XII AROUND THE RIM

It is one thing to read about the scorching heat of Death Valley, the great salt flats and sinks of Utah and Nevada, historic streams like the Truckee, Humboldt, and Snake, and the vast flat grasslands of the Great Plains. But it is another matter to experience them oneself.

The Great Basin was the only section of the Great American Desert that I did not know well when I began this study, and I knew that a land journey beyond the Rockies was an absolute necessity before this book could be completed. Accordingly, I headed west on Highway 66 in midsummer of 1964—with no special itinerary in mind, and with a graduate student as a companion. With an air-conditioned station wagon and a small camp trailer, I covered more than 6000 miles in four weeks. The trip was more leisurely than the time and distance might indicate, for as everyone who has traveled in the West knows, settlements and camping grounds often are far apart and traffic outside the few large cities is rarely a problem. Though we kept pretty well to a circular course around the

Hollon's Trips

━━━━━ 1964: Journey "Around the Rim"

▪▪▪▪▪▪ 1965: Journey into the heart of the Desert

rim of the Great American Desert, we managed to visit several major cities, as well as some of the most important reclamation projects of the interior.

During the course of the journey we camped in national forests, in tourist traps such as Lake Tahoe, along wilderness roads and mountain streams, and occasionally in a trailer park near the edge of a city. At every possible opportunity we talked with the local inhabitants—bank presidents, chamber of commerce directors, small shopkeepers, trailer court dwellers, lawyers, newspapermen, politicians, filling station operators, bartenders, scientists, federal employees, and itinerant workers. But mostly we drove for hours and days with little to occupy our thoughts except the unfolding landscape of distant mountains, the heat waves that bounced off the surface of the asphalt road ahead, or the dry alkali stretches of land on each side of the road.

The desert is difficult to describe without resorting to the shopworn clichés of clear skies, glorious sunsets, or sage, sand, and cactus. All of these phrases and others are apt descriptions, and thanks to air-conditioning these aspects of the desert can be appreciated today. No longer does the traveler need to look upon the desert as a place to be crossed before reaching civilization. And without the discomfort of heat and thirst, the stillness and freedom offer an escape from the problems of the world. After one has experienced it, he surrenders this contact with reluctance. At the same time, the desert can be depressing and lonely, but these are qualities that in retrospect one forgets quickly.

During the first day of our journey we drove across the hot flat lands of west Texas to Roswell, New Mexico, an oasis city on the west bank of the Pecos River. Roswell is an important starting point for a tour of the desert for two reasons: It is at the base of the Llano Estacado and at the extreme eastern edge of the Great American Desert. It is also the site of one of the experimental water-conversion plants built by the Office of Saline Water. This town, with 30,000 inhabitants, was chosen for the pilot plant because of its serious water shortage and because its deep wells contain a high concentration of minerals.

The new distillation plant looked smaller than we had expected, but it has the capacity of converting approximately a million gallons of water a day, or about one-tenth of the local household demand. The distilled water is piped to a selected section of the town, but users are not altogether pleased with the arrangement. They complain that it is so soft that washing the soap off after a shower is extremely difficult. Also, the absence of minerals leaves the water tasteless. (Incidentally, California emigrants raised this same objection a century earlier when they first drank the clear water of mountain streams. So accustomed were they to impurities that they considered water free of sand and minerals not only tasteless, but downright unhealthy.)

From Roswell we traveled southward along the Pecos Valley to Carlsbad, through one of the most extensive irrigation districts in the Southwest. Some two or three hours' drive west of the flat farm lands around Carlsbad and Artesia are the picture-post-card Sacramento Mountains, surrounded on all sides by the desert. Situated near the top, approximately 9,000 feet above the desert floor, is the small tourist town of Cloudcroft. The place is appropriately named, for the clouds seem to rest upon the ground, and throughout the summer there is a little rain almost every day. Its air is bracing by day and cold at night, and though the community depends heavily upon winter and summer tourists, it has a clean look about it and a relaxed atmosphere. We set up camp a half mile from town, and that night the constant patter of raindrops on the canvas-topped trailer proved more effective than a powerful tranquilizer. Except for minor disturbances from bears searching for food in the camp's garbage cans, it proved one of the most restful nights of the entire trip.

It is only an hour's drop from Cloudcroft to the Tularosa Basin, the region between the Sacramento Mountains and the Rio Grande. Here near Alamogordo is where the first atomic bomb was exploded. The famous White Sands National Mon-

ument is in the same vicinity, an hour's drive east of Las
Cruces. The latter city is the largest one on the Rio Grande
between Albuquerque and El Paso and the last important
settlement that we would see before reaching Tucson two or
three days later. At Lordsburg, near the Arizona line, we
turned southwest on Highway 80 to Douglas, Arizona. There
was no particular reason for detouring so far out of the way
en route to Tucson except that we had now resolved to keep
to the outer rim of the desert as much as possible. And you
cannot get much closer to the outer rim of the Great American Desert in the United States than Douglas. Although the
road map shows this arid section spotted with towns, for the
most part they are disappointingly small and in spite of their
colorful past they often are drab-looking places.

It took more than a week to work our way from Douglas to
Hoover Dam, near the opposite corner of the state. In between
we stopped off at Tombstone and its historic old mining camp,
thence to the Saguaro National Monument, San Xavier Del
Bac Mission, and the Desert Museum—all in the general vicinity of Tucson. Next we moved to Phoenix for two crowded
days of discussions and interviews with various people regarding the proposed Central Arizona Water Project, local and
national politics, and Arizona's industrial developments. Flagstaff, our next destination, is approximately 100 miles north
of Phoenix, in a region that contains some of the most beautiful scenery that the desert has to offer. Along Oak Creek Canyon, south of Flagstaff, are the red buttes, mesas, boulders,
streams, and steep canyons so familiar to the subscribers of
Arizona Highways. Indeed, this magnificent country has been
the subject of innumerable illustrated articles about the desert, to which even the best color photographs fail to do
justice.

Flagstaff is at the intersection of Highways 66 and 89, as
well as partially completed Interstates 40 and 17. Much of the
cross-country traffic between the East Coast and California
passes through here, and it also serves as a kind of jumping-
off place to the newly completed Glen Canyon Dam near the

Utah border, as well as the Grand Canyon to the north. Service stations, restaurants, and motels seem to operate at full capacity twenty-four hours a day. Situated as it is about half way between Gallup, New Mexico and Needles, California, Flagstaff likewise is an important headquarters for the Arizona Highway Patrol. Arizonans refer to this long strip of east-west highway as "Bloody 66," and the state police, who are assigned to each thirteen miles of road, rigidly enforce the speed limit. Even so, the accident rate is high, for by the time cross-country drivers have reached this section of the West they are fatigued from several days of driving. The probability of a traveler getting killed today is greater than it was when the Indians were collecting scalps from emigrants a century ago.

We deviated from our erratic circular course at Flagstaff to take a look at Lake Powell, the large reservoir formed by Glen Canyon Dam. From here we doubled back southward to view the Grand Canyon and the new desert cities that have been laid out in northern Arizona. So far, these places are long on roadside advertising and street markers but short on buildings and people. All along the highways leading north of Flagstaff there are signs offering land for sale at "$5.00 down and 5 years to pay" for an acre city lot. Developers also use such eye-catching phrases as "This space reserved for future generations," "Discover the pride of ownership," and "The basis of all wealth is land." Perhaps a few of these places will succeed, and great cities may some day be a reality in this section of the desert. But unless somebody provides more water than is presently available, it seems likely that most of the surveyed sites will never amount to more than a land speculator's dream.

From the south rim of Grand Canyon we doubled back to pick up Highway 66 at Williams and continue westward to Kingman, Arizona. Thence we turned northwest toward Boulder City, Nevada, the site of Hoover Dam and Lake Mead. Though we had seen desolate and forbidding country before, none of it could be compared with the barren landscape, hot dry air, and sparse vegetation of this corner of the desert. The

midday temperature at Hoover Dam registered 110°, and step-
ping out of an air-conditioned car was like walking into a furnace. But the view at Hoover Dam is worth the discomfort of
August heat, for it is truly one of the wonders of the western
world.

Two days in Las Vegas, a few miles west of Hoover Dam,
was more than enough to satisfy our curiosity. Las Vegas has
been described as "an oasis city of iniquity in a sea of moral
inhibitions," but I was glad that I saw it. Otherwise, I could
not have believed it really existed or have been so glad to
leave a place.

Our route then carried us toward Reno to the northwest,
along Highway 95, and through such desert settlements as Indian Spring, Beatty, Tonopah, Coaldale, Luning, Babbit, and
Weed Heights. The 450-mile stretch along the southwestern
edge of Nevada is long, depressing, and tiresome. It raised
thoughts about the future of this country and caused me to
wonder if it can ever be anything other than what it is—
sand and sage and ugly little towns whose main businesses are
service stations and rest stops for truck drivers. Perhaps because it has so little to recommend it, the Defense Department has set aside large sections of Nevada as a bombing and
gunnery range. At least it serves some useful purpose.

Wherever we stopped we found the natives of the small and
farflung towns friendly but rather listless, as if their entire
energies were expended in merely surviving the hot winds that
blow off the desert. A smog-like haze hung over Death Valley
as we passed along its eastern rim. Numerous signs near the
highway read "Goldwater Country," and whether they re-
flected the symbolism of Death Valley, or vice versa, was a
source of curiosity. Equally baffling were the stacks of used
truck and automobile tires lying every few miles along Highway 95. These, plus the weather-beaten shacks and occasional
automobile graveyards, helped break the monotony of the
landscape, but this would be a good place to start on the
campaign to beautify America. No matter in which direction
one looked there were always rough-looking, low-lying moun-

tains resembling giant rubble heaps rimming the distant horizon.

We arrived at the southern tip of Walker Lake, near Babbit, Nevada, and followed along its western shore for several miles. Like most lakes in the Great Basin, this one is shallow and brackish and has no outlet. Some distance beyond we turned at Silver Spur to the southwest on Highway 50 to visit Virginia City and the nearby state capital of Carson City. Suddenly the country became mountainous once again, and it offered a pleasant contrast to the area we had traversed. Lake Tahoe, which straddles the California-Nevada line, sits in a majestic setting surrounded by beautiful ponderosa pine forests. We were told by a resident that the region formerly had been stripped of its timber by sawmill companies, but CCC workers reforested it a generation ago and most of the pines are second-growth. The road that circles the lake is one continuous strip of casinos and tourist courts on the Nevada side, and golf courses, expensive vacation homes, clean beaches and private camp grounds on the California side. The cold blue waters of the lake, plus the bumper-to-bumper traffic and the evidence of wealth, makes one forget temporarily that the desert is less than an hour away.

From its source at Lake Tahoe we followed the Truckee River north to Reno, the "Divorce Capital of the World." This city is a slight improvement over Las Vegas as far as garishness and human refuse are concerned. Doubtless the University of Nevada is a contributing factor, though some maintain that it is because Reno draws most of its visitors from northern California—whereas Las Vegas depends heavily upon less sophisticated southern California. In both places, however, the dealers at the gambling tables looked more respectable than most of the customers.[1] But regardless of how much one has read about these desert havens of sin, they still do not seem real.

There are no camp grounds near Reno, so we had to park

[1] Gambling casinos in Reno use women dealers at the Black Jack tables, while Las Vegas employs men dealers exclusively.

our trailer in an overcrowded court next to the main highway. Trailers are a way of life in the desert, and most of the
permanent occupants at the cheaper courts are construction
workers or itinerant farm hands. Nearly all of the houses on
wheels are surrounded by clotheslines and perhaps a small
picket fence. There is little privacy, and noise from cross-
country trucks is incessant, especially at night. Most of the
run-of-the-mill courts are pretty shabby places, with an abundance of children who have no suitable place to play either inside or outside the trailer homes.

Two days is long enough to see Reno and then some. We
took Interstate 80 out of town, passed through the adjoining
city of Sparks and followed along the Truckee due east toward
Wadsworth. The Truckee is a beautiful stream, but the farther it flows from Lake Tahoe, the more brackish the water
becomes. At Wadsworth it makes an abrupt turn to the north
and eventually empties into Pyramid Lake, from which there
is no outlet. A few miles from Wadsworth on Highway 40 we
picked up the Humboldt River, which the intrepid Canadian,
Peter Skene Ogden, had explored more than a century and a
quarter before. Our route to the northeast for the next hundred miles paralleled this evil-tasting stream that had sustained thousands of emigrants in their arduous trek to the
California gold fields. And—although it will be of small comfort to them now—they certainly had my sympathies.

Here and there one finds a few oasis spots like Lovelock,
where water from the Humboldt is trapped for irrigation. But
for the most part this section of Nevada offers few signs of life
other than sage and a few other desert plants. No livestock
or houses are visible for miles and miles, and only an occasional sink where the Humboldt goes underground or a barren mountain takes one's mind off the monotony of the road.
Still, the desert country has a strange fascination that is difficult to describe, though the more I saw of its alkali soil, the
more I was beginning to appreciate it in theory rather than in
reality.

The only town in the northwestern quarter of Nevada

worthy of the name is Winnemucca. There Highway 95 leaves the Humboldt and turns straight north toward the southwestern corner of Oregon. Heretofore I had omitted this state from the Great American Desert, primarily because it is not contiguous with the Rocky Mountains and also because it is generally associated with the Pacific Northwest. But a few miles after leaving Nevada I realized completely the obvious truth—just as I had done a few days before while passing Death Valley—that the desert does not conveniently adhere to state lines drawn on a map. As a matter of fact, I soon discovered that fully one-third of Oregon qualifies as a true desert in almost every sense of the word.

A quick look at a road map will show that there are few settlements of any size in the large space between Winnemucca and Burns, Oregon. Burns is situated in almost the exact center of what is locally called the Oregon Desert, approximately 125 miles north of the Nevada state line and an equal distance from the western boundary of Idaho, formed by the north-south course of the Snake River. This arid country, like some of the barren portions of Nevada, once supported considerable vegetation and livestock, though I found this difficult to imagine.

The Oregon Desert is the least known of our arid regions, with good reason. This land has not been celebrated in books, magazines, or movies. And because it is off the main trails, few tourists or retired people seeking the open spaces have discovered its "charm." The federal government owns three-fourths of the area, and until recently wild horses outnumbered the human inhabitants. As has often been said about hell, the Oregon Desert might not be too bad a place to live if only it possessed more water and a more attractive climate.

A few herds of wild horses supposedly still roam the vast terrain, but we saw no evidence of them in the day it took to drive up to Burns and back eastward to Idaho. On the second lap of the journey we followed Highway 20 to Ontario, Oregon, and much of the way we ran alongside a rat-tail river called the Malheur. Such place names as Stinkingwater Mountain, Sage Hen Hill, and Poison Creek Summit pretty well describe the terrain. Ordinarily, it contains the type of land where one would expect to find a typical Indian reservation, since obviously few whites can make a living here. The fact that the federal government bypassed the opportunity to set aside such God-forsaken country for the Indians is perhaps more indicative of the inhospitable geography and climate than of bureaucratic conscience.

We crossed the Snake over into Idaho a short distance beyond Ontario. The country there changes dramatically; it is almost one continuous narrow strip of irrigated farm lands and green truck gardens clear to Wyoming. The Snake comes down from Jackson Lake in the Teton Mountains and winds its way westward in a great arc across southern Idaho. Southwest of Boise it turns straight north to form the common boundary of Idaho, Oregon, and a corner of Washington. En route it cuts through the famous Hell's Canyon, a 5500-foot gorge which is destined to become one of the great reservoirs of the Western Hemisphere.

We left the Snake soon after crossing it at the Idaho-Oregon boundary to visit the capital city of Boise, and did not pick it up again until we were a few miles below Mountain Home, Idaho. Thence we followed it all the way to Idaho Falls before turning northward to Butte, Montana. The river is swift and crystal clear and it irrigates one of the lushest valleys of corn, potatoes, sugar beets, and fruit orchards found anywhere on earth. Except in the ever-present uplands, where the irrigation waters cannot reach, it is easy to forget that much of Idaho belongs to the Great American Desert. The great arid reaches, however, are apparent from the air, and the natives of southern Idaho are quite aware that they live an oasis existence. For without the life-giving waters of the exotic Snake, this part of Idaho would be as depopulated as southeastern Oregon or northwestern Nevada. State officials whom we talked to at Boise invariably mentioned Idaho's need for more industry in order to balance its economy. So far, most of the local manufacturing is food-processing—seasonal industries that employ more women than men and generally at low wages. Though two large hydroelectric dams have been completed on the Snake at Anderson Ranch and Arrowrock, there is still need for additional power before extensive industrial growth is possible. Thus, most Idahoans strongly support the proposed high dam at Hell's Canyon. At the same time the state could do more to develop its tourist industry, especially since it contains so much magnificent scenery in the central and northern sections. Even so, the tourist trade brings in approximately $150,000,000 per year. It is one of Idaho's largest industries.

By the time the Snake River reaches Twin Falls, halfway across the southern part of Idaho, most of its waters have been depleted for irrigation. Then it miraculously gains new life from the Unknown River, which gushes forth from a thousand springs along a lava embankment. As it flows on toward an eventual rendezvous with the mighty Columbia, it is replenished by dozens of small tributaries at approximately the same rate that its water is withdrawn.

Idaho is one of the least known of our western states, and the bizarre sense of humor of its inhabitants came as somewhat of a surprise. This especially was demonstrated by the roadside signs. At most state borders, the traveler is greeted by billboards that say "Welcome to New Mexico, the Land of Enchantment," or "Welcome to Arizona, the Land of Opportunity." Idaho puts it more succinctly: "Refugees Welcome. No Inspection. No Dipping." We observed pithy comments such as these on roadside billboards: "Idaho skunks are not to be sniffed at"; "Sagebrush is free, stuff some in your car"; and "The eyes of Taxes are upon you."

Each desert state seems to have a proclivity for a distinct type of outdoor advertising, slogans, and general pronouncements. In New Mexico, for example, there are many bright yellow billboards advertising reptile gardens, along with historical markers and occasional warnings such as "Jesus Saves"; "Prepare to Meet Thy Maker"; and "Where will you be on

Judgment Day?" Arizona, on the other hand, appears more concerned with the present, judging by the profusion of slogans on the order of "Save America—Elect Barry Goldwater"; "Save our Republic—Impeach Earl Warren"; and "Communist Slavery we Deplore—Cuba Free in '64."

Nevada's highway advertising naturally emphasizes gambling casinos, motels, restaurants, and wedding chapels. "Complete Wedding, Including Flowers, Witnesses, and Recordings, $10," are commonplace signs posted around Las Vegas and Reno. A frequent advertisement for motels reads something like this: "Truckdrivers, Salesmen, and Divorcees Welcome." Several restaurants call attention to their "Famous Atomic Steaks," and various pawn shops inform the visitor about bargains in diamond rings, cameras, transistor radios, tape recorders, and binoculars. You also see in Nevada the slogan "The family that plays together, stays together," whereas in Utah the word is "prays" instead of "plays." Perhaps each word is as indicative of the character of the respective states as any other that can be found.

Service stations, private museums, and city chambers of commerce are the major outdoor advertisers in Montana and Wyoming. We saw a profusion of car bumper stickers which read: "Federal aid hell—it's *our* money!" Here, as in other parts of the West, the traveler is frequently advised to "Fill up with gas and oil—next service station 100 miles." Particular towns advertise their existence by claiming that they are on "the shortest route" or "the scenic drive" to some important place. And nearly every town of any size in Wyoming and Montana generously advertises its most important event, the annual rodeo or Wild West show. Since space along the right-of-way is so abundant, these and other roadside billboards often extend a hundred feet or more in length, with a single line of lettering large enough to be read at great distances and when driving at high speed.

The most distinctive signs along the Colorado highways, other than those referring to Jesus and Earl Warren (the first is definitely "in" and the second definitely "out"), are the anti-litter warnings. The Colorado Public Safety Department makes it clear that litterers are subject to a $100 fine. Apparently, the signs mean what they say, for Colorado gives the impression of being a clean state in this regard. Even the ghost towns look orderly, and one rarely ever sees the rubble and trash along the highway that is so obvious in some other parts of the arid West.

But let us renew our journey around the rim of the desert. At Pocatello, Idaho, the highway divides, with one fork turning almost due south toward Salt Lake City and the other north toward Butte, Montana. To go south would have caused us to miss one of my favorite states, Montana. Since I had crossed Utah from one end to the other on previous trips, and also because I wanted to maintain as wide a circular course as possible, we continued northward beyond Idaho Falls on Highway 91 until we ultimately reached Butte.

This city is situated on a spur of the continental divide. When I first visited it three years previously it was one of the ugliest places I had ever seen. Once a city of approximately 70,000 people, it then claimed less than 25,000 and had been a depressed area for several decades. Its streets were dingy, its curbs broken, and more than half the houses and buildings were cracked and tottering. The ragged, bleached hill on which it sits is a mile high, and there is an open mine pit near the center of the town a mile deep. Every other house and public building was vacant and dilapidated, with heaps of slag, dingy neighborhoods, and neon-lit "honkey-tonks" visible in all directions. Though Montana contains some of the most breath-taking scenery in the world, you did not find much of it around Butte. Furthermore, no one I had met there in 1961 had a kind word to say about either the town or the Anaconda Copper Company, which they held responsible for most of their geographic and human scars.

Upon arriving in Butte in late August, 1964, I was astounded at the transformation taking place. Instead of being a depressed area, Butte had undergone an astonishing rejuvenation. Everywhere one looked there were new buildings under construction or dilapidated ones being torn down. New paved streets and sidewalks were being laid, and a modern high school plant was being readied for the fall term. Industry was moving in, mining activities were expanding, and the population was approaching a 100 per cent increase over the 1960 census figure.

When we decided to bypass Utah in favor of Montana, we at first toyed with the idea of exploring the Lewis and Clark country near the headwaters of the Missouri River in the southwest corner of the state. But Montana is a large state, and however inviting this mountainous wilderness region was, we decided in favor of the more arid eastern section. Our route on Highway 10 took us out of sight of the northern Rockies within a few hours. We spent the night at Billings, and two days later, by the time we arrived at Miles City, near the eastern border of the state, we needed no further proof that Montana belongs to the Great American Desert.

Central and eastern Montana flattens out into a series of low-lying buttes some ten to fifteen miles apart, and each intervening valley looks like the one just passed. About the only visible crop is hay, which is harvested from native grass during the summer months and stacked inside specially built stockades to protect it from deer and elk. Like all sections of the Great Plains, this part is monotonous and lonely-looking, windy in summer and hellishly cold during the winter months.

We later regretted that we did not take the highway at Billings [2] that would have carried us south through the Crow Indian Reservation and the Custer battlefield—thence to Sheridan, Wyoming. Otherwise, our long trek across Montana served no particular purpose except to confirm the obvious,

[2] I had never been to Billings before, and because of its reputation as one of the coldest spots in winter in the United States, I had expected the worst. Instead, it turned out to be a bustling city surrounded on three sides by a caprock escarpment. The view of the city below, especially at twilight, is truly sublime.

and before we could work our way down to Wyoming we had to go all the way to Spearfish, South Dakota, and then double back. From Spearfish we followed Highway 14 westward to Buffalo, Wyoming, over one of the crookedest roads we encountered on the entire journey. Buffalo is at the foot of the Big Horn Mountains, and since I had driven through them on a previous trip during a severe fog and rainstorm, we unhesitatingly turned south toward home. The country between here and Colorado is very much like the northern plains in general, but the winds seem to blow stronger and without letup, even at night. If anyone ever did a study on "The Effects of the Population Explosion on Eastern Wyoming," it would be a thin book indeed.

The farther south we went, the drier the landscape became. Except for the irrigated strips along the Platte and Arkansas rivers, it was even drier in eastern Colorado. Cities all up and down the eastern slope of Colorado were rationing water, and wherever we stopped we heard considerable talk about falling water tables, disaster areas, burned-out crops, and the possibilities of another Dust Bowl.

As we continued through the drought area I recalled the storms of protest that came from the *Denver Post* and other Colorado boosters back in 1957 when Professor Webb included the state in the Great American Desert. Now, seven years later, after three or four seasons of little rainfall, few people were taking offense at the mention of the word "desert." Later that fall President Johnson declared most of the region a national disaster area. Meanwhile, the plight of Colorado farmers and ranchers had been dramatized in several national television specials, in which frequent reference was made to the historic Great American Desert. It was not the first time that the Great Plains were included in the desert, and doubtless it will not be the last.

The mountains gradually faded from view as we continued eastward from Pueblo, Colorado, on Highway 50. The late August heat would have been unbearable without air-conditioning, but the 150 miles along the Arkansas River to Lamar was another familiar and continuous strip of green fields of alfalfa, sugar beets, feed lots, truck gardens, corn, and wheat. This country resembles the Snake River Valley of Idaho and is a dramatic example of how irrigation in the midst of a drought-stricken area can make desert lands flourish. Farm towns such as Rocky Ford, La Junta, and Las Animas are not particularly attractive places, but they gave a definite appearance of prosperity in the summer of 1964. A mile or two beyond the river, however, there is a different story. There, the desert takes over immediately where the irrigation ditches leave off.

From Lamar to central Oklahoma is one day's easy drive, and after four weeks of almost constant driving and looking I was glad to be home. In retrospect the journey around the rim of the Great American Desert emphasized the fact that its natural geography is not laid out according to neat state lines. By turning my trailer a little further south, I would have found a more aggravated part of the desert in the triangular corner of west Texas and below the border. Likewise, by staying clear of southern California, I missed seeing the Colorado and Mojave deserts, two rather dry ones. The trip also made me realize that I needed to make a more thorough examination of the heart of the vast arid region while its extremities were still fresh in mind.

Meanwhile, several characteristics of the region that I have called the Great American Desert emerged from the long journey. One is the great distances between the few major centers of population, a fact that has to be experienced before it can be fully appreciated. This helps explain one of the greatest problems of the arid West, that the great distances produce high transportation costs, which in turn produce a high cost of living. Heretofore, production has remained largely in the form of raw materials such as metals, wool, lumber, cotton, sugar beets, wheat, and beef. Most of these products are shipped elsewhere for processing, while food and manufactured goods must be imported.

Until the 1920's the railroad thoroughly dominated transportation throughout the West. It played a major role in politics and economics, and it almost literally determined the existence or nonexistence of various towns and cities. Today, federal and interstate highways, automobiles, and trucks have reduced the railroads to secondary importance. This change has accelerated since World War II with the growth of commercial aviation, and the railroads—which once boasted of having built the West—are now struggling to remain in business. Airplanes and automobiles and buses have taken their passenger business, and trucking lines have taken over most of their freight hauling.

At the same time, the decline of the mining industry and the rerouting of highways have transformed many communities into ghost towns. The presence of these picturesque but abandoned places seem to emphasize the temporary existence that has so colored much of the history of the desert. Many of the hamlets and small cities that do survive depend heavily upon small businesses allied with automobiles and trucks— filling stations, ice houses, all-night cafes, motels, and trailer camps.

An invitation to teach at the University of Montana in the 1965 summer session gave me the opportunity to return to the Great American Desert sooner than I had anticipated. Consequently, I headed west for a second extensive trip—this time with my family, but without the trailer. My immediate destination was Flagstaff, Arizona, from which I turned north on Highway 89 toward Glen Canyon. Ten years previously there were no highways in this section of the desert, and to get from one bank of the Colorado at Glen Canyon to the other side required a detour by jeep of almost three hundred miles. Today a beautiful arch bridge spans the river a hundred yards below the dam. Also nearby is the neat-looking community of Page, Arizona, originally built as a camp for construction workers but now an excellent example of the permanent economic benefits that follow dam construction.

We crossed the Glen Canyon bridge and within a few hours

were in the "Stand-up Country" of southern Utah. Highway 89 turns abruptly northward at Kanab, and it continues in that direction across the entire length of the state. Running parallel to it is Highway 91, the main route from Salt Lake City to the north rim of Grand Canyon. It was along these two routes that the Mormons pushed their lines of settlement southward, and except for the area around Salt Lake City, it is the most densely populated part of Utah.

A chain of long narrow valleys extends from southern Utah to Glacier National Park in northwestern Montana for a distance of almost 1500 miles. These valleys lie within the trough of north-south mountain ranges, and they support intensive irrigated farming. For the most part the towns along the way are scattered fifteen to twenty miles apart and vary in population from one to two thousand people. Local economy depends heavily upon sugar beets, livestock, and truck gardening. There is little or no industry outside of the large cities such as Provo-Orem, Salt Lake City, and Ogden, and most of the farm crops are harvested by migrant Indian and Mexican laborers.

Our route eventually carried us beyond Idaho Falls, Idaho, where we turned at a place called Mud Lake and followed a desert road—parallel to the Continental Divide—in a northwest direction to Salmon. The road extends for a hundred miles through a strip of sage land that is almost devoid of human habitation. At Salmon we intercepted Highway 93 and crossed due north into the Bitterroot Valley of Montana. The country between there and Missoula is extremely mountainous and heavily forested. At almost every turn in the road one encounters an historical marker to Lewis and Clark, Alexander Ross, or other pioneer travelers. Except for the few trappings of civilization here and there, this wilderness area looks much as it did a century and a half ago. Indeed, the Lewis and Clark expedition appears almost as close in time as yesterday.

Before starting our return trip home in early August, we made several side journeys from Missoula to various wilderness areas along the Continental Divide and as far northward as the Canadian border in Glacier National Park. En route back to Oklahoma, we drove by way of Helena, Great Falls, and Lewistown, cities that I had missed the previous summer. From Billings we followed Highway 87 in a general southward direction to Sheridan, Wyoming, passing through the broken country of the Little Big Horn and by the site of the Custer Battlefield.

Below Sheridan the rolling landscape of the Great Plains presented all-too-familiar scenes. In eastern Colorado we retraced the route of the previous summer along the Platte and Arkansas rivers. The effects of a flash flood that had hit the Denver region six weeks earlier were unbelievable. Whole towns had been under water, new interstate overpasses had washed away, and thousands of acres of rich farm lands were damaged. Indeed, no more vivid evidence could be found of how much more destructive floods can be in an arid region than droughts.

My second trip likewise revealed to me the striking contrast between the heart and the periphery of the Great American Desert. Yet, as one views the arid West from both perspectives, he realizes more clearly how the Rocky Mountains and their lush green valleys are the underlying unity for many of the desert's characteristics. The valleys sustain most of the population, while the mountains capture life-giving rains and distribute them to the various parts by means of a poorly developed system of rivers and streams. These rivers and streams serve the great body of land in much the same way as a nervous system. And though the body is irregularly developed, it would be even less so without the all-important spine of mountains that hold it together.

XIII DESERT CITIES ON THE MARCH

More than a century ago Horace Greeley wrote of John Charles Frémont that "from the ashes of his campfires arose the great cities of the arid West." This statement contains more rhetoric than truth, for Frémont probably camped on the site of only three of the future cities of the desert: Boise, Pueblo, and Salt Lake City. While he passed close to present Denver, Ogden, Phoenix, Las Vegas, and Reno, his maps and writings had little or no direct influence on the location of any of them. Salt Lake City is the exception. Even though Brigham Young claimed to have seen "the place" in a vision, Frémont's previous description undoubtedly helped the vision along.

When the pathmarker entered the Far West in the 1840's, there were three small settlements already in existence that have since become major cities: Santa Fe, Albuquerque, and Tucson.[1] Today there are seventy-four cities in the eight arid

---

[1] This, of course, excludes Taos and other pueblos of New Mexico and Arizona that have been continuously inhabited for centuries.

states with a population of more than 10,000, and ten with a metropolitan concentration in excess of 100,000. Two of the larger cities, Phoenix and Denver, contain more than 50 per cent of their state's inhabitants, while percentages for Las Vegas and Salt Lake City are only slightly less. The proportion of urban to rural population in the arid West has been consistently greater than in the nation as a whole. The reasons are obvious, for when Anglo-Americans arrived in the mid-nineteenth century, the traditional eastern pattern of settlement was suddenly inverted.

Towns and cities in the East largely developed out of an agricultural society, and new territories and states that entered the Union before 1848 were dominated by the rural ideal. Professor Robert Athearn has pointed out in his *High Country Empire* that gold altered the nation's frontier movement: "Overnight it was an urban frontier, far in advance of the settler's frontier . . . Where there used to be settlements and few or no towns, now there was a town and no outlying settlement." Land along the mountain creeks and gulches was valued by the foot instead of the acre or quarter section. The mining industry by its very nature therefore was an urban affair, as was the cattle industry to a lesser extent.[2] Indeed, miners concentrated so close together that they not only could see and hear their neighbors, they could even smell them.

Because of the temporary nature of mining, most of the scattered settlements of the Great American Desert died an early death. There were notable exceptions, particularly Denver, but its ultimate survival depended upon trade and agriculture rather than mineral resources.

Of the sixteen largest oasis cities of the Great American Desert, only three owe their beginning to Spanish rather than Anglo-American pioneers. These, of course, are Santa Fe, Albuquerque, and Tucson. The first two are both located in the Rio Grande Valley of New Mexico, but otherwise they no

2 Cow towns and shipping points on the railroads sprang into existence long before the surrounding country filled up.

longer retain much in common. In fact, Santa Fe often refers to itself as the "City Different," and it takes great pride in its retention of Spanish and adobe architecture, narrow streets, and Indian culture. When entering the city, the visitor is struck by how hidden it is by mountains until he is almost upon it. Also, there is a surprising lack of billboards along some highway approaches, since local vigilantes equipped with power chain saws are not adverse to cutting them down in the dead of night.

Founded in 1609, two years after Jamestown, and given the name of *La Villa Real de las Santa Fe de San Francisco*, Santa Fe is the oldest capital city in the United States. It remained a sleepy enclave of Spanish civilization until Missouri traders discovered it in the 1820's. For more than half a century it continued as the focal point of the famous Santa Fe trade and the largest settlement in the Southwest. A decade and a half before the Civil War it became a part of the United States, but its population remained fairly static until 1920. In that year it stood at slightly more than 7000. This figure more than doubled during the next two decades and has increased since World War II to approximately 40,000.[3]

Considering the population explosion of other desert cities, the above figure is not too impressive. But Santa Fe would not be Santa Fe if it grew much larger, a fact of which its town fathers are acutely aware. Not only do they jealously protect historic buildings and homes and retain their crooked and narrow streets, they are careful to make new structures conform to the traditional style of adobe architecture. At the same time they encourage tourists to come in and industry to stay out. They also support four or five excellent museums, a flourishing colony of artists and writers, and one of the most successful smaller opera companies in the nation. Among distinguished writers who lived in or around Santa Fe at one time or the other were Willa Cather, Mary Austin, D. H.

[3] Statistics on the size of western cities vary considerably. All approximations cited here are for metropolitan centers and are based upon official United States Census reports.

Lawrence, and Oliver La Farge. Artists included John Sloan, one of the founders of the "ashcan" school of art, Reginald Marsh, and Gerald Cassidy.

A standard chapter of the growth of most western cities has been the coming of the railroads. As the Atchison, Topeka, and Santa Fe tracks approached from the east, Santa Fe residents demanded such a high price for the land along the pass through which the rails would have to go that the company bypassed the city in favor of Albuquerque. The fact that Albuquerque soon outstripped the capital in population and wealth did not seem to matter too much. Santa Fe considers its cultural opportunities, state-house politics, excellent restaurants, Indian and Spanish-American traditions, and delightful climate to be more than adequate compensation.

The sixty-two miles of superhighway between Santa Fe and Albuquerque is a short distance in space and time. It might as well be several thousand as far as similarities between the two go, for Albuquerque is a modern city while Santa Fe remains a way of life. The larger city was established almost a hundred years after Santa Fe, and was named for the Duke of Albuquerque. It did not amount to much until 1880, when the railroad came to town. Actually, the tracks of the Santa Fe Railroad missed the sleepy village of Albuquerque by one mile, and a new settlement grew up around the station. Gradually the two merged and continued as a sort of desert oasis for the next several decades. By 1940 Albuquerque had grown to approximately 35,000.

Suddenly the war brought military bases and civilian employees, and when the first atomic bomb was tested nearby in 1945, the population explosion that followed was almost as spectacular. Today approximately 300,000 people live in the metropolitan area, and except for the "Old Town" section near the river bank, much of the former Indian and Spanish cultural traditions has been absorbed or overwhelmed by the "Anglos." The new prosperity is based primarily upon the defense and research spending. The Sandia Corporation, a subsidiary of Western Electric, employs over 7000 people, most of whom are highly skilled. Another 21,000 people are employed in the more than one hundred government agencies located there.

Albuquerque is primarily a business town, not a cultural center. The University of New Mexico, however, is becoming one of the better institutions in the Southwest, and serves as a sort of cultural supermarket for the townspeople. Each year it sponsors a series of courses, concerts, art shows, public lectures, and plays, which are attended by thousands of local residents. At the same time the business section of Albuquerque is hardly distinguishable from any other modern city—smog, congested traffic, and all. And like most large oasis settlements, the population is in danger of outstripping its water supply. Water rationing is a common practice, and it sometimes begins as early as April and continues until October.

The Sandia Mountains rim the outskirts of Albuquerque on the east, and from the crest of these mountains, looking westward, the visitor is treated to one of the most spectacular views in the world. "You could set the Grand Canyon down there and have a hard time finding it," is a common New Mexican boast. But as you enter the city from the pass through the Sandia Mountains and continue westward on Central Avenue, which is Highway 66, you are treated to a ten-mile stretch of garish neon signs, used-car lots, filling stations, ice cream stands, and more than 200 motels, which range in price from three dollars a room to fifty dollars a suite. Beyond the Rio Grande the highway makes a dramatic ascent of more than a thousand feet within three miles before moving on into the flat and limitless horizon.

Of all the desert cities, none more closely resembles the ideal of a large oasis than Tucson. It is often referred to as the "other city of Arizona," but in many ways it is more picturesque, interesting, and relaxed than Phoenix. Tucson lies flat on the open desert plains some sixty miles north of the international boundary with Mexico, but the distant mountains are always in sight. It is a city of tile-roofed structures, with flat-topped Spanish-Indian architecture predominating.

This theme is also carried out in the buildings on the University of Arizona campus.

Father Kino founded *San Cosme del Tucson* in 1700, but it amounted to little for the next 200 years. Its Anglo-American history began in 1854 when the United States acquired it as part of the Gadsden Purchase. The first Butterfield stage arrived three years later, and the town was no longer isolated from the rest of the world. Still, the combination of desert heat and fierce Apaches did not encourage extensive emigration. "If the world was searched over," one Tucson visitor wrote of its local citizens in the 1870's, "I suppose that there could not be found so degraded a set of villains as then formed the principal society of Tucson. Every man went armed to the teeth, and street fights and bloody affrays were of daily occurrence. It was literally a paradise of devils."

But the city is quite different today. Tucson has taken on the relaxed atmosphere of respectability, acquired new industries, built beautiful new subdivisions, and attracted thousands of retired people to its outlying suburbs. Its population growth closely parallels that of Albuquerque, leaping from 35,000 in 1940 to more than 260,000 in 1960. Air-conditioning, airplanes, and excellent highways have opened it up to thousands of tourists who come each winter to bask in its eternal sunshine. They can also visit the nearby Saguaro National Monument, historic San Xavier del Bac, "Old Tucson," famous Desert Museum, several good art museums, a community playhouse, and the Tucson Opera.

Most of the postwar growth of Tucson is based upon the new aircraft and electronics industries, which require little water. Hughes Aircraft alone employs approximately 2000 people, many of whom are scientists or highly skilled technicians. Douglas Aircraft[4] and Davis-Monthan Air Force Base combined employ a similar number. Long-staple American-Egyptian cotton, alfalfa, and cattle are produced in the region. The city at the moment has an adequate supply of

[4] Douglas Aircraft closed its Tucson plant in the early 1960s.

water, but unless the Central Arizona Project is completed, Tucson stands the best chance of running out of water in the next ten years of any major city of the Great American Desert.

Phoenix is slightly better off for water because of the nearby Roosevelt Reservoir and other reclamation projects on the Salt and Gila rivers. And because it is close to the Colorado, it will benefit most from the Central Arizona Project if and when it is constructed. At the same time its long-range need for water is even greater than that of Tucson because its metropolitan area contains three times as many people, approximately 700,000. And its ground water is being depleted at a fearful rate.

Phoenix is located on the site of an ancient Hohokan city, but except for a network of former irrigation canals all traces of civilization had long since disappeared when Anglo-Americans passed through in the 1850's en route to California. One such traveler recorded his feelings in a terse comment: "After entering it, there is nothing to do but leave." A few years later one John Y. T. Smith located a hay camp at the center of what is now modern Phoenix, and by 1867 a few other white men had arrived to rebuild the ancient canals and irrigate native hay. One of the more literate of the group predicted that a new city would spring from the ashes of the old, hence the name Phoenix.

The growth of Phoenix was slow, even after the first railroad train arrived in 1887. Health seekers made up most of the new residents of the town before the end of the century, but the place took on new life in 1911 with the completion of the Roosevelt Reservoir. Within ten years much of the valley in which Phoenix lies was under irrigation, and the population had reached almost 30,000. By World War II the metropolitan area had grown to 65,000 and has since multiplied tenfold. According to the Phoenix Chamber of Commerce, in 1960 some 2500 people were moving into the city each month. This figure has dropped in the last five years, and though the city boosters still claim an impressive increase, they seldom mention the number of people who leave.

The electronics industries, irrigated farming, copper mining, federal agencies, and tourism are the basis of the local economy, but all except the last two have recently slacked off. Indeed, Phoenix has its share of unemployed people and ranks among the top cities in the country in rate of crime and juvenile delinquency. Also, industries and automobiles have created smog, which sometimes hangs over the valley for days, blotting out the bright sunshine. In 1963 Barry Goldwater's home town rejected urban renewal when it voted down a housing code for fear that it would involve distasteful federal participation. But two years later the downtown businessmen were having second thoughts, as growing numbers of customers were shifting their business to shopping centers on the perimeter of the city. Accordingly, Phoenix applied for some federal antipoverty funds in April 1965. "There is even tentative talk of applying for federal funds for urban renewal," the *National Observer* reported. "This sort of talk is most unusual."

Still, Phoenix presents an impressive sight from the air or from the top of a nearby mountain. The valley is one vast expanse of subdivisions and suburban communities, such as Tempe and Scottsdale, while the downtown area boasts some of the most modern skyscrapers between Dallas and southern California. Approximately six million tourists visit the place each year.

Phoenix has almost lost what trace of Spanish or Indian culture it ever possessed, but it has made the usual effort of modern western cities to acquire the trappings of a newer culture. Arizona State University at nearby Tempe has recently been upgraded from a teacher's college to a university, and it is one of the fastest-growing institutions of its kind in the United States. A fairly respectable symphony orchestra and several museums and art exhibits provide the city's cultural stimulus.

Like everything else in the desert, cities are far apart. You have to drive more than 200 miles in an almost straight northwest line from Phoenix before you reach another city worthy of the name. That is Las Vegas, and some might question the implication of "worthy" in relation to it. Nevertheless, its metropolitan area contains approximately 130,000 souls, lost or otherwise. The city can be described as being composed of two areas—the Strip and the downtown center. The first consists of a string of motels and pleasure palaces along the highway to Los Angeles, while the downtown center is made up of casinos, pizza parlors, wedding chapels, all-night coffee houses, and pawnshops.

Las Vegas began under quite different circumstances than these. Brigham Young sent a group of Mormons there in 1855 "to build a fort to protect immigrants and the United States mail from the Indians." The first report that came back to Salt Lake City from Elder John Steele was rather prophetic: "The country around here looks as if the Lord has forgotten it." Three years later the Mormons wisely abandoned the site, and federal troops took over the post and renamed it Fort Baker. They too eventually gave up, and Las Vegas reverted back to a watering place until 1905, when the Salt Lake Railroad acquired a right-of-way and laid out a town. It was incorporated in 1911, but remained a small town until work started on nearby Hoover Dam in the following decade. Gambling had been legal in Nevada from 1869 to 1910, and became legal again in 1931. This, together with Hoover Dam, started a small population boom, so by 1940 Las Vegas had grown to more than 8000 permanent inhabitants and could boast of several plush hotels and gambling casinos. But the real population explosion came after World War II, jumping to 65,000 by 1950 and doubling again before the next census.

Recently, Las Vegas has become a convention center, entertaining some 60,000 delegates annually at more than a hundred professional gatherings. Even medical associations have suddenly discovered its environment and climate especially inducive to learned papers and lectures. Currently, Las Vegas is courting smokeless industry, rebuilding its civic center, and promoting new tract homes. But the main action is still on the Strip. Tourism and gambling pay most of the cost of operation of a first-rate school system, hospitals, and city government. The state keeps a close watch on the casinos and periodically reviews gambling licenses to see that things are kept honest. "The odds are so much in favor of the house," Las Vegas residents maintain, "that there is no point in running a crooked game."

The story of the growth of Reno is only slightly less spectacular than that of Las Vegas. It was settled in 1858—thirteen miles from California—by a group of emigrants who did not quite make it to the "promised land." First named Lakes Crossing, the town was renamed after General Jesse Lee Reno in 1868, when the Central Pacific Railroad built a station on the site. The discovery of the Comstock Lode to the south insured the permanency of Reno, but its growth was slow until 1940. The census that year gave it slightly more than 21,000 people, compared to approximately 83,000 twenty years later.

Reno originally depended almost exclusively on mining, and there is still some activity in the general area. Thanks to the nearby Truckee River, it is moreover the center of an irrigated district that produces about one-tenth of the state's entire agricultural income. But the largest industries by far are gambling and motel operation. As it does in most western cities, the federal government provides a large number of steady jobs, especially at Stead Air Force Base, local offices of the Bureau of Land Management, Bureau of Mines, and the Forest Service.

Manufacturing is limited to light industries, and in its effort to provide a broader base for employment, the Reno Chamber of Commerce tries to play down the city's unofficial title of "Divorce Capital of the World." It insists that there are more marriages performed in Reno each year than divorces, which may or may not prove something. Recently the Nevada state legislature passed a bill exempting goods in warehouses from taxation. This means that Reno's close proximity to the big West Coast markets could make it a major distribution center. Meanwhile, unless sinning becomes unpopular with the general public, the chance of its being surpassed by any other local business activity appears remote.

Boise is comparable to Reno only in size. The Idaho capital gives the appearance of a clean, quiet, and respectably dull city—quite a change from its robust beginning a century ago. In 1864 a military post was established on the site, one year after the first miners came into the region. The town was incorporated that year as the capital of Idaho Territory and remained a trade center for the nearby gold fields at Idaho City and Silver City. As the gold fever died and the mines played out, Boise settled down to become a sleepy agricultural community and the seat of state government. Though its population doubled between 1940 and 1960 to around 70,000, it still depends upon agriculture as its main source of income.

Because of the availability of water in southwestern Idaho, local agriculture has been diversified to include grazing, dairying, fruit-growing, and lumbering. Industries consist largely of food-processing and meat- and fruit-packing plants, which predominantly employ women. Jobs for men therefore are scarce. Not only are the wages in the packing plants low, but the work is extremely monotonous. "Separating little potatoes from big potatoes is the hardest work I ever done in my life," an Idaho worker explained to me. "You've just got to make decisions all the time."

Some mining is still carried on around Boise, but at the present most of the mines are marginal. Aside from being an agricultural trade center, Boise also contains an attractive state capitol, a beautifully landscaped building of classical design in the heart of the city. Its quiet beauty, combined with wide streets and well-kept playgrounds and parks, belies the frequently heard remark that one of the greatest local problems is juvenile delinquency. Another surprising discovery about Boise is that there are a large number of Japanese residents, most of whom settled in the area after World War II and became prosperous farmers and leading citizens.

Idaho's second largest city, Idaho Falls, is situated on the Snake River in the opposite corner of the state, about forty miles due west of the Wyoming border. It too had its beginning during the gold rush of the early 1860's, only to fall into decline when the miners exhausted the placers. The

Union Pacific saved the small town of 1000 inhabitants when it established a division point there in 1881. It almost died a second time in 1887, when the division point was shifted to Pocatello. Many of the Idaho Falls residents moved away and literally took their homes with them. It started to grow again near the end of the century as irrigation developed on the Snake. Since 1920 the population has doubled each twenty years to a present figure of approximately 35,000—not large for a modern city, but impressive enough in a state whose population is no more than four people per square mile.

Idaho Falls boasts of being the home region of the famous Idaho potato, and the largest employers of the city are the potato processers. It is also a center for sugar beet processing, dairying, and the totally unrelated concrete industry. Some good jobs are provided by the Atomic Energy Commission and its National Reactor Testing Station, while the nearby natural wonders of Yellowstone Park, Grand Teton Park, Craters of the Moon, Sun Valley, and the numerous fishing streams furnish some of the most superb outdoor recreational opportunities in America.

Like Idaho, neither Montana nor Wyoming has any metropolitan centers that approach 100,000 inhabitants. The two that come closest in Montana are Billings and Great Falls, both of which in 1960 were in the vicinity of 75,000. Billings is unusual among cities in the northern section of the desert since its economy is based on oil as much as upon agriculture. "The shops, the cars, the clothes, everything seems to have the prosperous look of an oil town living on its depletion allowance credit card," a writer for *Holiday* magazine recently observed. The downtown district looks very much like that of any well-off community in Texas or some other part of the country. Thanks to the oil industry, the average income of the ordinary citizen is fairly high, and most homes have an up-to-date, middle-class look about them. The city is located at the base of an unusual caprock formation, and it is periodically blanketed with smog from three major oil refineries.

Billings is also the center of a sizable irrigated farming and livestock industry. Sugar beet milling and food-processing provide considerable employment, but not nearly enough to attract the large population that realtors and merchants would like. Even so, the growth of Billings since it was founded in 1882 has been impressive. It began as a railroad town, located on the Northern Pacific Railroad, and was named after the president of that company. The city quickly became an important shipping point for the livestock industry of the northern plains. An oil boom in the early part of the twentieth century brought in a new breed of residents, especially from Texas and Oklahoma, and by 1940 the population had increased to approximately 23,000. Since then the growth has been a phenomenal 300 per cent, and with the completion of Interstates 90 and 94 it should continue.

Some 200 miles northwest of Billings is the slightly larger city of Great Falls. This is the historic country visited by Lewis and Clark more than a century and a half ago, and they referred to it in their journals as "the Great Falls of the Missouri." The town, however, was not laid out until 1882, nor chartered until 1888. Its growth continued steadily until it approximated 30,000 in 1940. Since then, as with all other major population centers of the desert, development has been spectacular and today its size is somewhere in the neighborhood of 85,000.

Great Falls has much to offer and could become a sizable metropolitan area within the next decade or two. In all, five private power dams have been completed in the vicinity, and Montanans frequently refer to the place as the "Electric City." Thus, in addition to water for irrigated agriculture, Great Falls has the potential for considerable industrial growth. Smelters of the Anaconda Company currently produce about twenty-seven million pounds of zinc and twenty-five million pounds of copper per month. There is also a large wire and cable manufacturing plant there, plus a major oil refinery operated by Phillips Petroleum Company, several flour mills, a brewer, a terminal and gathering station for oil and gas pipelines, and a large ICBM base. In fact, the Minuteman missile complex around Great Falls covers an area larger than the state of Maryland and provides approximately 15 per cent of the jobs and an annual payroll of forty million dollars.

In spite of what the federal government is spending in the region, Great Falls is typical of other Montana cities in that it is extremely conservative and antifederal. Some of the natives around Great Falls resent the arrival of so-called outsiders, judging from a remark made to me: "As far as I am concerned the whole damn bunch can go home. I would like to see this country stay just as it was, but now all these new people, and industry, and military have just about ruined it."

If anyone doubts that Great Falls has changed during the postwar period, he needs only to be reminded that it now has its own symphony orchestra and symphonic choir. It also has a new college, and a museum that contains many of the paintings of Charles M. Russell, who is far more famous in Montana than Titian or Michelangelo. Many of the Russell paintings—Gilcrease Museum in Tulsa, Oklahoma, claims the largest single collection—used to hang in a local Great Falls saloon. This is where some local citizens feel that they still belong, since during his lifetime Russell was far more at home in a saloon than in a museum.

If all of the people in Wyoming were located in one metropolitan center, it would constitute a city about one-third the size of greater Denver. According to the 1960 census, Wyoming had 327,531 residents, with the largest concentration in Casper and Cheyenne. The first grew up around Fort Caspar (sic), a frontier post on the North Platte in the east-central part of the territory. The town itself began to take shape around 1888, to serve the surrounding livestock industry. The first oil well was brought in in 1894, and Casper remains an oil town today, Not far away is the famous Teapot Dome field, and the city itself supports three major oil refineries and four interstate pipeline companies. Several minor and a few major petroleum companies also maintain headquarters or divisional offices there. In a recent *U. S. News and World Report* the average worker's income was listed as approximately $6600.

Casper has grown from an isolated town of 11,000 in 1920 to an isolated city of approximately 45,000 in 1960, with most of its growth in the past twenty years. Being built upon oil, natural gas, and cattle, it does not have many cultural inducements. It comes as no surprise, therefore, that Casper is isolated more than geographically. But as long as one does not bring up the subject of the New Deal or the Great Society, Casper residents are among the most pleasant, generous, and friendly individuals that one will ever find.

Cheyenne is just barely inside the southeast corner of Wyoming, and since 1869 it has remained the "temporary" capital. The reason that it is temporary is because there is a clause in the state constitution which provides that "a majority of all votes cast in a referendum" is required to establish a permanent location for the capital. Since no city has received a majority in various referendums, the capital remains where it began. Cheyenne's growth since 1920 has closely paralleled that of Casper, and about half of its present 45,000 population is the result of the postwar boom.

The city was first surveyed by General Grenville M. Dodge in July 1867, while searching for a suitable transcontinental route for the Union Pacific Railroad. According to local tradition, when Dodge and his small party were surprised by a war party of Cheyenne Indians, he is supposed to have remarked to his fellows that "If we save our scalps, I've found the route for the railroad." Obviously the surveyors did save their scalps, for the Union Pacific reached present Cheyenne before the end of 1867 and the town served for several months as the base work camp for 10,000 railroad laborers. Cheyenne quickly earned a reputation as a "hell-on-wheels" city, a reputation of which some of its citizens still like to boast.

When the railroad workers moved on, cattlemen came in, and for the next several years Cheyenne advertised itself as a desirable market place for livestock. Ranching is still a mainstay of the region's economy, and the traditions of the Old West live on each year in Cheyenne's annual Frontier Days celebration. Three major railroads converge here, and there are various government activities. Nearby is Warren Air Force Base, which contains another large ICBM complex, a bombing range, and a veteran's hospital. In fact, Cheyenne is so dependent upon the federal government that some natives refer to themselves as "half free and half slave."

Denver and Salt Lake City so overshadow all other cities in Colorado and Utah that the lesser ones are frequently overlooked. Among these are Ogden and Provo-Orem in Utah and Colorado Springs and Pueblo in Colorado. Each of these cities exceed in size the largest urban centers of Idaho, Montana, or Wyoming. Their growth during the past two decades has been even more spectacular. The population of Ogden, for example, jumped from 44,000 in 1940 to 110,000 in 1960, while nearby Provo-Orem is almost as large. Ogden obtained a degree of immortality when the Union Pacific and Central Pacific railroads joined their tracks nearby in 1869 in the famous ceremony of the golden spike. It has remained an important railroad center to this day. Moreover, it lies in the heart of one of the most fertile irrigated farming districts in the United States.

A few miles south of Salt Lake City is Provo-Orem, two pioneer Mormon settlements that recently have grown together into a metropolitan center with a population of more than 100,000. Provo is the home of Brigham Young University, which was founded by the Mormon Church in 1875 and currently boasts of a beautiful campus of modern architecture and an enrollment of 15,000 students. Its twin city of Orem, on the other hand, has recently acquired the Geneva Works of the United States Steel Corporation, the largest plant of its kind west of the Mississippi River and east of California.

Pueblo likewise is a steel and railroad center of approximately 118,000 people. It was near there that the explorer Zebulon Montgomery Pike erected a log stockade in 1806, the first building by an Anglo-American in the Great American Desert, and indeed among the first two or three such structures built by Anglo-Americans west of the Mississippi. Whereas Pueblo today has a substantial payroll from railroad shops and heavy industry, Colorado Springs to the north has long been known as a tourist and health resort center. It is also the home of Colorado Springs College. In 1960 the city's population exceeded 140,000 which represented an increase of more than 300 per cent during the postwar period. The United States Air Force Academy, various military installations, and other government spending projects account for much of this increase.

As previously noted, more than half the people in Colorado reside in the metropolitan area of Denver. Often referred to as the "Metropolis of the Mountains," Denver actually lies on a high plain just east of the Front Range of the Rockies. While the mountains rise up spectacularly to the west, the city itself is no more mountainous than Dallas, Texas. Historically, it is not quite as old as its mountain neighbor, Salt Lake City, and it began under entirely different circumstances. Gold, rather than religion, was its counterstone, but the mining industry just barely lasted long enough for Denver to reach maturity as an agricultural and trade center.

When gold was first discovered on Cherry Creek cannot be documented as accurately as the find that James Marshall made on January 24, 1848, that touched off the rush to California. But gold was discovered near Denver by various prospectors in 1858, and by the next year three mining camps had been started at the junction of Cherry Creek and the South Platte River: Denver, Auraria (sic), and Highland. When Colorado became a territory in 1861 the three mining camps united to form Denver City. The name Denver came from the Governor of Kansas Territory, James William Denver.

The Union Pacific, Eastern division, which started westward building from the Kansas City area, operated from 1869 to 1880 as the Kansas Pacific. It reached Denver in August, 1870. There it made connection with the Denver Pacific, which had already built to Cheyenne, to give Denver its much desired railroad outlet. Still later the Denver and Rio Grande Railroad brought a more direct connection with Salt Lake City. Subsequent gold and silver discoveries in the central Rockies and the thriving cattle and agricultural industries established the capital city of Colorado as the most important trade center between Chicago and San Francisco.

By 1920 the city claimed over 250,000 inhabitants. Forty years later, the total was near 925,000. Almost two-thirds of the increase came between 1940 and 1960. Most of it resulted from the many war industries that were located in the region during and after World War II. Recently the manufacture of ballistic missiles and "space hardware" has added considerably to the local economy. Today, the city is surrounded by a complex of military installations. The principal ones are Lowry Field and Lowry Bombing Range. Also, the Air Force Academy is located near the foot of Pike's Peak between Denver and Colorado Springs. Denver has an important government mint and is the headquarters for dozens of regional federal offices, so many in fact that it is often referred to as the "Nation's Other Capital."

Denver is the banking, financial, and shopping center of the West and the gateway to the Rocky Mountains. Major oil, uranium, and pipeline companies maintain offices there, and there are packing plants, food processors, and manufacturers of hundreds of other products. Denver's splendid hotels and restaurants and its many airline connections make it one of the most attractive convention cities in the West. Colorado's numerous parks, forests, trout streams, and winter sports contribute to the city's third or fourth largest business, tourism. Denver also is a cultural center, with excellent museums, a symphony orchestra, symphonic choir, theaters, the University of Denver, and the nearby University of Colorado at Boulder.

Even though Denver occasionally has to resort to water rationing, its proximity to the watershed of the Rockies places it in a more favorable position than almost any other large city of the Great American Desert. Its tremendous population growth, however, has brought problems, which the city has partly solved by constructing a new reservoir and by bringing water from the west side of the Continental Divide by means of a system of tunnels through the mountains.

Salt Lake City is situated in the heart of the Great American Desert and, next to Denver, it is the largest and most important in the eight-state region. The city is also the first major community between the 98th meridian and the Sierra Nevada whose origin is strictly Anglo-Saxon. The story of its founding has already been told in Chapter VI. It was laid out on a magnificent scale in 1847, and except for the national capital at Washington, D.C., it is the only large city in America that was carefully developed according to plan. Spread over a valley that is surrounded on all sides by mountains, Salt Lake City presents a memorable panorama from the distance. The heart of the city is no less disappointing, for its wide streets, well-kept parks, manicured lawns, multi-hued flower gardens, and orderly buildings seem to fulfill Brigham Young's famous pronouncement that "This is the place."

Salt Lake City has two notable areas visited by nearly all tourists: Temple Square and Capitol Hill. The building that houses the state government, with its classical style of architecture and copper dome, is the most prominent landmark. The beauty of its grounds would be a credit to the best Parisian landscape artists. Temple Square is even more impressive, not so much because of its landscaped gardens as its seclusion in the heart of a large city. A high stone wall encloses the magnificent temple, tabernacle, museum, and other structures and monuments and shuts out all traffic noise from the nearby streets. The tabernacle contains one of the largest pipe organs in the world and is probably the most historic Anglo-American structure in the West.

The downtown section of Salt Lake City surrounds Temple Square, and from there the wide streets extend outward to the far-flung suburbs. At the corner of each downtown block cool water constantly bubbles forth from drinking fountains, as if to remind the visitor that this desert oasis has an unlimited supply. In the heart of the city are nine large banking companies and a branch of the Federal Reserve, evidence that Salt Lake City is the financial and service center for the Great Basin region. On its periphery are processing plants for the variety of mineral, agricultural, and livestock products of the area. These include coal, copper, iron, silver, phosphate, gilsonite, lead, sugar beets, vegetables, beef, fruits, wheat, and poultry. And at nearby Orem the large plant recently built by the United States Steel Company, together with the other local heavy industries, employ over 35,000 people and, when the wind is from the south, supply Salt Lake City with a thick cover of smog.

Salt Lake City was destined to become the dominant city of the region even before the transcontinental railroad reached there in 1869. In fact, at that time it already was a city of more than 60,000—by far the largest between St. Louis and San Francisco. Today it is exceeded only by Denver and Phoenix, its population having grown from 150,000 in 1940 to 350,000 in 1960. Though the Church of Latter Day Saints no longer has the religious monopoly it formerly enjoyed, Salt Lake City still draws heavily upon its Mormon heritage. Its Tabernacle Choir is world famous, its people have one of the highest literacy rates in the nation, and its crime rate is one of the lowest. Because the Mormons were lovers of plays, Salt Lake City has always supported good theaters. It is also the home of the University of Utah, perhaps the leading state institution in the Great American Desert next to the University of Colorado.

Until a few decades ago the Great American Desert was a land of cactus, sage, cattle, sunshine, farms, sleepy hamlets, and wide, open spaces. All of these are still present, but the surge of recent events is drastically transforming large islands of the desert world into a predominantly business and industrial society of sprawling cities connected by a network of jet airlines and superhighways.

The newer cities and towns of the desert still have a temporary look about them. Most are man-made oases where the people are struggling for more water and industry with all their ingenuity. Scattered around the periphery of Phoenix, Tucson, Albuquerque, Denver, Salt Lake City, Las Vegas, and

Reno are cluttered eyesores of trailer courts, neon signs, used-car lots, giant billboards, and jerry-built housing developments, only a few steps removed from the slums. Most western cities have taken on a look of uniformity, largely the result of by-passes and connecting freeways built out to the new interstate highways. Along with these developments, however, have come modern banks and insurance buildings, giant supermarkets, schools, plush motels, sprawling industrial plants, and exclusive residential areas. This phenomenal growth of cities is perhaps the most outstanding characteristic of the "Great American Desert Now," in contrast to the "Great American Desert Then."

XIV THE CHALLENGE OF THE FUTURE

The future of the Great American Desert still depends upon water. Fortunately, the nation has accumulated more than a hundred years of experience in developing this valuable resource for the arid regions of the West. The technical problems are largely conquered, or at least modern tools have brought them within sight of solution. Also, dams and reservoirs have proved effective in capturing stream flow. Yet, impressive as these engineering achievements are, they cannot by themselves solve all the inherent problems of aridity. New sources of water have to be discovered, greater storage facilities built, watersheds protected more completely, pollution and sedimentation of the streams reduced, and the many human problems resolved.

With the knowledge now available, the capital to accomplish these things will somehow be found. But much will remain to be done. We need to reduce water losses through evaporation and *phreatophytes*, develop efficient saline-water-conversion procedures, and perhaps alter the climate itself. Otherwise, the alternative to President Kennedy's challenge "to conquer the desert" will be another costly lesson in consequences.

Finding new sources of supply and making better use of water already available could be one of the greatest achievements of the twentieth century. Real estate developers already have discovered that arid land, sunshine, and space are very salable items. Currently they are promoting whole new towns in some of the driest areas of North America, complete with swimming pools, golf courses, and artificial lakes. During 1963, land speculators opened more than 300 subdivisions in the Mojave Desert of California alone. Promotional literature invariably assures the prospective buyer of a new town lot that "plenty of water will soon be available."

With each advance in the struggle for more water, there has been a corresponding increase in population and a demand for still more water. And no sooner are old myths regarding the desert shattered than new ones are created. It is common belief today, for example, that science and technology will provide dramatic solutions to the water problems of the arid West. More especially, that the answer will be found in the conversion of salt and brackish water into fresh water. The nontechnical press has been overly optimistic in dramatizing recent developments in converting sea water, and millions of Americans are convinced that the problem has already been solved. They believe that it is only a matter of time before fresh water will be pumped by atomic power from the Pacific Coast or the Gulf Coast into the heart of the desert.

Research and development are proceeding at accelerated rates, but providing fresh water from saline sources at a cost comparable to that of natural supplies is at present unrealistic for the Great American Desert. Yet, since the idea has received so much publicity, it needs careful examination.

It is impossible to trace accurately the history of man's effort to separate fresh water from salt, but undoubtedly it began several thousands of years ago. Today, in a few arid regions of the world, various conversion processes are producing fresh water from the sea at relatively low cost. And practically all large ocean vessels are equipped with desalting plants. But the United States did not apply its knowledge of water purification to the arid lands of this country until 1952. In that year Congress appropriated two million dollars for water conversion research for a five-year period and designated the Secretary of the Interior to carry out the legislation. The Secretary immediately established the Saline Water Conversion Program under the direction of a small group of scientists.

Work had proceeded to such an extent by 1958 that Congress appropriated additional funds to construct five saline water-conversion plants at strategic locations across the country: "Such plants shall be designated to demonstrate the reliability, engineering, operation, and economic potential of the sea and for brackish water conversion processes which the Secretary shall select from among the most promising of the presently known processes, and each plant shall demonstrate a different process." Approximately 200 cities and communities requested consideration as a site for a plant. According to law, at least one plant designed for the treatment of brackish water had to be located in the northern Great Plains and another in the arid areas of the Southwest. The Secretary chose Webster, South Dakota, and Roswell, New Mexico.[1]

In selecting the various processes for individual pilot plants, the Saline Water Commission considered seventeen methods. The five eventually chosen included two types of distillation and one process each by electrodialysis, vapor compression, and freezing. The electrodialysis and freezing plants at Webster, South Dakota, and Wrightsville Beach, North Carolina, are capable of producing 250,000 gallons of fresh water each day, while the capacity of the other plants approximates a million gallons.

The first two processes represent large scale and ingenious improvements in distillation—trapping condensed steam and

[1] In addition, there are a few private and municipal plants in operation. Buckeye, Arizona, a town of 3000, depends entirely upon demineralized domestic water.

turning it into fresh water. The third process, electrodialysis, is based upon the principle of ion exchange, whereby mineral particles migrate through a membrane until the water on one side is nearly fresh and that on the other side more salty. The fourth method represents a new adaptation of the principle of vacuum or compression, while the last is based on the fact that ice formed through freezing is composed of nearly pure water.

By the summer of 1964 the various pilot plants were in production and supplying fresh water to nearby communities at relatively high cost. For example, the plant on the edge of the Great American Desert at Roswell was converting the brackish underground water of the Pecos Valley at about $1.50 per thousand gallons. Its output contributes approximately 10 per cent of the domestic consumption of the community, but it costs almost ten times as much as city water from deep wells. In Freeport, Texas, the 1,000,000-gallon-a-day plant was reducing the mineral content of the Gulf of Mexico water from 35,000 to 50 milligrams per liter of water. The cost varies from $1.00 to $1.25 per thousand gallons, but the Saline Water Commission is optimistic that here and elsewhere it eventually will vary from thirty to forty cents.

These figures may appear impressive to the layman, but it must be remembered that not many towns and cities in the United States pay as much as thirty cents for a thousand gallons of water. Irrigation farmers rarely pay more than five cents per thousand. The differential between conversion and natural water is in fuel costs, and some arid countries already are experimenting with unconventional sources. One of the oldest, of course, is the sun.[2] Atomic power might ultimately provide another cheap source of energy.

Short of a dramatic technical breakthrough in inexpensive fuel and in water transportation, it now seems highly unlikely

[2] A University of Arizona graduate student, Carl N. Hodges, has invented a method of desalting with heat from the sun. With a grant from the Department of the Interior, Mr. Hodges has set up a pilot plant at Puerto Penasco in Sonora, Mexico, on the Gulf of California, to test the worth of his ideas. Progress is expected to be slow.

that converted sea water will ever be used at great distances beyond the point of manufacture. A glance at a topographical map of the United States explains why, for converted sea water would have to be pumped uphill, and in most cases this means an elevation of several thousand feet. The cost of moving water from the Pacific over the Sierra Nevada into central Nevada or Utah, for example, would be prohibitive—perhaps four or five dollars per thousand gallons. On the other hand, converting sea water for towns and cities along the coast would relieve much of the demand for water now taken from inland streams and reservoirs.[3]

In recent years Secretary of the Interior Stuart Udall has warned his fellow Westerners repeatedly against the inefficient use of water already available. He therefore proposes integrating fresh surface and ground water supplies with great new saline-water-conversion plants on a regional basis. This means that the water-short states will have to co-operate with one another if they expect to prosper. Otherwise, in Udall's words, "they will surely shrivel separately."

Though conversion of saline and brackish water offers considerable promise, it is only one phase of an accelerated arid-zones research program now under way. Several institutes, symposiums, and international conferences have been held in the United States since 1956 to exchange ideas and to consider proposals regarding aridity. The University of Arizona has had an arid-lands program since 1958, the University of Texas is studying ways to deal with that state's inadequate water supply, and recently the University of Nevada established a Desert Research Institute for the same purpose. Meanwhile, some twenty universities of the eight desert states have started to pool their facilities in a concentrated research project. Hope-

[3] In August 1965, President Johnson stated that the nation "has lingered too long under the impression that desalting sea water is a far-out and distant goal," and he announced his determination "to make the great breakthrough before 1970." The Administration's target is to build plants, within five years, with a daily capacity of 100 million gallons each for the nation's biggest cities, as well as ten million-gallon plants for smaller communities by 1968.

fully an "arid-zone mentality" is slowly evolving, somewhat like the shift in attitude that created the European Common Market.

In relation to the total task to be accomplished, however, progress in the struggle to conquer the desert so far has been small. Wild speculation, unsupported claims, and extreme statements have raised false hopes, just as they did throughout the nineteenth century. The job of providing adequate water for the arid lands of the West is no less formidable today than splitting the atom or sending a man to the moon appeared to previous generations. Consequently, scientists are reviving a few old ideas and exploring dozens of new ones.

Modern professional rain-makers, for example, are carrying out a vast number of seeding operations, in which silver iodide is dispensed into the atmosphere from smoke generators on the ground. Though these experiments have produced more controversy than rainfall, it appears fairly certain that additional water can be secured from the sky rivers that flow over arid lands. The task is to make the clouds surrender their moisture at the right place and at the desired time. For the past several summers the Arizona Institute of Atmospheric Physics has been dispersing silver iodide vapor from airplanes into promising clouds. In the process the Institute has made many fundamental discoveries about what goes on inside a cloud when rain or snow or hail is formed; also, that nature herself provides a variety of precipitation mechanisms.

Perhaps man will learn to emulate nature, and if he cannot make it rain in one way, he might ultimately control the weather in another. Meanwhile, the search continues for various techniques to trigger precipitation artificially. One of the most unusual and ambitious ever undertaken is centered on a sandy mesa ten miles south of Yuma, Arizona. A number of scientists there, under the auspices of the Esso Research and Engineering Corporation, are treating large blocks of sandy earth with black asphalt material capable of absorbing up to 90 per cent of the solar heat falling on it. They speculate that if the heat can be radiated back into the atmosphere to warm and expand the air and generate powerful updrafts, then the latter will push the moisture-laden currents moving in from the ocean up to higher levels. There the cloud vapor could condense into rain and fall upon a district many times the expanse of the "pavement."

Unless man does learn to control the climate or to develop cheap conversion water, he will be forced to make better use of the supply already available. It is seldom realized that the water withdrawn from streams and wells in the arid and semi-arid regions of the United States is equivalent to the amount that supports 150 million people in the humid areas of the country. Most of the moisture in the West, however, is lost through evaporation, transpiration, and outright wasteful consumption. Lake Mead, for example, loses its upper six feet of water each year through evaporation. This, combined with losses from the other great reservoirs of the arid West, exceeds 25 million acre-feet per year, or about one-third of the total amount impounded. Fortunately, the knowledge of how to reduce these losses is already available and is being applied in restricted places.

For the past several years the Bureau of Reclamation has been working with a substance called hexadecanol, a low-cost alcohol. When sprayed on water, it forms a surface film of molecules a millionth of an inch thick. Where the film can be maintained, evaporation is reduced by almost two-thirds. Unfortunately, a strong wind will drive the molecules against the shore and the effect is lost. But scientists of the Water Laboratory of the Bureau of Reclamation have learned to combine the hexadecanol with other substances to form a white waxy solid. Lumps of the mixture are submerged all around the edge of a lake, where they dissolve, thus releasing the hexadecanol, which bubbles to the surface and forms a protective film.

Various types of soil sealants also are proving practical in reducing evaporation, subsurface pipes are replacing open ditches, and, near Lubbock, Texas, experiments are currently being conducted in watering crops below the surface. In other arid regions of the West experiments are under way whereby black polyethylene strips are laid in furrows. Small holes are punched into the covering at regular intervals by machines for "potted" seeds or young plants. Though the results are not yet conclusive, the effort shows considerable promise in controlling soil temperature and evaporation.

One of the best hopes at the moment for providing more water is to create patches in the desert for harvesting areas. Water harvesting is nothing new. The British obtain most of their water on Gibraltar by collecting runoff from the rocky slopes in corrugated iron aprons, as do the people in most of the Caribbean Islands. The Ácoma Indians depend partly upon runoff water captured in natural basins on top of the rock mesa that has been their home for centuries. In 1964, many farmers and ranchers of New Mexico, Nevada, Colorado, Wyoming, and Montana were receiving emergency assistance from the Department of Agriculture because of a prolonged drought. Much of the grazing and farm land in these states is located in extremely low rainfall areas, and many of the water harvesting methods being tested could prove invaluable.

Experts estimate that at least 90 per cent of the total rain that falls on the desert eventually is lost by evaporation. A little goes for the support of plant life, but only a tiny fraction ever reaches the natural underground reservoirs, or aquifers. At Granite Reef, Arizona, experimenters are trying out various chemicals on large surface areas, as well as butyl rubber, aluminum foil, polyethylene sheeting, and several other plastics. Costs for different water repellents vary from three to eighty cents a square yard, and these repellents are capable of harvesting anywhere from 30 to 100 per cent of the rain falling on the covered area, depending upon atmospheric conditions and the type of storm. This means that harvested water will cost more than three times what is now considered a reasonable price for water used for irrigation purposes. But once harvested water is really needed, users will have no alternative.

Next to evaporation, the greatest water thief in the arid

region is the *phreatophyte,* or "water-wasting" plant. The most common *phreatophyte* in the West is the all-but-worthless juniper. Throughout west Texas, New Mexico, Arizona, Nevada, Utah, and Colorado, farmers, ranchers, and water experts universally condemn this small evergreen tree. Indeed they should, for junipers occupy some 60,000,000 acres of land, and each plant, with its long tap root, absorbs more moisture than most thirty-foot trees do. Snow and ice are retained on the branches until most of their moisture is lost to the atmosphere. Furthermore, juniper forests are so dense that they choke out forage for cattle and greatly reduce the yield of recoverable water.

Throughout west Texas an eradication program has been going on for more than thirty years, and in north-central Arizona a $75,000,000 scheme is now under way to clear juniper trees from some 7,000,000 acres of land. Wherever the plants have been removed in large test areas, grass has come back and runoff has increased appreciably. On one Indian reservation stripped of juniper growth, springs are reported running again for the first time in years. But eradication is expensive. About the only way junipers can be destroyed permanently is to "bulldoze" them over with huge tractors, allow the dead trees to dry for a year, and then destroy the skeletons by fire. The federal government so far has borne most of the cost in the prolonged anti-juniper fight, and by its very magnitude the program captures the imagination. Nevertheless, many other water-saving devices are also being tried. Some success has been achieved in artificial recharge of underground reservoirs and the introduction of relatively salt-tolerant crops in areas where the underground water has a high saline content.

One great difficulty is the attitude of the public and the local governments toward water. Most desert cities provide lower rates for higher levels of water use and thus encourage wasteful consumption. It is not uncommon for as much as 40 per cent of the annual supply to go to lawns and shrubs, a practice that most cities cannot afford indefinitely. One sign of change among urban communities is the trend in Albuquerque, Phoenix, Tucson, Salt Lake City, and elsewhere toward colored gravel or pebbles in place of grass. Furthermore, private homes and public buildings more and more are being landscaped with large boulders and low-water-consuming native plants. Though private swimming pools and artificial lakes are increasing throughout the region, stricter ordinances are being passed regarding recirculation of the water, plastic covers for the pools, and chemically treated soil to reduce seepage from the lakes.

Perhaps the most dramatic, costly, and ambitious plan for bringing water to arid lands ever conceived by man is the Alaskan River Diversion Project, popularly known as NAW-APA (the North American Water and Power Alliance). NAWAPA provides for the collection of surplus waters from the Fraser, Yukon, Peace, Athabasca, and other rivers of Alaska and western Canada. Through a complex system of canals, tunnels, rivers, lifts, aqueducts, and reservoirs, water would be distributed to the parched areas of Canada, the western United States, and northern Mexico. The mammoth plan was first suggested by the Ralph M. Parsons Company, engineers-constructors of Los Angeles, and it is now receiving serious consideration by the Special Senate Subcommittee on Western Water Development. The estimated cost exceeds 80 billion dollars and time for completion is thirty years, or approximately the same as that for constructing the present federal interstate highway system.

To reach northern Mexico, Alaskan and Canadian water would have to travel a distance equal to that between Sweden and Egypt. Parsons believes that the project would supply an additional 4.3 billion acre-feet of storage, or almost twice the present available water resources in the seventeen western states. This would be distributed among all of the eight desert states, except Wyoming, plus the rim states of Oregon, California, Nebraska, Kansas, Oklahoma, and Texas. Moreover, there should be enough left for Mexico alone to develop eight times as much new irrigable land as the Aswan High Dam will provide Egypt.

The heart of the plan is a 500-mile-long reservoir extending down from western Canada into northern Montana and the Rocky Mountain Trench. Water from the upper extent of the Trench will be diverted southwestward to Vancouver in one direction and eastward across Canada to Lake Superior in another. Not only would these giant canals deliver irrigation water to the Canadian Plains and provide hydroelectric power along the way, but they also would make possible a navigable waterway from the Pacific to the Great Lakes and thence via the St. Lawrence Seaway to the Atlantic.

Water for use in the Great American Desert would come from the overflow of the Rocky Mountain Trench. It would move through the Sawtooth Lift in Montana and northern Idaho to supplement the flow of the Columbia and Snake rivers and thus double their hydroelectric power potential. From the Snake in southern Idaho, the Sawtooth Tunnel would carry surplus water to the newly created Lake Nevada near the common borders of Utah, Nevada, and Idaho. Diversion aqueducts would distribute part of the supply from Lake Nevada to a series of reservoirs and lakes across the Great Basin into southern California and Baja California. The remainder would continue through central Utah, via Lake Powell on the Colorado and Lake Navajo in north-central Arizona, where ultimately it would be distributed to southeastern Arizona, northern Mexico, southern New Mexico, and across the Continental Divide into eastern Colorado.

The engineering problems involved in the project could be less complex than acquiring the necessary land and altering outmoded state water laws and practices. It is difficult to see who will pay for all this, but desperation breeds daring. By the end of this century, with the demands for water in the West expected to increase threefold, the problem will be acute enough to require a giant-size project like NAWAPA to remedy it. Certainly, an effort of such magnitude would materially affect business and labor and give great impetus to industrial development. It would increase land value, encourage tourism and recreation, broaden the tax base, and provide several billion dollars annually from the sale of hydroelectric power. With adjustments, it could be integrated with existing federal projects into one system.

Even if NAWAPA were completed by the year 2000, it probably would still fall short of supplying the total needs for the arid West. For this and other reasons, some experts believe that the long-range solution is the curtailment, if not outright elimination, of irrigated agriculture. They argue that, no matter how efficient irrigation becomes, it will never approach the values that are attainable through the use of the same water for other purposes, particularly for industry. Furthermore the traditional fields of agriculture, mining, and ranching, to which all arid countries must devote their initial efforts, do not offer a long-term basis for support of developing societies with rising economic standards.

Irrigation already consumes most of the available water in the Great American Desert and produces 75 per cent or more of the value of all agricultural crops. Even though the secondary income and employment produced by this type of agriculture are considerable, it still demands careful re-evaluation. As population and the competition for land and water increase,[4] agriculture may be forced to relinquish its current pre-eminent position. Encroachment by interstate highways and urban development already has taken some of the best irrigable lands in the West. In most cases farmers have sold their land to the government, or leased their water rights to industry at a higher annual income than they had received from farm crops.

In 1956, at an international conference on arid lands held in Albuquerque, New Mexico, Louis Koenig of the Southwest Institute, San Antonio, startled the delegates with the dramatic statement that "irrigation is not an appropriate use of that

[4] The projected population figures by the United States Census Office for the year 2000 for the region west of the 98th meridian, excluding the three states on the Pacific Coast, is approximately 45 million. This represents twice the present figure for the mountain and plains states within the Great American Desert.

valuable resource, water." Koenig observed that the hinterlands of practically every civilization have first been opened for agricultural and other extractive industries. As civilization advanced, the rural areas were gradually taken over and converted to urban and industrial uses. "This situation was satisfactory as long as adequate rainfall permitted appropriate use of land for either agriculture or industry." In the absence of adequate rainfall, Westerners have resorted to irrigated agriculture, when actually "agriculture at best is a marginal use of water."

Koenig backed up his argument with the statement that the water that supports one worker in arid-land agriculture will support sixty or seventy workers in manufacturing. He therefore advised Westerners to look forward immediately to industrial rather than agricultural expansion:

> The railroad trains run in both directions. Let the humid region ship food into the arid, since with the arid lands reaching the limit of their water supply, the humid regions can produce more efficiently anyway and have by no means reached the limit of their capabilities. . . . If we can ship cotton, we can ship cameras; if we can ship radishes, we can ship radios; if we can ship watermelons, we can ship watches. Only then can the arid lands provide employment and a continuing high standard of living, both for the present inhabitants and for the many who are swelling their numbers seeking the favorable climate and the living which the land can afford.

Undoubtedly, most people who are engaged in irrigated agriculture would strongly oppose a systematic conversion of any part of their water rights to industrial and other nonagricultural uses. But the potential advantages of developing practical means for reallocating some of the water now used in agriculture are so great that it certainly cannot be ignored in the future. If, for example, only one million acre-feet of water now being used for irrigation in the West could be transferred to industrial uses, the value of the increased production would almost equal the present three-billion-dollar total of all irrigated crops. According to Peter C. Duisberg, an arid-lands specialist of El Paso, this means that only a small proportion of agriculture would need to be replaced, and the individual farmers who retired land and transferred water rights would be well compensated: "The remaining farmers would have increased markets and services as new population and industry entered the area."

In places like central Arizona and New Mexico, where many farmers already face a crisis because of declining water tables, such reallocation of water could be a salvation. In other places, particularly in the wheat belt of the Great Plains, farmers are producing far more special crops than the domestic market can consume. If sufficient farm lands were taken out of production it would be possible to re-establish a satisfactory balance. Such action perhaps would require a whole new concept of land laws and the regulation of surface and ground water as a unit. There are many indications that the individualistic Westerners are not ready to accept changes necessary if the desert's resources are to be utilized to the fullest. But failure to do so will surely result in more physical waste and ruin.

Naturally, not everyone agrees that irrigated agriculture should be reduced, even though at present the nation is producing a surplus of some crops. They point out that this should not be considered a serious liability as long as there are human beings on the edge of starvation anywhere in the world. Surpluses as we know them today will disappear, they believe, under the impact of the increasing population of the United States itself. Therefore, even full utilization of water available for irrigation in the West will be insufficient to meet the requirements of the future.

But the need for additional water is not the only immediate challenge of the desert. It is also important that the colder arid regions of Idaho, Montana, and Wyoming be developed. These areas possess some of the most magnificent scenery in the world, abundant energy resources, large stretches of underdeveloped space, superior summers, and unlimited winter sports possibilities. If a few disadvantages can be overcome, they might easily repeat the phenomenal growth experienced by the Southwest during the past two decades. At present the greatest barrier to year-round living is the idea that the winters are cold and unpleasant, a belief not shared by all who live there. Already, central heating by natural gas has made indoor living in subzero weather completely comfortable. Lessons learned from arctic and antarctic regions and from the national space program have resulted in light, comfortable clothing for out-of-doors. In addition, improved machinery for removal of winter snow and ice offers excellent opportunities for collecting water for subsequent use in the dry months.

It has been only a hundred years since the railroads pushed across America to connect the two oceans. But before then, crossing the desert and mountains of the West posed a real threat to life, and only the hardy and adventurous even considered such a possibility. The twentieth century has brought automobiles, hard-surfaced roads, trucks, buses, propeller-driven airplanes, and jets. Now the traveler can cross while taking a short nap, imbibing one or two martinis, or viewing a first-run movie. On the road it takes longer, and the experience is often much more rewarding.

In spite of these tremendous advances, the Great American Desert finds itself today in a dilemma. The question is: How much of its scenic and recreational facilities can remain unimpaired while the economic resources are expanding? Or to put it another way: How can the Great American Desert be integrated into the national economy without drastically altering the landscape?

The arid West is viewed by some as a huge playground or sanctuary for those cramped up in the cities most of the year. To them, the greatest challenge of the future is to preserve the region's scenery and outdoor recreational facilities. As the work-week decreases and longer annual paid vacations become universal, more and more people turn to the desert and mountains in their leisure time. During the past twenty years the number of visitors to national parks, wilderness areas, and national monuments has multiplied tenfold. Some estimate that such activities will increase twenty to thirty times more before the year 2000. As this happens, pressure to develop the public lands of the arid regions for further recreational uses is inevitable.

At the same time, the people of the region must continuously cope with droughts and floods, sporadic runoff of mountain streams, diminishing ground water and timber supplies, and extremes of heat and cold. Here, the problems of the rest of the country, to say nothing of the rest of the world, are projected on a wide screen. Here too, is virtually the last area in the United States in which our booming population can find living space. In the past Americans have demonstrated an infinite capacity to deface the environment in the name of progress. Reversing this tradition, and taking collective action that will aid the individual without impairing his freedom, might very well become the overwhelming challenge from here on.

Meanwhile, man inevitably remains the trespasser in the Great American Desert, but he cannot abandon it for the simple reason that he no longer has any other place to go.

BIBLIOGRAPHICAL NOTES

I WHAT IS THE GREAT AMERICAN DESERT?

Edmund C. Jaeger, *The North American Deserts* (Stanford: Stanford University Press, 1957) provides a concise and interesting discussion of the five North American deserts and their subdivisions, with considerable attention to the plant and animal life of each. Earlier works by Jaeger relating to the desert are *The California Deserts: A Visitor's Handbook* (Stanford: Stanford University Press, 1933), and *Our Desert Neighbors* (Stanford: Stanford University Press, 1950). More detailed geographic information on the arid lands of North America is found in C. Langdon White and Edwin J. Foscue, *Regional Geography of Anglo-America* (New York: Prentice Hall, 1954), and Preston E. James, *A Geography of Man* (New York: Ginn and Company, 1959). James emphasizes the effect of geography on man and his adaptation to the climate.

James C. Malin, *Geology and Geography; Grassland Historical Studies: Natural Resources Utilization in a Background of Science and Technology* (Lawrence: James C. Malin, 1950) does a scholarly and original job of combining the geological history of the Great Plains with its recorded human history. A more classical work along similar lines is Walter P. Webb, *The Great Plains* (Boston: Ginn and Company, 1931). Easy to read is Paul B. Sears, *Deserts on the March* (Norman: University of Oklahoma Press, 1935). Sears, a botanist, vividly describes the effects of civilization in disturbing the balance of nature in arid regions of the American West, particularly the Great Plains.

Climate as a factor in Great Plains settlement is covered fully by the sociologist Carl Frederick Kraenzel, *The Great Plains in Transition* (Norman: University of Oklahoma Press, 1955). Robert G. Athearn, *High Country Empire: The High Plains and Rockies* (New York: McGraw-Hill, 1960) discusses the geographic features that make the section of the Great American Desert that is drained by the Missouri River a region within a region. Individual essays in *Regionalism in America* (Madison: The University of Wisconsin Press, 1951), edited by Merrill Jensen, also stress the climatic and geographic factors that contribute to regionalism.

For additional reading on individual sections of the Great American Desert the following books are recommended: Lynn I. Perrigo, *Our Spanish Southwest* (Dallas: Banks Upshaw and Company, 1960); Gloria Griffen Cline, *Exploring the Great Basin* (Norman: University of Oklahoma Press, 1963); Leonard J. Arrington, *Great Basin Kingdom: An Economic History of the Latter Day Saints, 1830–1900* (Cambridge: Harvard University Press, 1958); W. Eugene Hollon, *The Southwest: Old and New* (New York: Alfred A. Knopf, Inc., 1961); Morris E. Garnsey, *America's New Frontier: The Mountain West* (New York: Alfred A. Knopf, Inc., 1950); and W. Storrs Lee, *The Great California Deserts* (New York: G. P. Putnam's Sons, 1963).

Among the more specific and technical works are Clifford M. Zierer (ed.), *California and the Southwest* (New York: John Wiley & Sons, 1956); Nevin M. Fenneman, *Physiography of Western United States* (New York: McGraw-Hill, 1931); Lyman David Benson and Robert A. Darrow, *The Trees and Shrubs of the Southwestern Desert* (Tucson: University of Arizona Press, 1954); J. W. Wright (ed.), *Rainfall and Tree Growth in the Great Plains*, by Ernst Antevs (Baltimore: Lord Baltimore Press, 1938); Gilbert F. White (ed.), *The Future of Arid Lands: Papers and Recommendations from the International Arid Lands Meetings* (Washington, D.C.: The American Association for the Advancement of Science, 1956); Carl Hodge and Peter C. Duisberg (eds.), *Aridity and Man: The Challenge of the Arid Lands in the United States* (Washington, D.C.: The American Association for the Advancement of Science, 1963); Wynne Thorne, *Land and Water Use* (Washington, D.C.: The American Association for the Advancement of Science, 1963).

Older books that are still useful include Paul Fountain, *The Great Deserts and Forests in North America* (New York: Longmans, Green, and Company, 1901); Ellsworth Huntington et al., *Climatic Factor as Illustrated in Arid North America* (Washington, D.C.: Carnegie Institute of Washington, 1914); Forrest Shreve, *Vegetation of a Desert Mountain Range as Conditioned by Climatic Factors* (Washington, D.C.: Carnegie Institute of Washington, 1915); and Arthur Jerome Burdick, *The Mystic Mid-region, the Deserts of the Southwest* (New York: G. P. Putnam, 1904).

Scientific and popular articles that have been written on the desert during the past century probably exceed a thousand. Certainly the most recent, controversial, and significant one is Walter Prescott Webb, "The American West, Perpetual Mirage," *Harper's* (May 1957). Among others that supplied background material for this chapter, and one of the most excellent descriptions of the desert ever written, is Mary Austin, "A Land of Little Rain," *Atlantic* (January 1903). Another is Sharlot M. Hall, "When Spring Comes to the Desert," *Out West* (June 1905). Similarities of the Great American Desert to the Egyptian deserts are pointed out in the pioneer essay by Johannes Walther, "The North American Deserts," *The National Geographic Magazine* (February 1893).

Several dated but significant essays on plant and animal life in the desert are available, including: Raymond J. Pool, "Glimpses of the Great American Desert," *Popular Science* (March 1912); W. C. Mendenhall, "The Colorado Desert," *The National Geographic Magazine* (August 1909); Frederick V. Coville, "The American Deserts," *The National Geographic Magazine* (April 1904); Daniel T. MacDougal, "Botanical Features of the North American Deserts," *The National Geographic Magazine* (August 1910); Ernest Ingersoll, "Plant Life in the Desert," *Harper's* (March 1905); Frank H. Spearmen, "The Great American Desert," *Harper's* (July 1888); Frank W. Blackmar, "The History of the Desert," Kansas State Historical Society *Transactions* (1905–1906); William T. Marshall, "Animal Life in the Great Desert," *Popular Science* (December 1890); H. L. Shantz and Raphael Zon, "Grassland and Desert Shrub," *Atlas of American Agriculture* (Washington, D.C.: Department of Agriculture, 1924); F. E. Lloyd, "Vegetation in Western United States,"

Popular Science (February 1905); A. T. Sweet, "How Plants Tell the Soil Story," *Nature Magazine* (February 1934); G. W. James, "Strange Creatures of the American Sahara," *Suburban Life* (November 1908); and "Climate and Settlement of the Arid Region," *Yearbook of the Department of Agriculture, 1941.*

II THE ORIGINAL OCCUPANTS

A beautifully illustrated and well-written account of the original inhabitants of the Great American Desert is found in *The American Heritage Book of Indians,* edited by Alvin M. Joseph, Jr. (New York: American Heritage Publishing Co., Inc., 1961). Harold S. Gladwin, *A History of the Ancient Southwest* (Portland, Me.: Bond Wheelwright Co., 1957) traces the evolution of the early foragers and hunters of the Stone Age in California, Arizona, New Mexico, and Texas to the arrival of the Spaniards in the sixteenth century. Other readable accounts of ancient civilizations in the southern section of the Great American Desert are Edgar L. Hewett, *Ancient Life in the American Southwest* (Indianapolis: Bobbs-Merrill Company, 1930), and Adolph Bandalier and Edgar L. Hewett, *Indians of the Rio Grande Valley* (Albuquerque: University of New Mexico Press, 1937).

Commentaries on the primitive tribes of the Great Basin are found in *Life, Letters and Travels of Father Pierre-Jean De Smet, S.J. 1801–1873,* 4 volumes, edited by Hiram M. Chittenden and Alfred T. Richardson (New York: Francis P. Harper, 1905). Also useful are Dale L. Morgan, *Jedediah Smith and the Opening of the West* (Indianapolis: Bobbs-Merrill Company, 1953), and *Peter Skene Ogden's Snake Country Journals, 1824–25 and 1825–26,* edited by E. E. Rich and A. M. Johnson (London: Hudson's Bay Record Society, 1950). More general are two books by Clark Wissler, *The American Indian* (New York: Oxford University Press, 1938), and *Indians of the United States* (New York: Doubleday, Doran and Co., 1949). Frederick W. Hodge (ed.), *Handbook of the American Indians North of Mexico* (Washington, D.C.: U.S. Government Printing Office, 1912) contains a mine of information on the origin and location of various tribes. Considerable information on primitive tribes of the desert states likewise is found in *The Works of Hubert Howe Bancroft* (San Francisco: The History Company, 1889–1901).

Practically every individual tribe has had its biographer, but historians have had to depend upon the archeologist and anthropologist for pre-Columbian information. Among the most significant periodical articles in this regard are Charles C. Jones, Jr., "Antiquity of North American Indians," *North American Review* (January 1874); Victor F. Lotrich, "Points of Antiquity from Twelve States," *Colorado Magazine* (1939); Lewis H. Morgan, "Indian Migrations," *North American Review* (1869, 1870); Jonas M. Poweshiek, "Agriculture of American Aborgines," *Annals of Iowa* (1955); Joseph B. Thoburn, "The Tropical and Sub-Tropical Origin of Mound-Builder Cultures," *Chronicles of Oklahoma* (March 1938) and D. E. Worcester, "The Weapons of American Indians," *New Mexico Historical Review* (July 1945).

Three significant articles that describe the Indian's adaptation to desert living are Frederick V. Coville, "Desert Plants as a Source of Drinking Water," *Smithsonian Report* (Washington, D.C.: U.S. Government Printing Office, 1903); Richard B. Woodbury, "Indian Adaptations to Arid Environments," *Aridity and Man* (Washington, D.C.: The American Association for the Advancement of Science, 1963); and N. B. Johnson, "The American Indian as a Conservationist," *Chronicles of Oklahoma* (No. 3, 1952). The Indian utilization of the buffalo for food, clothing, and shelter is described in innumerable books and magazines. One such classical work is M. S. Garretson, *The American Bison* (New York: New York Zoological Society, 1938).

III   THE WHITE MAN'S ARRIVAL

Every general textbook on the American West contains one or more chapters on Spanish explorations and settlements in the New World. Individual chapters in Walter Prescott Webb, *The Great Plains* (Boston: Ginn and Company, 1931), and Ray Allen Billington, *Westward Expansion: A History of the American Frontier* (New York: The Macmillan Company, 1949) are as concise and clear as any treatments available. More general and extensive are the works of Herbert E. Bolton. Much of Bolton's scholarly work is in the form of edited journals of various explorers, including *Spanish Exploration in the Southwest, 1542–1706* (New York: C. Scribner's Sons, 1916); *The Colonization of North America*, with Thomas Maitland Marshall (New York: The Macmillan Company, 1920); and *Anza's California Expedition*, 5 volumes (Berkeley: University of California Press, 1930). Two popular biographies by the same author are *Coronado, Knight of Pueblo and Plains* (Albuquerque:

University of New Mexico Press, 1949), and *The Padre on Horseback; A Sketch of Eusebio Francisco, S.J., Apostle of the Pimas* (San Francisco: The Sonora Press, 1932). Several accounts of Cabeza de Vaca's adventures have been published. An easy one to read is Morris Bishop, *Odyssey of Cabeza de Vaca* (New York: The Century Company, 1933). Another is Cleve Hallenbeck, *The Journey of Fray Marcos de Niza* (Dallas: University Press, 1949), which tells the story of Cabeza de Vaca's Negro companion. The original documents of Oñate's colonizing efforts in New Mexico have been translated by George P. Hammond, *Don Juan de Oñate, Colonizer of New Mexico, 1596–1628* (Albuquerque: University of New Mexico Press, 1953). The movement of population northward from Mexico into the Great American Desert is touched upon by Hubert H. Bancroft, *History of North American States and Texas*, 2 volumes (San Francisco: The History Company, 1884–89). More specific is George P. Hammond and Agapito Rey (eds.), *Expedition into New Mexico Made by Antonio de Espejo, 1582–1583* (Los Angeles: The Quivira Society, 1929). Spanish efforts to control her subjects of the arid region of North America is described in Sidney B. Brinckerhoff and Odie B. Faulk (eds.), *Lancers for the King: A Study of the Frontier System of Northern New Spain* (Tucson: The Arizona Historical Foundation, 1965).

Significant articles relating to mission life include John Francis Bannon, S.J., "Black-Robe Frontiersman: Pedro Mendez, S.J.," *Hispanic American Historical Review* (Febraury 1947); Sylvester Baxter, "The Father of the Pueblo," *Harper's* (June 1882); Herbert E. Bolton, "The Black Robes of New Spain," *Catholic Historical Review* (October 1935); George P. Hammond, "Pimeria Alta after Kino's Time," *New Mexico Historical Review* (July 1929); Richard J. Morrisey, "Early Agriculture in Pimeria Alta," *Mid-America* (1949); Philip Wayne Powell, "Presidios and Towns on the Silver Frontier of New Spain, 1550–1580," *Hispanic American Historical Review* (May 1944); and Charles Wilson Hackett, "The Revolt of the Pueblo Indians of New Mexico in 1680," *Southwestern Historical Quarterly* (October 1911).

IV THE NORTHERN MYSTERY

Several references to books and articles relating to the explorations of Father Kino and Juan Bautista de Anza already have been made. Not as well known are the explorations of the Spanish missionaries

Garcés, Domínguez, and Escalante. Scholarly studies, however, have been produced on each by Herbert E. Bolton: *The Early Explorations of Father Garcés on the Pacific Slope* in *Anza's California Expedition* (previously cited), and *Pageant in the Wilderness: The Story of the Escalante Expedition to the Interior Basin, 1776* (Salt Lake City: Utah Historical Society, 1950). Previously, Elliott Coues edited Garcés's journal, *On the Trail of a Spanish Pioneer: The Diary and Itinerary of Francisco Garcés,* 2 volumes (New York: Francis P. Harper, 1900). Pedro Font was rescued from history's limbo by Frederick Teggart, *The Anza Expedition of 1775–1776; The Diary of Pedro Font* (Berkeley: University of California Press, 1913).

Numerous biographies of early Anglo-American explorers who tried to solve the riddle of the "northern mystery" have been published, in addition to various edited journals. Lewis and Clark have received the most attention, first by Elliott Coues, *The Journals of Lewis and Clark,* 4 volumes (New York: Francis P. Harper, 1893), followed by Reuben G. Thwaites, 8 volumes (New York: Dodd, Mead and Company, 1904–1905), and more recently by Bernard De Voto (Boston: Houghton Mifflin, 1953). The Pike journals likewise were edited by Elliott Coues, *The Expeditions of Zebulon Montgomery Pike, To Headwaters of the Mississippi River, Through Louisiana Territory, and in New Spain, During the Years 1805-6-7* (New York: Francis P. Harper, 1895). Much new material on each of these explorers has since been appearing regularly in book form during the past decade. The two most recent are Donald Jackson's extensive collection of *Letters of the Lewis and Clark Expedition, With Related Documents, 1783–1854* (Urbana: University of Illinois Press, 1962), and Richard Dillon, *Meriwether Lewis* (New York: Coward-McCann, Inc., 1965).

Stephen H. Long perhaps is the most neglected of the early western explorers, primarily because most of his journals were lost. The standard narrative of Long's explorations is Edwin James, *An Account of an Expedition from Pittsburgh to the Rocky Mountains,* in Reuben G. Thwaites (ed.), *Early Western Travels, 1748–1846,* 32 volumes (Cleveland: Arthur H. Clark, 1904–1906). Thanks to his own prolific pen and a host of admirers and detractors, the exploits of John Charles Frémont have been well publicized. Frémont's *Report of the Exploring Expedition to the Rocky Mountains in the Year 1842, and to Oregon and North California in the Years 1843–44,* 28th Congress, 2nd session, House Executive Document 166 (1845), covers his two major expeditions into the heart of the Great American Desert. All of Frémont's biographers have borrowed heavily from this document.

The activities of other desert travelers and observers during the early nineteenth century are adequately treated in Harrison Clifford Dale, *The Ashley-Smith Explorations and the Discovery of a Central Route to the Pacific, 1822–1829* (Cleveland: Arthur H. Clark, 1918); Bernard De Voto, *The Course of Empire* (Boston: Houghton Mifflin, 1952); Lawrence J. Burpee, *The Search for the Western Sea* (London: Alston Rivers, Ltd., 1908); Edmund William Gilbert, *The Exploration of Western America, 1800–1850* (Cambridge, England: Cambridge University Press, 1933); Dale L. Morgan, *The Humboldt, Highroad of the West* (New York: Farrar and Rinehart, 1943); *Jedediah Smith and the Opening of the West* (Indianapolis: Bobbs-Merrill, 1953); and Gloria Griffen Cline, *Exploring the Great Basin* (Norman: University of Oklahoma Press, 1963).

By far the most significant article relating to the "northern mystery" and more especially to the mythical Buenaventura River is C. Gregory Crampton and Gloria Griffen (Cline), "The San Buenaventura, Mythical River of the West," *Pacific Historical Review* (May 1956). Other articles on similar subjects include C. Gregory Crampton, "The Discovery of the Green River," *Utah Historical Quarterly* (October 1952) and "The Myth of El Dorado," *The Historian* (Spring 1951); Herbert E. Bolton, "Escalante in Dixie and the Arizona Strip," *New Mexico Historical Review* (January 1928); Lewis F. Byington, "The Historic Expedition of Colonel John C. Frémont and Kit Carson to California in 1843–44," *Quarterly of the Society of California Pioneers* (September 1931); Cecil J. Alter, "Father Escalante's Map," *Utah Historical Quarterly* (January–April 1941); Frederick V. Holman, "Life and Services of Peter Skene Ogden," *Oregon Historical Quarterly* (December 1923); and T. A. Rickard, "The Strait of Anían," *British Columbia Historical Quarterly* (July 1941).

V   THE FIRST EXPLOITERS

The standard general works on the fur trade are Hiram M. Chittenden, *The American Fur Trade of the Far West*, 3 volumes (New York: The Press of the Pioneers, 1935); Clarence A. Vandiveer, *The Fur Trade and Early Western Exploration* (Cleveland: Arthur H. Clark, 1929); and more recently Paul Chrisler Phillips, *The Fur*

262 THE GREAT AMERICAN DESERT

Trade, 2 volumes (Norman: University of Oklahoma Press, 1961).
Indeed, I pondered so many books and articles on the subject of
the fur trade that I find myself unable to improve upon the 79-
page list supplied by the late Professor Phillips, for the simple
reason that Phillips includes just about everything that had been
done before 1960. Meanwhile, production of additional fur trade
literature continues unceasingly, including a 7-volume work currently being edited by LeRoy R. Hafen, *The Mountain Men and
the Fur Trade of the Far West.*

For conciseness and readability, it would be difficult to improve
upon individual chapters on the fur trade found in Ray Allen
Billington, *Westward Expansion: A History of the American Frontier* (New York: The Macmillan Company, 1949); Robert G. Athearn, *High Country Empire: The High Plains and Rockies* (New
York: McGraw-Hill, 1960); and LeRoy Hafen and Carl Coke Rister,
Western America (New York: Prentice Hall; 1941).

The coming of the missionaries to the Far West is covered in
F. G. Young (ed.), *Correspondence and Journals of Nathaniel J.
Wyeth, 1831–1836,* in *Sources of the History of Oregon,* I (Eugene,
Ore.: University Press, 1899); Cornelius J. Brosnan, *Jason Lee, Pro-
phet of the New Oregon* (New York: The Macmillan Company,
1932); and A. J. Allen, *Ten Years in Oregon* (Ithaca, N.Y.: Mack,
Andrus and Co., 1848). Plains travel is described by LeRoy R.
Hafen (ed.), *Overland Routes to the Gold Field* (Glendale, Calif.:
Arthur H. Clark, 1942). Also, good general accounts of overland
migration are found in J. C. Bell, *Opening a Highway to the Paci-
fic, 1838–1846* (New York: Columbia University Press, 1921); W. J.
Ghent, *The Road to Oregon* (New York: Longmans, Green and
Co., 1929); Jay Monaghan, *The Overland Trail* (Indianapolis:
Bobbs-Merrill, 1947); and Rockwell D. Hunt, *John Bidwell, A
Prince of California Pioneers* (Caldwell, Idaho: The Caxton Print-
ers, 1942). The Donner episode is told by George R. Stewart, Jr.,
Ordeal by Hunger: The Story of the Donner Party (New York: H.
Holt and Co., 1936). Popular books on the westward movement are
legion, such as Dorothy Gardiner, *West of the River* (New York:
Thomas Y. Crowell, 1941), and Ina Faye Woestemeyer, *The West-
ward Movement* (New York: Appleton-Century Co., 1939).

Two fascinating articles relating to covered wagon trains crossing
the desert are Ralph K. Andrist, "Gold!" *American Heritage* (December 1962) and George R. Stewart, "The Prairie Schooner Got
Them There," *American Heritage* (February 1962). Articles in schol-

arly journals describing the hardships of the trail number in the thousands. Among those consulted by the author in the writing of this chapter are James Abbey, "California. A Trip across the Plains in the Spring of 1850," *Magazine of History* (XLVI); Louise Barry (ed.), "Overland to the Gold Fields of California in 1852: The Journal of John Hawkins Clark, Expanded and Revised from Notes Made During the Journey," *Kansas Historical Quarterly* (August 1942); Ralph P. Bieber, "California Gold Mania," *Mississippi Valley Historical Review* (June 1948); John W. Caughey, "Southwest from Salt Lake in 1849," *Pacific Historical Review* (No. 2, 1937); William Clark, "A Trip Across the Plains in 1857," *Iowa Journal of History and Politics* (April 1922); LeRoy R. Hafen, "George A. Jackson's Diary, 1858–1859," *Colorado Magazine* (1942); and Charles Kelley, "Gold Seekers on the Hastings Cutoff," *Utah Historical Quarterly* (1952).

VI THE MORMON CONQUERORS

Every general work on the American West contains one or more chapters on the Mormons, and no more concise or readable summary has been done than Ray Allen Billington, *Westward Expansion* (previously cited). The bibliography of that work would be difficult to improve upon. Of the general histories, the best is Thomas F. O'Dea, *The Mormons* (Chicago: The University of Chicago Press, 1957). The most comprehensive official history of the Church is Brigham H. Roberts, *A Comprehensive History of the Church of Jesus Christ of Latter-Day Saints*, 6 volumes (Salt Lake City: Deseret Book Company, 1930). A highly critical account is William A. Linn, *The Story of the Mormons* (New York: The Macmillan Company, 1923).

Brigham Young has been the subject of several biographies. One of the most laudatory is by a daughter, Susa Y. Gates, *The Life Story of Brigham Young* (New York: The Macmillan Company, 1930). Reasonably objective and popular is M. R. Werner, *Brigham Young* (New York: Harcourt, Brace & Company, 1925).

Early Mormon settlements in the Great American Desert are well described by Andrew L. Neff, *History of Utah, 1847–1869* (Salt Lake City: Deseret News Press, 1940), and Hubert H. Bancroft, *History of Utah, 1540–1886* (San Francisco: The History Company, 1889). Expansion of Mormon settlements is described by Leland H. Creer, *The Founding of an Empire: The Exploration and Colonization of*

Utah, 1776–1856 (Salt Lake City: Bookcraft, 1947); Milton R. Hunter, *Brigham Young the Colonizer* (Salt Lake City: Deseret News Press, 1940); and Nels Anderson, *The Mormon Frontier in Utah* (Chicago: University of Chicago Press, 1942).

Significant articles on the Mormons include two by Leonard J. Arrington, "The Desert Agricultural and Manufacturing Society in Pioneer Utah," *Utah Historical Quarterly* (1956), and "The Mormon Cotton Mission in Southern Utah," *Pacific Historical Review* (August 1956). Also, there are James R. Clark, "The Kingdom of God, The Council of Fifty and the State of Deseret," *Utah Historical Quarterly* (1958); Leland H. Creer, "The Evolution of Government in Early Utah," *Utah Historical Quarterly* (1958); Katherine Fullerton Gerould, "Salt Lake: The City of the Saints," *Harper's* (June 1924); Dale L. Morgan, "The State of Deseret," *Utah Historical Quarterly* (April, July, and October 1940); and T. Edgar Lyon, "Orson Pratt: Pioneer and Proselyter," *Utah Historical Quarterly* (1956).

The most scholarly and objective economic history of the Mormon settlements is Leonard J. Arrington, *Great Basin Kingdom: An Economic History of the Latter-Day Saints, 1830–1900* (Cambridge: Harvard University Press, 1958). Arrington devotes considerable discussion to the pioneer work by Mormons in developing irrigation. Other studies related to early irrigation practices in the Great Basin are Richard J. Hinton, *Irrigation in the United States —Progress Report for 1890* (Senate Executive Documents: 51st Congress, 2nd Session); Frederick Haynes Newall, *Irrigation in the United States* (New York: Thomas Y. Crowell, 1902); William R. Van Dersal, *The American Land: Its History and Its Uses* (New York: Oxford University Press, 1943); and Mont H. Saunderson, *Western Land and Water Use* (Norman: University of Oklahoma Press, 1950).

VII   DEATH AND SURVIVAL IN THE DESERT

It is a fairly safe assumption that few subjects have been more thoroughly examined by historians, sociologists, anthropologists, and popular writers than the western Indians. Most of the studies, however, have been written from the white man's view, since the Indians themselves left few records and documents. The University of Oklahoma Press alone has published more than sixty volumes in its "Indians of America Series" during the past thirty years. As a general survey, few books can surpass the previously mentioned *Book of Indians* (American Heritage Publishing Company, 1961) for readability, beautiful illustrations, and current status of the various western tribes. Accounts of plains warfare are found in Frederic L. Paxson, *Last American Frontier* (New York: The Macmillan Company, 1910); Robert G. Athearn, *William Tecumseh Sherman and the Settlement of the West* (Norman: University of Oklahoma Press, 1956); James H. Cook, *Fifty Years on the Old Frontier* (New Haven: Yale University Press, 1923); and Jacob P. Dunn, *Massacre of the Mountains: A History of the Indian Wars of the Far West* (New York: Harper and Brothers, 1886). More popular books on the same subject are two by Paul I. Wellman, *Death in the Desert* (New York: The Macmillan Company, 1935), and *Death on the Prairie* (New York: The Macmillan Company, 1934). An excellent survey of warfare in the Southwest is found in Edward E. Dale, *The Indians of the Southwest: A Century of Development under the United States* (Norman: University of Oklahoma Press, 1949). More specific accounts are in Ruth M. Underhill, *The Navajos* (Norman: University of Oklahoma Press, 1956); C. L. Sonnichsen, *The Mescalero Apaches* (Norman: University of Oklahoma Press, 1959); Carl C. Rister, *The Southwestern Frontier, 1865–1881* (Cleveland: Arthur H. Clark, 1928); and Rupert N. Richardson, *The Comanche Barrier to South Plains Settlement* (Glendale: Arthur H. Clark, 1933).

Warfare on the northern plains is covered in L. E. Textor, *Official Relations between the United States and the Sioux Indians* (Palo Alto, Calif.: The University, 1896); George E. Hyde, *Red Cloud's Folk: A History of the Oglala Sioux* (Norman: University of Oklahoma Press, 1937); George E. Hyde, *A Sioux Chronicle* (Norman: University of Oklahoma Press, 1956); Grace R. Hebard and A. R. Brininstool, *The Bozeman Trail*, 2 volumes (Cleveland: Arthur H. Clark, 1922); Edgar I. Stewart, *Custer's Luck* (Norman: University of Oklahoma Press, 1955); and Chester A. Fee, *Chief Joseph* (New York: Wilson-Erikson, Inc., 1936).

The standard work on the development of Indian policy is Loring B. Priest, *Uncle Sam's Stepchildren: The Reformation of United States Indian Policy, 1865–1887* (New Brunswick, N.J.: Rutgers University Press, 1942). A more emotional and influential argument for reform was voiced in Helen Hunt Jackson, *A Century of Dishonor* (New York: Harper and Brothers, 1881).

Among the dozens of articles from which material for this chapter was drawn are Randolph C. Downes, "A Crusade for Indian Reform, 1922–1934," *Mississippi Valley Historical Review* (December 1945); William T. Hagan, "Private Property, The Indian's Door to Civilization," *Ethnohistory* (No. 2, 1956); N. B. Johnson, "The American Indian as Conservationist," *Chronicles of Oklahoma* (No. 3, 1952); Stanley Pargellis, "The Problem of American Indian History," *Ethnohistory* (No. 2, 1957); D. E. Worcester, "The Weapons of American Indians," *New Mexico Historical Review* (July 1945); Donald J. Berthrong, "Federal Indian Policy and the Southern Cheyenne and Arapahoes, 1887–1907," *Ethnohistory* (No. 2, 1956); Dorothy M. Johnson, "Ghost Dance: Last Hope of the Sioux," *Minnesota History Bulletin* (Summer 1956); Thomas Le Duc, "The Work of the Indian Claims Commission under the Act of 1946," *Pacific Historical Review* (February 1957); and Dorothy Van de Mark, "The Raid on the Reservations," *Harper's* (March 1956).

VIII   THE CATTLEMEN'S INVASION

Like the fur traders and the Indians, the cattle industry has been thoroughly covered by students of western history. Good brief accounts of the origin of ranching in Texas can be found in Ray Allen Billington, *Westward Expansion: A History of the American Frontier* (previously cited); Rupert N. Richardson and Carl C. Rister, *The Greater Southwest* (Glendale: Arthur H. Clark, 1935); Carl C. Rister, *The Southwestern Frontier, 1865–1881* (Cleveland: Arthur H. Clark, 1928); and Walter P. Webb, *The Great Plains* (Boston: Ginn and Company, 1931).

The classical economic studies of the range cattle industry are Ernest S. Osgood, *The Day of the Cattlemen* (Minneapolis: The University of Minnesota Press, 1929); Louis Pelzer, *The Cattleman's Frontier* (Glendale: Arthur H. Clark, 1936); and Edward E. Dale, *The Range Cattle Industry* (Norman: University of Oklahoma Press, 1929). More recent, though confined principally to the cattle industry on the northern plains, are three monographs by Maurice Frink, W. Turrentine Jackson, and Agnes Wright Spring, published as a single volume under the title of *When Grass Was King* (Boulder: The University of Colorado Press, 1956).

Cow towns are described in Robert Athearn, *High Country Empire* (previously cited); F. B. Streeter, *Prairie Trails and Cow Towns* (Boston: Chapman and Grimes, 1936); and Robert M. Wright, *Dodge City, the Cowboy Capital and the Great Southwest* (Wichita:

Wichita Eagle Press, 1913). The extension of the cattle frontier over the Northwest is described in Harold E. Briggs, *Frontiers of the Northwest* (New York: D. Appleton-Century Co., 1940). Wayne Gard, *The Chisholm Trail* (Norman: University of Oklahoma Press, 1954) represents the most scholarly work on the cattle drives, while Andy Adams, *Log of a Cowboy* (Boston: Houghton Mifflin, 1903) is one of the few fictional works on the subject which deserves the approbation of classical.

Histories of many of the famous western ranches have been written, and studies of some of the lesser-known ones are currently being published by the University of Texas Press. Individual cattle kings such as Charles Goodnight, Major George W. Littlefield, John Chisum, George Slaughter, and Granville Stuart likewise have had their biographers. For penetrating analyses of cattle kings and cowboys see Lewis E. Atherton, *The Cattle Kings* (Bloomington: Indiana University Press, 1961), and Joe B. Frantz and Julian E. Choate, Jr., *The American Cowboy: The Myth and the Reality* (Norman: University of Oklahoma Press, 1955).

Periodical literature on the ranching industry runs the gamut from pioneer reminiscences to carefully annotated, technical discourses. The following are but a sampling: Harold E. Briggs, "The Development and Decline of Open Range Ranching in the Northwest," *Mississippi Valley Historical Review* (March 1934); Edward E. Dale, "The Ranchman's Last Frontier," *Mississippi Valley Historical Review* (June 1923); C. R. Fay, "The Success of Cooperation among Livestock Producers in the United States of America," *Southwestern Political and Social Science Quarterly* (March 1929); Robert S. Fletcher, "The End of the Open Range in Eastern Montana," *Mississippi Valley Historical Review* (September 1929); T. R. Havins, "The Passing of the Longhorn," *Southwest Historical Quarterly* (July 1952); Lewis Pelzer, "A Cattleman's Commonwealth on the Western Range," *Mississippi Valley Historical Review* (June 1926); J. A. Rickard, "The Hazards of Ranching on the South Plains," *Southwest Historical Quarterly* (April 1934); and Orin J. Oliphant, "The Eastward Movement of Cattle From The Oregon Country," *Agricultural History* (January 1946).

Two articles on sheep ranching are Harold E. Briggs, "The Early Development of Sheep Ranching in the Northwest," *Agricultural History* (July 1937), and Edward N. Wentworth, "Trailing Sheep from California to Idaho in 1865: The Journal of Gorham Gates Kimball," *Agricultural History* (April 1954).

IX BLOSSOM LIKE THE ROSE

Most of the sources for Chapter IX are found in periodical literature published in various scientific, scholarly, and popular maga-
zines throughout the past century. However, a few books did prove
invaluable, foremost of which is Henry Nash Smith, *Virgin Land:
The American West as Symbol and Myth* (Cambridge: Harvard
University Press, 1950). Smith traces the transformation of the
Great American Desert to the Great American Garden and the ac-
companying hopes, frustrations, and crushing disappointments.
John Wesley Powell, *Report on the Lands of the Arid Regions:
With a More Detailed Account of the Lands of Utah* (Washington,
D.C.: U.S. Government Printing Office, 1879) must also rank as one
of the most significant reports ever published on the American
West.

Mary Wilma M. Hargreaves, *Dry Farming in the Northern Great
Plains, 1900–25* (Cambridge: Harvard University Press, 1957) deserves praise as a definitive study of an otherwise "dry" subject. The
problems of the prairie farmers are discussed in Fred A. Shannon,
The Farmer's Last Frontier (New York: Rinehart and Company,
1945), and Everett Dick, *The Sod House Frontier, 1854–1900* (New
York: D. Appleton Century Co., 1937). Essential to an understand-
ing of man's efforts to conquer a hostile environment is Walter P.
Webb, *The Great Plains* (previously cited). Significant chapters on
the same subject also are found in Robert Athearn, *High Country
Empire,* and Ray Allen Billington, *Westward Expansion* (both pre-
viously cited). Two standard works on the Populist movement are
Solon J. Buck, *The Agrarian Crusade, Chronicles of America Series*
(New Haven: Yale University Press, 1921), and John D. Hicks, *The
Populist Revolt* (Minneapolis: The University of Minnesota Press,
1931). A more recent and somewhat more critical evaluation of the
Populists is Richard Hofstadter, *The Age of Reform: From Bryan
to F.D.R.* (New York: Alfred A. Knopf, Inc., 1955).

Among the periodical literature pertinent to this chapter, the
most significant by far is Henry Nash Smith, "Rain Follows the
Plow: The Notion of Increased Rainfall for the Great Plains, 1844–
1880," *The Huntington Library Quarterly* (February 1947). Two
others that deserve special mention are Walter Kollmorgen, "Rain-
makers on the Plains," *Scientific Monthly* (February 1935), and
Clark C. Spence, "The Dyrenforth Rainmaking Experiments: A

Government Venture in 'Pluviculture,'" *Arizona and the West* (Autumn 1961). Also highly significant and well documented is Ralph C. Morris, "The Notion of a Great American Desert East of the Rockies," *Mississippi Valley Historical Review* (September 1926).

Pioneer articles relating to man's effort to conquer the desert include Frank H. Spearman, "The Great American Desert," *Harper's* (July 1888); Howard Miller, "Preliminary Report on the Possibilities of the Reclamation of the Arid Regions of Kansas and Colorado by Utilizing the Underlying Waters," U.S. Department of Agriculture *Bulletin* (1892); Herbert Quick, "Desert Farming Without Irrigation," *World's Work* (1906); Ray Stannard Baker, "The Great Southwest," *The Century Magazine* (May 1901); C. J. Blanchard, "Millions for Moisture," *The National Geographic Magazine* (April 1907); and George W. Julian, "Our Land Policy," *The Atlantic Monthly* (March 1879).

Of more recent origin are L. C. Archer, "Growing Grain on Southern Idaho Dry Farms," *Farmer's Bulletin* (1916); H. P. Gould and O. J. Grace, "Growing Fruit for Home Use in the Great Plains Area," *Farmer's Bulletin* (1916); N. C. Donaldson, "Grains for Montana's Dry Lands," *Farmer's Bulletin* (1916); J. W. Jones, "Grains for Utah Dry Lands," *Farmer's Bulletin* (1917); L. R. Breithaupt, "Grains for the Dry Lands of Central Oregon," *Farmer's Bulletin* (1917); R. B. Cowles, "Let's Make the Desert Yield," *Natural History* (March 1951); R. T. Dickson, "Challenge of Arid Lands," *Science Monthly* (February 1956); "Dry Land," *Scientific American* (June 1955); Thomas Rowe, "Are the Prairies Doomed," *Canadian Magazine* (April 1937); "Future of Arid Lands," *Scientific American* (September 1955); and Frank Cameron, "American Desert Comes to Life," *Reader's Digest* (January 1961).

X   LESSONS IN CONSEQUENCES

Much of the story of irrigation and reclamation has come from federal government sources, particularly the various divisions of the Department of the Interior and the United States Senate's Select Committee on National Water Resources Activities in the United States. The earliest government document of significant importance, of course, is the much-referred-to *Report of the Lands of the Arid Regions* by John Wesley Powell. Most scholarly writers on the subject since 1879 have borrowed heavily from Powell. Another pioneer work is Frederick Haynes Newell, *Irrigation in the United*

States (New York: Thomas Y. Crowell, 1902), which discusses various aspects of irrigation in the West around 1900.

Four important and recent secondary sources that furnished general background material for "Lessons in Consequences" are Wallace Stegner, *Beyond the Hundredth Meridian* (Boston: Houghton Mifflin, 1954); Roy M. Robbins, *Our Landed Heritage: The Public Domain, 1776–1936* (Princeton: Princeton University Press, 1942); Mont H. Saunderson, *Western Land and Water Use* (previously cited); and Vernon Carstensen (ed.), *The Public Lands: Studies in the History of the Public Domain* (Madison: The University of Wisconsin Press, 1963).

Among other secondary sources are Donald C. Swain, *Federal Conservation Policy, 1921–1933* (Berkeley: University of California Press, 1963); Samuel P. Hays, *Conservation and the Gospel of Efficiency: The Progressive Conservation Movement, 1890–1920* (Cambridge: Harvard University Press, 1959); J. Frederick Dewhurst and Associates, *America's Needs and Resources* (New York: The Twentieth Century Fund, 1955); Robert S. Kerr, *Land, Wood, and Water* (New York: Fleet Publishing Corporation, 1960); William R. Van Dersal, *The American Land: Its History and Its Uses* (New York: Oxford University Press, 1943); and J. Russell Smith and M. Ogden Phillips, *North America: Its People and the Resources, Development and Prospects of the Continent as the Home of Man* (New York: Harcourt, Brace & Company, 1942).

Invaluable to this study are three works published by the American Association for the Advancement of Science—symposiums in which internationally known arid-land and water specialists participated. The first conference, held in Albuquerque, New Mexico, resulted in Gilbert F. White (ed.), *The Future of Arid Lands: Papers and Recommendations from the International Arid Lands Meetings* (Washington, D.C.: 1956). The various papers, or individual chapters, cover the broad area of arid lands and suggestions for future use of them. At Denver in 1961 another symposium emphasized water uses in the Intermountain West. Wynne Thorne (ed.), *Land and Water Use* (Washington, D.C.: 1963) is the result. Two years later at Buenos Aires a series of papers summing up the United States' experience in arid lands resulted in Carl Hodge and Peter C. Duisberg (eds.), *Aridity and Man: The Challenge of the Arid Lands in the United States* (Washington, D.C.: 1963).

In recent decades the Bureau of Reclamation has issued hundreds of booklets and pamphlets on various dam and reclamation projects.

However, *Reclamation Project Data* (Washington, D.C.: U.S. Government Printing Office, 1961) is an authoritative reference on all major water developments in the American West. For more complete information on the Colorado River and similar basin storage projects see individual booklets available through the Department of the Interior.

The story of southern California's efforts to pipe water from desert streams is interestingly told in Robert Glass Cleland, *From Wilderness to Empire, A History of California* (New York: Alfred A. Knopf, Inc., 1959). Considerable information and propaganda on the Central Arizona Project has been issued by the Arizona Planning and Resources Board. More ponderous but more complete information, however, is contained in *Central Arizona Project: Hearings before the Subcommittee on Irrigation and Reclamation of the Committee on Interior and Insular Affairs, United States Senate,* 88th Congress, 1st and 2nd Sessions (Washington, D.C.: United States Government Printing Office, 1963).

A partial list of selected articles pertinent to this chapter include Angus M. Woodbury, "Colorado Dam Controversy," *The Scientific Monthly* (June 1956); James C. Malin, "Dust Storms," *Kansas Historical Quarterly* (May, August, November 1946): Thomas H. Langevin, "Development of Multiple-Purpose Water Planning by the Federal Government in the Missouri Basin," *Nebraska Historical Magazine* (March 1953); Richard H. Leach, "The Interstate Compact, Water, and the Southwest," *Southwestern Social Science Quarterly* (December 1957); Alfred B. Sears, "The Desert Threat in the Southern Great Plains; The Historical Implications of Soil Erosion," *Agricultural History* (January 1941); Oliver Knight, "Correcting Nature's Error: The Colorado-Big Thompson Project," *Agricultural History* (October 1956); and Richard L. Neuberger, "Hell's Canyon, The Biggest of All," *Harper's* (April 1939).

XI DESERT POLITICS

In addition to the various western newspapers cited in this chapter, much of the material was drawn from personal interviews and observations by the author: A rereading of John Gunther's *Inside U.S.A.* (New York: Harper and Brothers, 1947) revealed the surprising parallel between the pressure groups and political philosophies in the desert states two decades ago and those of the present. Far more valuable and timely summaries of politics in the region, and especially in the individual states, are found in Frank H. Jonas (ed.), *Western Politics* (Salt Lake City: University of Utah Press, 1961).

Earl Pomeroy, *The Pacific Slope* (New York: Alfred A. Knopf, Inc., 1965) contains some fresh observations on recent political developments in Utah, Idaho, and Nevada. I have also borrowed some information on politics in the upper Great Plains states of Colorado, Wyoming, and Montana from Robert G. Athearn, *High Country Empire: The High Plains and Rockies,* and from my own *Southwest: Old and New* (New York: Alfred A. Knopf, Inc., 1961) for the desert states of Arizona and New Mexico. K. Ross Toole, *Montana: An Uncommon Land* (Norman: University of Oklahoma Press, 1959) contains a frank and interpretative treatment of that state's turbulent politics.

Three articles of interest dealing with western isolationism and conservatism are Ray Allen Billington, "The Origins of Middle Western Isolationism," *Political Science Quarterly* (March 1945); William G. Carleton, "Isolationism and the Middle West," *Mississippi Valley Historical Review* (December 1946); and O. Douglas Weeks, "Republicanism and Conservatism in the South," *Southwestern Social Science Quarterly* (December 1955).

XII   AROUND THE RIM

XIII   DESERT CITIES ON THE MARCH

Nearly all of the subject matter for Chapters XII and XIII came as a result of extensive travel throughout the Great American Desert during recent years. The idea of a firsthand examination of the physical geography of the region and the character of the people who live there was inspired by John Steinbeck's fascinating best-seller, *Travels With Charlie.* Otherwise, in the journey "around the rim" of the desert, I charted each day's course from road maps and recorded my impressions of the people and the landscape. In some formal interviews with especially knowledgeable individuals I took extensive notes on the spot.

Though I am familiar with all sixteen of the desert cities covered in Chapter XIII, I have had to rely upon brochures published by local chambers of commerce and state planning and resources boards or commissions for statistical data on population and industrial growth. This type of literature generally is on the optimistic side, yet it often represents the most recent and accurate information available. The Research Department of the Valley National Bank, in Phoenix, Arizona, regularly publishes up-to-date statistics on most of the major cities of the Great American Desert. Popular magazines such as *U. S. News and World Report, Holiday, Saturday Evening Post, Reader's Digest,* and *Time* contain innumerable articles on the subject of American cities from which I have obtained scattered material. The pioneer story of each of the desert cities discussed here is found in individual state histories, regional historical quarterlies, and in scholarly western history survey books.

XIV THE CHALLENGE OF THE FUTURE

Material for this chapter is largely based upon government documents, newspaper clippings accumulated over a five-year period, personal interviews, periodical literature, and speeches by specialists in the Department of the Interior. The following books did supply some general background information: Carl F. Kraenzel, *The Great Plains in Transition* (Norman: University of Oklahoma Press, 1955); Paul Sears, *Deserts on the March* (Norman: University of Oklahoma Press, 1947); Nathaniel Wollman (ed.), *The Value of Water in Alternative Uses* (Albuquerque: University of New Mexico Press, 1962); and Marion Clawson, Burnell Held, and Charles Stoddard, *Land of the Future* (Baltimore: Johns Hopkins Press, 1963).

A clearer insight on the problems associated with land and water uses was obtained from interviews with Gladwin Young, Deputy Administrator, Soil Conservation Service, and Charles F. MacGowan, Director, Office of Saline Water (April 25, 1962).

Various methods of saline water conversion are described and illustrated in the United States Department of the Interior *Saline Water Conversion Report for 1963* (Washington, D.C.: U.S. Government Printing Office; 1963). Since 1963 voluminous publications in the form of brochures and bulletins have been issued by the Department of the Interior on the progress in saline water conversion at the various demonstration plants currently in operation. In addition, more than thirty reports resulted from extensive studies on Water Resources Activities in the United States by the Select Committee on National Resources, United States Senate, 88th Congress, 2nd Session. Six of these are especially pertinent: "Future Needs for Reclamation in the Western States" (Committee Print No. 14),

"Evaporation Reduction and Seepage Control" (Committee Print No. 28), "Application and Effects of Nuclear Energy" (Committee Print No. 27), "Present and Prospective Means for Improved Reuse of Water" (Committee Print No. 30), "Population Projections and Economic Assumptions" (Committee Print No. 5), and "Future Water Requirements for Municipal Use" (Committee Print No. 7).

Two miscellaneous government bulletins are "Facts about Wind Erosion and Dust Storms on the Great Plains," Department of Agriculture Bulletin No. 394 (1961), and "Windbreaks in Conservation Farming," Department of Agriculture Bulletin No. 759 (1958).

Among the hundreds of technical and scientific articles published during the past decade are Edward S. Deevey, "The Human Population," *Scientific American* (September 1960); Lewis Koenig, "The Economics of Water Sources," *The Future of Arid Lands*, edited by Gilbert F. White (previously cited); "The Challenge of the Future," *Aridity and Man*, edited by Carl Hodge (previously cited); and L. E. Meyers, Jr., "Water Harvesting," *Proceedings, Nevada Water Conference, 16th* (Carson City: Department of Conservation and Natural Resources and Nevada State Reclamation Association, 1963).

Newspapers in general have tended to overdramatize recent developments in finding new sources of water for arid lands. Editorials and feature articles on the conservation of water, pollution of streams and lakes, and future plans and projects appear regularly in such western newspapers as the *Denver Post*, Albuquerque *Journal*, Oklahoma City *Times*, Salt Lake *Tribune*, and *Arizona Republic*. A list of the major articles in these newspapers alone for the past ten years would extend to several pages. However, an excellent synthesis of the postwar achievements and the water research currently under way is the extensive article by Ernest Douglas of Phoenix, Arizona, "Using Ingenuity in a Fight to 'Harvest' Water," *The National Observer* (January 4, 1965).

INDEX